The African Experience
in Colonial Virginia

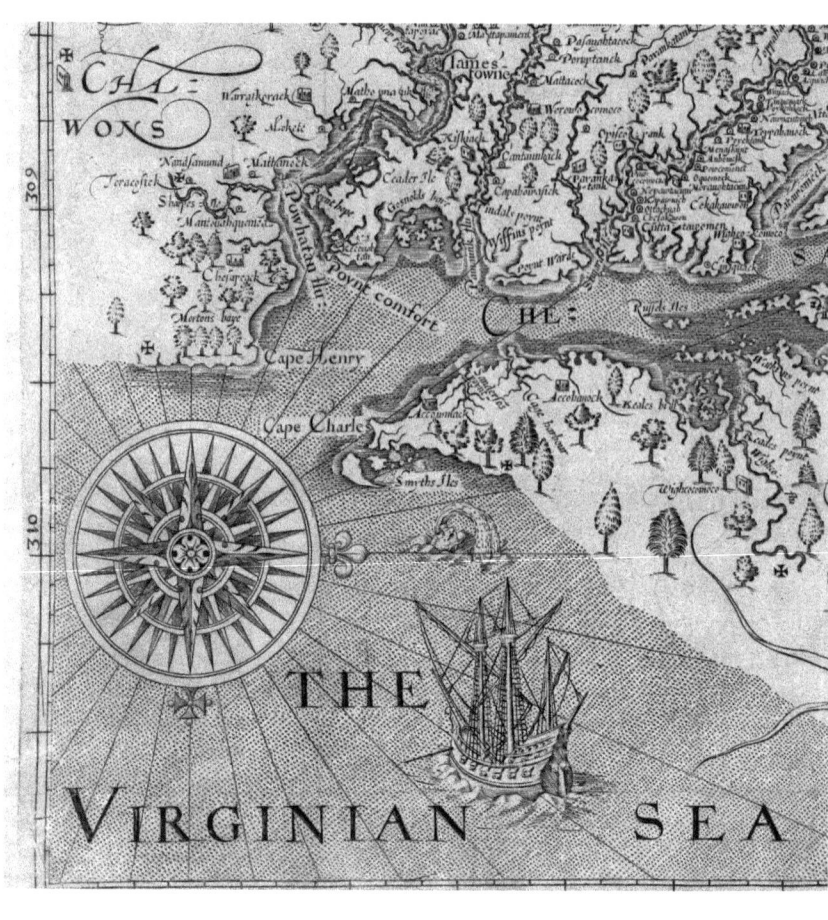

The African Experience in Colonial Virginia

Essays on the 1619 Arrival and the Legacy of Slavery

Edited by
Colita Nichols Fairfax

Foreword by Justin E. Fairfax

McFarland & Company, Inc., Publishers
Jefferson, North Carolina

Frontispiece: **Map of the Region of Point Comfort, Virginia ca. 1624. J. Smith, & W. Hole, 1624 (Library of Congress).**

Library of Congress Cataloguing-in-Publication Data

Names: Fairfax, Colita Nichols, editor. | Fairfax, Justin E., writer of foreword.
Title: The African experience in Colonial Virginia : essays on the 1619 arrival and the legacy of slavery / edited by Colita Nichols Fairfax ; foreword by Justin E. Fairfax.
Other titles: Essays on the 1619 arrival and the legacy of slavery
Description: Jefferson, North Carolina : McFarland & Company, Inc., Publishers, 2021 | Includes bibliographical references and index.
Identifiers: LCCN 2020050499 |
ISBN 9781476678085 (paperback : acid free paper) ∞
ISBN 9781476640020 (ebook)
Subjects: LCSH: African Americans—Virginia—History—17th century. | Slavery—Virginia—History—17th century. | African Americans—Legal status, laws, etc.—Virginia—History—17th century. | Virginia—Race relations—History—17th century. | Virginia—History—Colonial period, ca. 1600-1775. | Collective memory—Virginia.
Classification: LCC E185.93.V8 A37 2021 | DDC 306.3/6209755—dc23
LC record available at https://lccn.loc.gov/2020050499

British Library cataloguing data are available
ISBN (print) 978-1-4766-7808-5
ISBN (ebook) 978-1-4766-4002-0

© 2021 Colita Nichols Fairfax. All rights reserved

No part of this book may be reproduced or transmitted in any form or by any means, electronic or mechanical, including photocopying or recording, or by any information storage and retrieval system, without permission in writing from the publisher.

Front cover image: Landing of 20 African captives at Jamestown from Dutch man-of-war, 1619 © 2020 Everett Historical/Shutterstock

Printed in the United States of America

McFarland & Company, Inc., Publishers
Box 611, Jefferson, North Carolina 28640
www.mcfarlandpub.com

To Anthony (Antoney), Isabell(a), William, the first African family in the English North American framework, to Angeloa/Angela, and all of those Africans who forge a life with their cultures, philosophies, ideologies, values, customs, traditions, ingenuity, benevolence, and languages in Colonial Virginia in 1619. Their pioneering will to survive is important in the study of history and culture. Their survival in the face of abject human neglect and hate is a testimony to the enduring spirit of all African people trapped in the horrors of enslavement. Yet they dared to exist on their cultural terms when they could. This body of work honors them.

Table of Contents

Acknowledgments   ix

Foreword
    Justin E. Fairfax   1

Introduction
    Colita Nichols Fairfax   3

The "Middle Passage": The Enforced Migration of Africans Across the Atlantic
    Paul E. Lovejoy   15

Race and Constructions of "the Negro" in Colonial Virginia
    Anthony Q. Hazard, Jr.   55

The Other Amazing Grace from a Slave Ship
    James A. Forbes, Jr.   69

1619: A Conceptual Worldview Marker in Africana Cultural Memory Studies
    Christel N. Temple   80

Twin Events of Summer 1619 in Tidewater Virginia, and the Prospect for Government of, for, and by the American People: A Commentary
    Peter Wallenstein   101

Engendering Slavery in Virginia: An Examination of Blacks' First Century in the Old Dominion
    Maureen Elgersman Lee   107

"Wash Me and I Shall Be Whiter Than Snow": A Living
Historiography of African Women and Christianity in
the Virginia Colony
  VALERIE M. JOYCE   120

What Life? Experiences of Enslaved Africans in Virginia
  COLITA NICHOLS FAIRFAX   137

Posttraumatic Slave Syndrome, the Patriarchal Nuclear Family
Structure and African American Male-Female Relationships
  NOELLE M. ST. VIL, CHRISTOPHER ST. VIL and
  COLITA NICHOLS FAIRFAX   153

Vestiges of Slavery: The Occupational Segregation of
Black Women
  RHONDA VONSHAY SHARPE   166

Building a Nation: United States Black Founders, Racial
Ideology and the Crisis of Black Citizenship
  LAGARRETT J. KING   182

Epilogue: E Pluribus Unum, *Out of Many, One*
  SOPHIA A. NELSON   197

About the Contributors   201

Index   205

Acknowledgments

I am immensely rich with family and friends. Words are almost insufficient to explain the level of intimate support, nurture and love I have received throughout my lifetime. To complete this project would not have occurred without the enduring levels of encouragement, and guidance. Each contributor in this volume is a unique person in the field where they labor. They have created inroads to changing society to push the boundaries of knowledge. Paul E. Lovejoy, Anthony Q. Hazard, Jr., Peter Wallenstein, Valerie M. Joyce, Maureen Elgersman Lee, Noelle and Christopher St. Vil, Rhonda Vonshay Sharpe and LaGarrett King are stellar scholars who saw the value in the project and I thank them so much for participating. The Rev. Dr. James A. Forbes, Jr., whom I have known for all of my life, graced my home as a child and shared an abiding friendship with my late father, added sage wisdom to the meaning of this work. For all of my life, I was privilege to hear scholarly social justice discourse between theologians, which propelled me to think deeper about my own purpose in life. I thank you for who you are to my family and to me. Ni'ngatho muno!

Dr. Christel N. Temple and I are extended family from the Richmond community, and are graduate school classmates. As she shared her brilliance in literary criticism, I learned how to think differently about artistry and prose in my work as a social scientist. I thank her for the role she has played in my life. I thank one of my mentors Dr. Daudi Azibo, a singular thought leader; I have benefited from him as a graduate student and growing researcher. Sophia A. Nelson became a seriously supportive figure in the development of this body of work. An extremely knowledgeable woman, passionate about the beauty of America in all of its racial colors, she saw the value in this work. I thank her for whom she is. Asante sana!

My parents have been the most powerful and influential people in my life. Although my father, the late Dr. Paul Nichols, has departed this life, his larger than life form remains with me through every endeavor. I received my interest in history and genealogy from my mother, Mrs. Brenda Dabney

Nichols. I thank you Mama for all you poured into me to carve my own intellectual pursuits in my own way.

In addition to my role as a professor at Norfolk State University, I co-chaired the City of Hampton 2019 Commemorative Commission, with Lt. Col. Claude Vann, III (ret). He is my new big brother and our work as a team to elucidate for citizens the Point Comfort narrative in the development of the Virginia colony, was rewarding. A strong community advocate, I thank Mr. Vann for reminding me that community work is necessary.

The bounty of goodness that I experience every hour of each day is in the form of my beloved husband, Anthony E. Fairfax, and our beautiful daughters Layla and Natalie. Family is everything and I have everything in family. My love with you Tony is an enduring love that surpasses all understanding, and the late nights and early mornings when I had to work on this book. I am thankful for you and our girls.

Foreword

Justin E. Fairfax

The Commonwealth of Virginia provides a microcosm for analyzing where America has been, where it is going, and how it decides to move forward. At every historic stage of the country's development, Virginia has played a pivotal role—for better or for worse.

The August 1619 landing of African people aboard the ship *White Lion* at Point Comfort in present-day Hampton is perhaps the most poignant and monumental historical moment, given the complex legacy and reality of race relations in America. Yet Virginia also was the "Mother of Presidents" in the early years of America, including our first president, George Washington. And it was the state that elected the first popularly elected African American governor in our nation's history—L. Douglas Wilder.

Today, Virginia is moving in the direction of a multicultural society in which American ideals provide an opportunity for everyone to thrive if we stay true to those ideals. Yet we must never forget that it was the presence, sacrifices, and contributions of those Africans who made it possible for later generations to push for expanded definitions of freedom and liberty for themselves and others—ensuring that we honor inherent and inalienable rights for people across America. Virginia has come to recognize the importance of the early pioneering roles that this population had in building the foundation of what would become both Virginia and America.

My family's story speaks to this reality.

Just moments before I was sworn into office as Virginia's 41st Lt. Governor, my father handed me a remarkable document. It was a copy of a manumission document from June 5, 1798, by which Thomas Fairfax, the 9th Lord Fairfax, freed my great-great-great grandfather Simon Fairfax from slavery—over 60 years prior to the Civil War. We don't know much about Simon, but we do know that of the nearly 100 slaves that Thomas Fairfax freed, Simon was one of the first two.

Simon's ancestors honored his legacy with their own important accomplishments across the generations. As I held a copy of the manumission document in my breast pocket at my inauguration, I contemplated what Simon might have thought of the possibility of that inauguration. He could not have set foot in the Virginia Capitol as a slave and yet here was his great-great-great grandson being sworn in as the second-in-command of the government of the Commonwealth of Virginia.

I have since seen the original signed manumission paper in the records of the old Fairfax County Courthouse. Truly this manumission document and the document on my office wall certifying my election as lieutenant governor shows that all things are possible if people follow the better angels of their nature.

This collection provides the reader with scholarly information and commentary about the lives and humanity of Africans who came to the Virginia colony against their will in 1619. It explores cultural memory, the brutal realities of their lived experiences, and analyzes the vicissitudes of their labor, with particularly emphasis on the experiences of women.

This book is unique in that it includes a discussion of the psychological impact upon generations of Africans who were not only enslaved, but their progeny who would be free. It provides us with lessons to view these historic figures as pioneers, heroes, founders, and not only as enslaved, helpless, captive people.

I am delighted to know that this book will educate and re-educate the public about what happened in 1619, and what should be happening in 2019. The scholars who have contributed to this book offer us new insights and analyses to reframe our thinking about 1619 and about the strong people who walked off of the ship *White Lion* into an unimaginable future.

I commend Colita Nichols Fairfax for spearheading this project that provides the reader with nuanced viewpoints that will give our Commonwealth and country the tools to consider the beginning of America in a different way. I hope that this book will become a primer for all people who believe in what America can be and should be for all—a Commonwealth and country that can rise together.

Justin E. Fairfax was elected lieutenant governor of the Commonwealth of Virginia on November 7, 2017. He is a prominent lawyer, political figure, philanthropist, and community leader. He graduated from Duke University in 2000 with a degree in public policy studies and earned his Juris Doctorate in 2005.

Introduction

Colita Nichols Fairfax

> I've known rivers:
> I've known rivers ancient as the world and older than the flow of human blood in human veins.
> —Langston Hughes, 1920

Scene—1619

The historical narrative that set the scene for how Africans are depicted in the unfolding paradigm of what would become America, is a stale, routine deposit with soulless expression:

> About the latter end of August, a Dutch man of War [*White Lion*], of the burden of a 160 tunnes arriued at Point Comfort, the Comandors name Capt Jope, his Pilott for the West Indies, one Mr. Marmaduke an Englishman. They mett with the Treasurer in the West Indyes, and determined to hold consort ship hitherward, but in their passage, lost one the other. He brought not anything but 20 and odd Negroes, which the Governor and Cape Merchant bought for victuals (whereof he was in greate need as he pretended), at the best an easyest rates they could [Sluiter, 1997, 395].

John Rolfe's journal contains a description of a business transaction of human beings for food. The names of the Englishmen are listed. The names, ethnicities, ages, beliefs, philosophies, languages, titles of the Africans are not. The faceless Africans. The Africans are not considered as "founders, pioneers, frontiers-folk, originators, contributors, innovators," yet are needed to advance the economic productivity of the colony to advance a settler project of England, as mere workers. Throughout the Virginia colony, there were clusters of settlements where Africans were placed to work and serve those in power. For example, in Kecoughtan (Elizabeth City County, which is present-day Hampton; Stensvaag, 1985), Flowerdew Hundred Plantation, Warrasquoke, Jamestown, etc., Africans were dispersed for labor. After the aboriginal people, the Kecoughtan, were slaughtered in 1610, ushering in Elizabeth City County, other aboriginal people would have their existence and cultural way of life tested over and over, such as the Powhatan, Mattaponi, Pamunkey, Chickahominy, Potomac, Chesapeake, Rappahannock, Appomattox, Nansemond, Cheroenhaka, and several others. Yet the Anglo-Powhatan War devastated many of these villages (Beckley, 2008, 75). The aboriginal people would find their way of life upended, and many of their people enslaved. It should not be forgotten that they were the first group of people enslaved in the Virginia colony.

The Africans who disembarked the ship *White Lion* were from the Angola region. Their ethnicity was either Kimbundu or Kikongo. They were skilled people in farming, herding, textile weaving, blacksmithing, and musicality. They were a spiritual people with a philosophy, a worldview of family, rituals, beliefs, ideologies. They may have been exposed to Christianity, and may have been baptized as Christians. Wisdom and art were esteemed highly and children were cherished. These Africans hailed from nation-states that evolved political, religious and military institutions. This society was hierarchical, well organized and inhabitants had many skills in areas such as trade, metalworking, animal husbandry and agriculture. They used proverbs in the form of Anansi tales passed down through generations as Brier Fox and Rabbit folk stories. They created the stringed box–like device that we call the banjo. Women were leaders, as evidenced of the historic figure Queen Ana Njinga (Nzinga) Mbande (1583–1663), who ruled over Ndongo and Matamba, whose "outstanding accomplishments and decades-long reign was comparable to that of Elizabeth I of England" (Heywood, 2017, 1). In fact, millions of Africans enslaved in Brazil were from Angola, as the Africans who disembarked the ships *White Lion* in August 1619 and *Treasurer* in 1620 at Point Comfort, present-day Hampton, "were from Ndongo, Matamba and Kongo" (Heywood, 2017, 255), kingdoms in Angola. The presence of African people is not only due to the expansion of the colony as a settler project, but it speaks volumes to what they contributed. Although the Africans who landed in 1619 originated from Angola, the forced migration of African people transferred centuries of knowledge in mathematics, religion, governance, military and societal organization frameworks, creative production in literacy and movement such as the Ring Shout and Cake Walk, medicine/science, astronomy, metallurgy, architecture, engineering, and navigation (Moore, 2010; Rogers, 1980; Van Sertima, 1976). Many ancient societies in Africa engaged in seafaring expeditions, settling in parts of the Americas.

Enslavement is a phenomenon in which every civilization in the world participated. It predates European forays into the Americas, developing into a more exploitative, inhumane and racial enterprise that had previously existed in Europe, Africa or the Americas (Guasco, 2014). The Spanish settled St. Augustine, Florida, in 1565, and African people had been in the Americas against their will for 500 years before 1619. Enslaving the aboriginal people in Virginia, and trading African people for food in 1619 were normal business transactions for the English. Given that enslavement predates the 1619 context, one may take the posture that the English knew to develop codified laws to subjugate and suppress Africans, and the development of codified Black Codes in the 1600s simply legitimated the enterprise of enslavement. There has been an incredible amount of discussion about whether the Africans who landed in 1619 were free, indentured or enslaved. The reality is that those Africans were forced captives who were kidnapped and trafficked across the Atlantic Ocean for the purpose of advancing a settler colonial project in Virginia. Vaughan explains that "[t]he evidence of the decade ... shows with alarming clarity that blacks from the outset suffered from a prejudice that relegated them to the lowest rank in the colony's society, and there are strong hints that bondage for blacks did not follow the same terms as for whites" (Alden, 1972, 477). The March 1620 Census records 32 Africans; 15 males and 17 females in the Virginia, who were aboard the *White Lion* and *Treasurer* ships (Vaughan, 1972, 472). An example is here: "Nine of them lived in James City, seven at Percy's Hundred, three at Elizabeth City, two at Warrasquoke, one in the 'Neck of land near James City,' and one at 'Elizabeth Citty beyond Hampton River'—a fairly wide geographical distribution of black laborers" (Vaughan, 1972, 473). A 1625 muster in Elizabeth City (formerly Kicotan, now Hampton), lists that Antoney (Negro) and Isabella (Negro) (Dorman, 2004), had William their child baptized. Antoney and Isabella labored in the household or on the land of Capt. William Tucker. The child William is often described as the first African child born in America; however, there is a second child listed in the 1625 muster at Flowerdew Hundred, and no records indicate which child was born first. John Pedro also resided in Elizabeth City County, "owned" by Francis West. Given this information, the reader must reconcile that there was not a concentrated group of Africans "arriving" at or "living in" Jamestown. Africans were placed where their owners lived, and where they were needed for the economic survival of the colony. The settlement of Jamestown did not have a community of Africans in 1619 or shortly thereafter. Furthermore, present-day Hampton is able to account for at least 4

Africans, which shows its historical relevancy in the development of the Virginia colony. More to the point, Africans were isolated throughout the colony, based upon who owned them. After surviving the harrowing Middle Passage, the extremely painful journey of enduring the journey across the Atlantic under incomprehensible sadistic and brutish conditions, these Africans lived the rest of their lives in social and cultural isolation in colonial Virginia.

In 1619, this scene is not for the development of a multicultural, multiethnic, multiracial nation. It presents a blueprint that demonstrates the true purpose of African people in the settler colony, that despite their gifts, intellect and genius, they were to be used as laborers, regarded as property without human and legal rights. Though there are names of free Black men, such as John Phillip and Anthony Johnson (Vaughan, 1972), in the colony, their "freedom" was individualized. The ability to gain one's freedom was not provided to every African who was among the first groups to land in 1619. The first governor of the Colonial Virginia, George Yeardley, was the first person to own enslaved Africans. Most landowners who would ascend to the House of Burgesses, and become sainted members of the General Assembly in Virginia are those who enslaved the aboriginal people of what would become Virginia and African people.

Impact of 1619

The City of Hampton's 2019 Commemorative Commission has worked since 2014 to educate the public about the landing of African people in present-day Hampton. The impact of year 1619 to the developing Virginia colony and what would become America, has been thrust into public memory. With the development of commemorative activities, the public is engaged about the landing of Africans to the shores of Virginia, and what would become of them. The following epochs of enslavement, Jim Crow segregation, and urbanization of African descendants must be included as significant points of study, because the history of human suffering, marginalization, systemic bloodthirstiness and hatred continues to undermine the American experience for Black people for 400 years. "The long-term biopsychosocial effect that circumscribing public policy and governing around wealth, maleness, and whiteness would have on American people who were poor, female, disabled, or members of one racial population has been reinforced and legitimized" (Davis, 2004, 229). The trauma induced has not been erased.

Secondly, of special interest to the impact of the presence of Africans in 1619 is citizenship; "the Naturalization Act of 1790 narrowly outlined the parameters or desired features of American citizenship, decreeing privileges of citizenship and the right to vote enjoyed only by Wealthy White men" (Davis, 2004). The Africans who disembarked from the ships *White Lion* and *Treasurer* were not regarded as human beings and neither were their descendants for generations. The status of chattel property followed them for decades, until 1868 (Chambers, 2013). The passage of the 14th Amendment, which granted Black people citizenship rights, did not transform the human experiences of generations following those who disembarked in 1619. Only after the issuance of the Emancipation Proclamation, Due Process (Civil War) amendments—13th, 14th and 15th—another 100 years of legalized apartheid, and the Civil Rights Laws of the 1960s, would citizenship and citizenship rights secure a contiguous life for people of African descent:

> In theory, citizenship is the foundation on which that attempt rests. However, the nature of American citizenship was not clear at the Founding and remains somewhat unclear. Whether American citizenship is supposed to be rights-based with a focus on the rights owed to citizens by the community, and obligations owed by citizens to the community, or belonging-based with a focus on making sure that every citizen is thoroughly connected to the community through implicit connections to fellow citizens, and the community that augment any formal rights and obligations that attend, citizenship status is not clear [Chambers, 2013, 512].

Citizenship status has undermined and underscored access to resources, meaningful crisis interventions, choices of educational training and economic business supports. Labels such as servants, enslaved, concubines, contraband, subjects have been applied to Black people, but not necessarily the term citizen; "the stratification of our welfare system that distributes benefits according to race and gender also differentiates between two classes of inhabitants—citizens and subjects" (Roberts, 1996, 1576). Moreover, and even more concretely, the lack of citizenship rights have reverberated into the lack of livable resources to thrive and be inclusive, the lack of opportunity for an equal education, the absence of equality for predominantly Black educational, benevolent, agencies and civic institution, and an absence of wealth-attainment circumstances. The obscene vicissitude of poverty, deprivation, impecuniousness, that touches almost every extended African American family, speaks to how citizenship rights are and or not applied, following a 400-year pattern of human treatment. Black people are still suffering from this crime (enslavement), because we have not been allowed to find our way back to the sense of cultural identity, and continuity, which would transform us into a unified and whole people, and have not been able to function in the world with a collective consciousness that naturally imparts a strong sense of cultural roots (Ani, 1997).

Next, popular culture does not include a discussion about how Angola was left bereft of its people in the criminal enterprise of kidnapping. People began to go missing without any warning. Family members, friends, cohorts, business partners, leaders, and particularly children were taken from kingdoms in Angola. For centuries, people were kidnapped primarily by having their villages and homes raided when they were unprepared to defend themselves (Nunn, 2008). Such predatory behavior weakened relationships, boundaries and legalities between ethnic groups and nation-states, which allowed for further raiding and kidnapping of people for centuries (Nunn, 2008). So not only did the 1619 moment bring in a new framework for colonial Virginia, it was a catalyst for what would happen to parts of Africa impacted so heavily by this national kidnapping enterprise. "While the population and resources of the New World were developed, as a result of the overseas slave trade, the African continent deprived of its most vital resource—humans—was underdeveloped" (Mukhtar, Kara, Abba & Ahmed, 2014, 223). Agriculture and industry were seriously affected by mass kidnapping, because children and people in their prime who would have contributed to the development of their societies, both in industry and in family. Therefore the population of West Africans societies was largely depleted, leaving societies with either relatively too young or too old persons to develop their respective societies (Mukhtar et al., 2014, 224).

Lastly, it is an indisputable fact that every time the African American community existed on their own cultural terms, they were victimized and murdered with barbaric methods that were sanctioned by government. Examples of such barbarity include the New York City Draft Riot of 1863; Knoxville, Tennessee, community in 1919; Greenwood community in Tulsa, Oklahoma, known as "Black Wall Street," which was annihilated in 1921; and the Rosewood, Florida, massacre of 1923. In these communities and thousands across America, a network of economic business districts accompanied schools, institutions of higher learning, benevolent and training centers, fraternal orders, health institutions, religious denominations and institutions with a heavy social justice emphasis, where the socialization of young people was peer-based, extended family structured, led and ordained by elders. These efforts were engaged to not only develop people and inculcate their sensibilities of who they were as cultural beings, but these efforts were created in the face of Segregation, which isolated and excluded Black people from the public sector, resources, power and opportunity. The impact of 1619 is not only of that year, but how what happened in that year became the fate of those early Africans and their progeny in colonial Virginia and ultimately in America.

How This Collection Informs Knowledge About 1619

This text elucidates elements of the global enterprise of enslavement, racism, and capitalism that has underscored bestial inhumanity and obscene profits for those benefiting from it. Scholars provide perspectives that address forgotten and ignored narratives about the early landscape of the "settler colony," with important outcomes for social policy, cooperative economics, work and profit, personhood, psychological realignment, spiritual awareness, resource development, curriculum and pedagogy, institution building, community development processes, and literary and creative production. Not just a text for the ivory tower, the wider population will benefit from its dividends, by being posed newer questions and information with ignored facts and information about the year 1619. African American historiography "is a distinct area of inquiry, within the discipline of history, with Black people as its primary focus to reveal their thought and activities over time and place" (Harris, 1982, 118). This body of work is not reactionary, nor does it seek to only "synthesize a broader narrative or only critique the effects" (Prout, 2007, 16–17) of the phenomenon studied. This text represents an analytical concept I have developed entitled "social justice historiography." I posit that social justice historiography is an activity where a range of historical discourses employs methods, techniques, and procedures, to critically examine historical data to address systemic power relationships that constrain political, economic advancement, cultural solvency and group independence. This framework challenges a legacy of conventional discourses that are failing to foster curative measures and approaches in institutions attending to generational collateral afflictions. A redemptive outcome of this exchange is to offer the reader alternative paradigms and frameworks that attend to societal healing, through appropriate ontological approaches that transform institutional behavior, disrupt exploitative economic systems and attend to cultural mis-orientation. The reader is not left without hope. Each essay reflects social justice historiography, written by a thought-leader who pushes the boundaries of the story of people of African descent and places a proper context of the year 1619. Reframing this discussion is not simply telling the story as an "English" story, but it is an international and aboriginal parable. The need to engage in corrective narratives that will address the presence of and intersection with the rich aboriginal cultures of Virginia are important and remains hidden in public discussion. In addition to the Introduction, the editor provides an analysis of the lived experiences of enslaved people in Virginia, who lived through a portion of the twentieth century, so that the reader will hear from the actual voices of those enslaved. I also illustrate what happened to them after Emancipation, with a particular emphasis on their economic and life trajectories that impaired generations, including my own.

I was fortunate to secure permission to include an earlier published article of Paul E. Lovejoy, entitled "The 'Middle Passage': The Enforced Migration of Africans Across the Atlantic." This contribution exposes the reader to another aspect of enslavement, which is the heinous journey in a slave ship as a commodity, sacredly referred to as "The Middle Passage." The reader is exposed to not only the cruelty of the journey, but the global changes that this enforced migration created. He explains how western African countries were depopulated, as well as impacts of repopulated areas in the Americas and Caribbean islands, due to the phenomena of kidnapping people to labor for the economic advancement of European countries and America. Though there were African individuals who participated in this global enterprise, not one African country or economy benefited.

Anthony Q. Hazard, Jr.'s essay, "Race and Constructions of 'the Negro' in Colonial Virginia" provides a discussion about the legal framework in developing an alternative identity to African. Understanding the creation of a "Negro" that was not African, bereft of history, philosophies, languages, etc., that supported how Africans would be used in the colony. Negroes were not citizens, but were subjects, subhuman, non-human, unequal in every human aspect, to be governed by a legal framework that justified the American brand of enslavement. Seldom do we learn of the ethnicity of those Africans who arrived in 1619, because their identities were deliberately erased and continue to be erased from public memory. The host of Black Codes, Slave Codes and other forms of local and state laws carry the verbiage Negro or Negress in order to attach these Africans to this identity legally and psychologically.

Nationally renowned theologian James A. Forbes, Jr., who was recognized by *Newsweek* in 1996 as one of the twelve "most effective preachers" in the English-speaking world, issues a commentary about the spiritual resilience, courage, and tenacity that those Africans carried with them across the Atlantic which underscored their survival. These methods of survival which were inherited by their progeny are only heralded in words, but not in tangible resources, opportunities, or access to institutions that underscore quality of life variables. He admonishes quadricentennial commemorations to not only reexamine the transgressions of intergenerational racial violence, but to overturn vestiges of ill-gotten gains. Forbes artistically offers a portrayal of the lamentations of those Africans in song and prose, which were undoubtedly offered over and over to the God of their understanding. African people are not only asking "How come we are here?," but everybody regardless of race should ask what is the purpose of their own lives, given the presence of the vestiges of suffering due to the system put in place when the "20 And odd" disembarked.

Africana studies scholar Christel N. Temple presents a theoretical lens to the 1619 encounter based upon public cultural memory, which means that a group has the capacity to share in and meditate upon a memory that shapes them collectively. She explains that Black cultural mythology attends to the method of how memory collectively forges identity. She provides examples to show how powerful memory is, not only in ways of surviving. This liberation method is used by leaders who engage in remembrance activities that are cultural foundations. This method does not stay in the moment of trauma and dysfunction, but it ushers in critical engagement in order to transform into a cultural authentic communitarianism of rituals and enlightenment activities. Not only does engagement in this intervention help with what is remembered or remembered accurately, it opens a space for accuracy and meditation. This intervention becomes a first-person intervention, where the person places their self in the historic moment of what happened to them personally, making the intervention sacred and intimate.

Award winning historian Peter Wallenstein offers implications of the 1619 historical moment. He instructs the reader to recognize that perspective has a great deal to do with understanding the historical moment of 1619, but that historical moments compete with one another. He honestly explains how the beginning of government was not for everyone, but for a fraction of the population in the Virginia colony, laying the framework for how government would function. He includes the role of laboring that the majority of those who were inhabiting the new colony were doing, with their progeny inheriting a sentence of noncitizenship, which have endured since then.

Canadian-born historian Maureen Elgersman Lee reminds us that African men and women had equal work responsibilities, yet women had the burdensome responsibility of bearing and rearing children in bondage. Black Codes in the 1600s determined the status of children, adding an extra layer of identity and freedom that became gendered. This was a different trajectory from English custom, where the status of the father determined the status of his children. By using gender to identify the status of children, the government decided for African children what their status would be, and it placed the burden of identity solely upon African women. This painful frontier is a result of the manipulation and control of family life and mothering.

This text includes performance scholarship from Valerie M. Joyce. In a monologue, Joyce chronicles the life of Mary, an enslaved woman in Norfolk, found guilty of her own rape, and who was publicly humiliated for it through the employment of Christianity. Joyce explains the methods in developing her production as living historiography. Focusing on Mary's voice, the reader learns more intimately about the impact of enslavement, with particular emphasis on how sex was defined separately for White men and African women. Living historiographies highlight the voices of historic women who are able to articulate for themselves so that we may learn from their perspectives, their realities. As we reflect upon the 1619 moment, the experiences of African women are important to include, especially given the wide attention the year 1620 occupies in the annals of history, as the year that White women arrived in the colony.

The editor's essay reveals the lived experiences of enslaved Africans in Virginia. Given that 1619 ushered in the perpetual enslavement of African people in North America, it is tantamount to capture for the reader the horror and misery of their lives from their perspectives. This essay documents that after 1619, successive generations of enslaved Africans were enslaved and brutalized in a global economic and racial enterprise that has even impacted generations of the twentieth and twenty-first centuries. There were enslaved Africans who lived well into the twentieth century, bringing their sorrows yet indefatigable spirits of survival to the collective memories that may be used for socialization, sacred and cultural instruction to remember, to heal, to be restored.

Wife and husband team Noelle M. St. Vil and Christopher St. Vil worked with the editor on an earlier version of a theoretical examination of posttraumatic slave syndrome, a psychological diagnosis developed by Dr. Joy DeGruy. DeGruy examines intergenerational behavioral and cultural trauma emanating from enslavement, post-enslavement and contemporary urbanization and state violence. St. Vil, St. Vil and Fairfax examine African American marriage patterns that follow patterns of trauma by applying the PTSS framework. For centuries, African people biologically and ontologically (one's state of being) had their cultural sensibility maligned by anti–African socialization, resulting in mis-oriented behaviors and cognitive processes that are exhibited today. An application of PTSS addresses male-female relationships for appropriate redress and intervention.

Labor economist Rhonda Vonshay Sharpe juxtaposes the labor experiences of women in enslavement with contemporary patterns of work. She explains that the domestic work of enslaved women mirrors contemporary work experiences and wages. She explains that positions of work within enslavement, Jim Crow Segregation and the twenty-first century remain sullied by race and gender limitations. She explains the impact of occupational segregation in the marketplace with consequences African American women experience, as a direct result of labor experiences experienced by their ancestral mothers in the Virginia colony. Regardless of educational attainment and skill-based attainment, African American women will experience occupational segregation with particular emphasis on traditional caregiving roles, impacting their wages, salaries, benefits, resources and quality of life variables in the twenty-first century.

Educational scholar LaGarrett J. King revisits the narrative of 1619 as a narrative filled with nostalgic Founding episodes of courageous Englishmen forging their way into a world to discover and create a country, minimizing the physical, mental and cultural impact that the invasion had upon indigenous people. He adds to the narrative that Africans should also be regarded as Founders and that the roles these Black Founders played as builders, creators, and articulators of philosophical and democratic principles of freedom, humanity, fairness, equality, social justice and agency. King challenges disjointed K–12 curriculums across America that maintain this imprecise and power-based narrative that restricts the human imagination to envision people of African descent as equal to those settlers of the colony.

Political strategist, opinion writer and attorney Sophia A. Nelson encourages the reader to consider what this 400th moment should be about in 2019. She is admonishing the reader to use this text to enact *e pluribus unum*. She is honest about the divisions in America, based heavily in the legacy of enslavement and the tantalizing folklore of the Virginia colony, and the need for a collective will to bring America to embody the lofty language in America's sacred documents. She admonishes the reader to engage with each essay for a re-assessment of how America came to be, on the backs of African people, and to use this new knowledge to become a re-awakened, civically engaged populace. This is not a text for a bookshelf. It is a text with a social justice historiographical framework, to re-educate, liberate, and authorize the reader to change institutional and societal patterns of social, economic and political behavior initiated in 1619.

REFERENCES

Ani, M. (2007). *Let the Circle Be Unbroken: The implications of African spirituality in the Diaspora*. New York: Nkonimfo Publications.

Beckley, J.R. (2008). How cultural factors hastened the population decline of the Powhatan Indians (Master's Thesis, Virginia Commonwealth University).

Chambers, H. (2013). Slavery, free blacks and citizenship, *Rutgers Law Journal*, 43, 487–513.
Davis, K.E. (2014). Social work's commitment to social justice and social policy, In T. Bent-Goodley & K.E. Davis (eds.), (2004). *The color of social policy* (pp 229–241). Alexandria, VA: CSWE.
Dorman, J.F. (ed.) (2004). *Musters of the inhabitants of Virginia 1624/1625, in adventurers of purse and person: Virginia 1607/1624/5*. 4th Edition, Baltimore: Genealogical Publishing, Inc.
Guasco, M. (2014). *Slaves and Englishmen: Human bondage in the early modern Atlantic world*. Philadelphia: University of Pennsylvania Press.
Harris, R.L. (1982). Coming of age: The transformation of Afro-American historiography, *The Journal of Negro History*, 67, 2, 107–121.
Heywood, L. (2017). *Njina of Angola: Africa's warrior queen*. Cambridge, MA: Harvard University Press.
Hughes, L. (1926). *The Weary Blues*. New York: Knopf Books.
Moore, A. (2010). Cross-cultural perspectives on the creation of American dance, 1619–1950 (Master's Thesis, Hofstra University).
Mukhtar, H.Y., Kura, S.M., Abba, Y., & Ahmed, M.A. (2013). The slave trade, colonialism and Africa's underdevelopment. *International Journal of Innovative Research and Development*, 2(2), 220–228.
Nunn, N. (2008). The long-term effects of Africa's slave trades. *The Quarterly Journal of Economics*, 123(1), 139–176.
Prout, J. (2007). Reconstructing our national narrative: American historiography at a crosswords, *Madison Historical Review*, 4, 2, Retrieved on December 4, 2018, https://commons.lib.jmu.edu/mhr/vol4/iss1/2/?utm_source=commons.lib.jmu.edu%2Fmhr%2Fvol4%2Fiss1%2F2&utm_medium=PDF&utm_campaign=PDFCoverPages.
Roberts, D.E. (1996). Welfare and the problem of Black citizenship, *Faculty Scholarship*. 105, 1283, pp 1563–1602. Retrieved on December 3, 2018, http://scholarship.law.upenn.edu/faculty_scholarship/1283.
Rogers, J.A. (1980). 100 amazing facts about the negro with complete proof. Middletown, CT. Wesleyan University Press.
Sluiter, E. (1997). New light on the '20. and Odd Negroes' arriving in Virginia, August 1619. *William and Mary Quarterly*, 54, 2, 395–398.
Stensvaag, J.T. (Ed.) (1985). *Hampton, from the sea to the stars: 1610–1985*. Norfolk, VA: The Donning Company.
Van Sertima, I. (1976). *They came before Columbus: The African presence in ancient America*. New York: Random House.
Vaughan, A.T. (1972). Blacks in Virginia: A note on the first decade. *William and Mary Quarterly*, 29, 3, 469–478.

The "Middle Passage"
*The Enforced Migration of Africans Across the Atlantic**

PAUL E. LOVEJOY

A Defining Migration

The transatlantic movement of enslaved Africans to the different parts of the Americas was the defining migration of the Western Hemisphere after 1492, influencing all parts of the Atlantic world, from western Europe to the Pacific shores of the Americas. The resulting migration created the African Diaspora, as it has become known. The settlement of Africans and the history of their descendants included many people who were in fact of mixed racial background, incorporating people of European and Amerindian background, and more recently people of Asian background as well. Between 1500 and 1860, about 12 million people are known to have left the shores of Africa destined for the Americas, and to a much lesser extent to Europe, although not everyone made it alive, and some died soon after arrival. Despite heavy loss of life during what has been called the "Middle Passage," many more Africans crossed the Atlantic than Europeans. The transportation of enslaved Africans constituted the largest single migration of people before the middle of the nineteenth century. From the sixteenth to the nineteenth centuries, the great majority of people moving from the Old World to the New World were black people. When gender is taken into consideration, then it can be said that far more black girls and women were forcibly taken to the Americas than the number of European girls and women who migrated, at least before the middle of the nineteenth century.

---

*This work was originally published in 2005–2007 by ProQuest LLC. The actual publication cannot be traced nor any proof of copyright identified. Although the copyright cannot be traced, this disclaimer fully acknowledges the original publication.

It follows, therefore, that the immigrant women who mothered America were disproportionately of African descent, and that they came under conditions of slavery, and not voluntary migration. While there is considerable debate over attempts to estimate the number of enslaved Africans who crossed the Atlantic, the broad parameters of this massive demographic movement are well understood, in large part because of a concerted effort of scholars to track every voyage that took Africans to the Americas (Eltis, Behrendt, Richardson, and Klein, 1999—it should be noted that this database is being expanded; also see Eltis, 2001). W.E.B. Du Bois recognized the basic problem of estimating the number of people in his pioneering Harvard dissertation of 1895 (Du Bois, 1895). Subsequently Philip D. Curtin reviewed the stereotypes and guesses that had characterized the study of the slave migration, demonstrating the possibilities of reasonably accurate estimates, despite warnings by David Henige of the inevitable difficulties of using incomplete and often inaccurate information (Curtin, 1969; Henige, 1986; also see Inikori, 1981, pp. 10–22). The trade lasted about 400 years, from the late fifteenth century until the middle of the nineteenth century. As shown in Table I, which charts the movement of 11.3 million people of the estimated 12 million who left Africa, it can be seen that the demographic movement was largely confined to the period 1700–1860 with over half (53.8 percent) of all Africans transported across the Atlantic in the eighteenth century, and another 30.6 percent transported in the nineteenth century.

Table I: Slave Exports from Africa: The Atlantic Migration

Period	*Number of Enslaved Africans Identified*	*Percent*
1450–1600	409,000	3.6
1601–1700	1,348,000	11.9
1701–1800	6,090,000	53.8
1801–1867	3,466,000	30.6
Total Known Population	11,313,000	

Source: Paul E. Lovejoy, Transformations in Slavery: A History of Slavery in Africa *(Lovejoy, 2000a, p. 19).*

That is, the number of people in the first 200 years or so of this migration was relatively small, with less than four percent of the total number of people moved before 1600, and about 12 percent moved in the seventeenth century, and much of this number transported in the late seventeenth century. The vast majority of enslaved Africans crossed the Atlantic from the last two decades of the seventeenth century through the middle of the nineteenth century, a period of 170 years. Undoubtedly, these estimates will be revised, but it is unlikely that the revisions will alter the conclusion that the overwhelming majority of Africans came to the Americas after 1700.

In the context of the transatlantic migration of enslaved Africans, the size and significance of immigration to North America has to be kept in perspective. For the transatlantic trade as a whole, for an estimated 11.8 million people who were sent into slavery from Africa, less than one twentieth (or five percent) of the total reaching the Americas came to what is now the United States. Ten times as many went to Brazil alone, with the Caribbean islands receiving about the same numbers. Nonetheless, the number of people today who trace African ancestry in the United States is so large that it can seem as if the size of the initial migration was much larger than was actually the case.

In order to understand the movement of such a large population across the Atlantic, it is essential to recognize that it was initiated by European countries, although the migration could not have taken place without the cooperation and full involvement of African countries. Otherwise there would not have been a migration in which there were many more Africans than Europeans in the early centuries of the colonization of the Americas, including North America. Moreover, how else can it be explained that many more African females arrived in the Americas than European women than by looking for African reasons as well as European designs, for it is African women who were most crucial in the demographic growth of the Americas. Among immigrants, African women more likely mothered the generations born in the Americas before the end of the nineteenth century than European women, because there were more African women than European women before the large-scale migration of Europeans after the middle of the nineteenth century.

Table II: Proportion of Females Among Enslaved Africans Crossing the Atlantic (Percent)

Region	1651–1675	1676–1700	1701–1725	1726–1750	1751–1775	1776–1800	1801–1825	1826–1850	1851–1867
Senegambia	—	27.0	31.0	21.3	37.8	31.6	46.8	32.6	—
Sierra Leone	—	23.2	31.9	—	41.4	34.8	32.0	28.1	—
Windward Coast	—	—	—	39.7	38.4	33.0	26.3	25.7	—
Gold Coast	42.7	46.8	32.9	32.2	37.9	34.2	28.1	28.7	—
Bight of Benin	41.3	41.0	36.0	40.8	46.2	34.3	24.3	34.9	27.7

Region	1651–1675	1676–1700	1701–1725	1726–1750	1751–1775	1776–1800	1801–1825	1826–1850	1851–1867
Bight of Biafra	50.3	41.1	48.3	24.6	39.9	42.6	35.0	34.3	—
West Central	—	40.1	26.2	32.8	32.5	35.2	29.1	26.8	24.7
South East Africa	—	—	—	47.3	—	28.5	30.5	19.4	13.2
Origin Unknown	38.5	40.6	34.5	33.6	43.4	30.1	31.3	24.8	27.3
Average	45.0	41.3	33.9	33.8	38.5	45.1	31.2	31.7	24.5

Data derived from: David Eltis, Stephen Behrendt, David Richardson, and Herbert Klein, The Atlantic Slave Trade: A Database on CD-Rom *(Eltis et al., 1999)*

As Table II demonstrates, there were many more African males taken to the Americas than females, whether women or girls. Slave traders generally tried to get twice as many males as females, but their ability to attain these quotas varied over time and over geographical regions of the African coast. In the earliest periods, when the numbers of Africans crossing the Atlantic were relatively few, the proportion of females was very high, between 41 and 45 percent, but for the first two-thirds of the eighteenth century the proportion was about one-third, and in the nineteenth century it was even less, perhaps 31 percent. In the last quarter of the eighteenth century, when the slave trade was at its height, the proportion of females was about 45 percent, as in the early period (Eltis and Engerman, 1992; Eltis and Engerman, 1993; Geggus, 1989).

Moreover, an analysis of where girls and women came from overwhelmingly shows that they were from areas close to the Atlantic coast, especially in the cases of the Bight of Biafra, the Bight of Benin before about 1800, the region of Sierra Leone, and the Angola and Congo regions of west central Africa. Hence the mothers of the generations of blacks born in the Americas usually came from coastal areas of Atlantic Africa rather than from the interior.

Regional Origins of the Migration

The regional origins of the enslaved population in Africa are outlined in Table III. The enslaved population came from all parts of the Atlantic coast of Africa, from Senegambia to southern Angola, and some enslaved people came from southeastern Africa, especially in the nineteenth century.

Table III: Regional Origins of Enslaved Africans Destined for the Americas (Sample Size: 7,911,688)

Region	1601–1650	1651–1700	1701–1750	1751–1800	1801–1850	1851–1867
Senegambia	536	17,836	54,714	139,977	30,440	—
Sierra Leone	—	2,834	4,962	132,378	66,076	898
Windward Coast	—	180	9,092	135,653	16,454	—
Gold Coast	82	35,478	155,631	345,886	80,597	—
Bight of Benin	519	134,219	374,509	399,630	209,612	12,795
Bight of Biafra	488	48,897	92,854	581,187	217,488	295
West Central	51,775	45,343	310,203	696,868	898,272	54,665
South East Africa	244	7,289	8,991	38,032	225,947	10,557
Origin Unknown	16,917	106,959	771,812	557,010	691,281	117,747
Total Sample	70,561	399,242	1,781,305	3,027,302	2,436,321	196,957

Data derived from: David Eltis, Stephen Behrendt, David Richardson, and Herbert Klein, The Atlantic Slave Trade: A Database on CD-Rom *(Eltis et al., 1999).*

Based on records for about eight million people, there are some clear patterns that help to explain the probable cultural and ethnic backgrounds of the displaced population (for a discussion of ethnicity and the origins of enslaved Africans, see Lovejoy, 2002, pp. 9–42; Law, 1997b; Hair, 1967; Hall, 2005; Gomez, 1998; Bühnen, 1993). The most important feature of the demographic structure is the central role played by the west-central African regions of Angola and the Kingdom of Kongo. This region was important very early in the trade, when the numbers of Africans were relatively small by comparison with the period after the late seventeenth century, and west central Africa remained an important source of people until the end of the trade in the nineteenth century. Together, perhaps as many as 40–45 percent of all enslaved Africans came from this region, and since people in this area spoke one or another of the closely related Bantu languages, they shared many cultural features.

The second most important source of slaves was the region of the Bight of Benin (the "Slave Coast" of European accounts but often referred to as the "Mina" coast), stretching westward as far as the Gold Coast. But this area, unlike west central Africa, only became important at the end of the seventeenth century and was associated with the political history of various states in the interior of the Gold Coast and the Bight of Benin, including the Akan states (Akwamu, Asante, for example) and the Gbe states (Ouidah, Allada, and Dahomey). Moreover, by the end of the eighteenth century, large numbers of Yoruba also came from this region, especially as a result of the consolidation of Oyo in the interior. The Bight of Biafra—the region of the Niger River delta and the Cross River estuary—became important in the 1730s and remained a significant source of immigrants for the slave trade for about 100 years. Most of the people of this area were Igbo or spoke Igbo as a second language, although a significant minority of the people were Ibibio.

Other areas of the coast—Senegambia, Sierra Leone, the "Windward" Coast between Sierra Leone and the Gold Coast—were important at specific periods, usually relating to political events in the interior and along the coast. However, the total number of enslaved persons from these parts of western Africa was relatively small by comparison with the Bight of Benin, the Bight of Biafra, and west central Africa. Finally, the enslaved population from southeastern Africa was culturally and linguistically similar to other parts of Bantu Africa. It should be noted that the coastal origins of a large percentage of the enslaved population is unknown. However, circumstantial evidence allows for a reasonably accurate understanding of the ethnic and cultural backgrounds of the enslaved population.

As noted above, the proportion of males and females among the deported population is known with some precision, the ratio of two males for every female being the standard aim of many European slaving firms, although the proportions changed over time and by coastal region. Moreover, it is also possible to know the approximate age composition of the enslaved population. There were many children—meaning those below the age of puberty—but very few infants. As shown in Table IV, the number of children, and especially boys, increased over time, and many of the enslaved during the last decades of the trade were children.

Table IV: Proportion of Children Among the Enslaved Africans Crossing the Atlantic (Percent)

Region	1651–1675	1675–1700	1701–1725	1726–1750	1751–1775	1776–1800	1801–1825	1826–1850	1851–1867
Senegambia	—	5.4	9.1	12.0	30.2	16.7	25.7	19.7	—
Sierra Leone	—	7.3	6.5	—	34.3	25.5	41.1	41.9	—
Windward Coast	—	—	—	35.3	42.7	24.9	34.5	29.3	—
Gold Coast	6.4	8.8	17.5	15.1	21.4	19.4	38.0	46.2	—

Region	1651–1675	1675–1700	1701–1725	1726–1750	1751–1775	1776–1800	1801–1825	1826–1850	1851–1867
Bight of Benin	6.5	12.3	19.6	26.1	19.3	14.5	22.5	36.1	18.8
Bight of Biafra	12.8	9.7	23.9	18.4	34.3	19.7	29.7	39.3	—
West Central	—	19.8	24.5	32.1	30.4	18.3	41.0	52.9	41.6
South East Africa	—	—	—	—	—	29.6	47.0	62.4	—
Origin Unknown	9.1	18.1	22.9	23.7	27.1	34.5	46.0	29.6	—
Average	10.5	11.3	19.3	22.6	28.8	22.2	42.6	40.7	35.9

Data derived from: David Eltis, Stephen Behrendt, David Richardson, and Herbert Klein, The Atlantic Slave Trade: A Database on CD-Rom *(Eltis et al., 1999)*

The proportion of children was relatively small in the early period, before the great expansion in numbers after the end of the seventeenth century, being five to ten percent of the enslaved population for many places in the seventeenth and even the early eighteenth centuries. However, the proportion of children in the nineteenth century from both west central Africa and southeastern Africa was over 40 percent and in the last decades of the trade as high as 60 percent, and the greatest numbers were boys.

The Middle Passage

Many accounts describe the horrors of the notorious "Middle Passage." Conditions onboard ship were usually crowded; sickness was a major problem, killing many of the enslaved and the crews of the slave ships as well, and shortages of food and drinking water were chronic. Misjudgments in rations, weather problems, and slave resistance onboard ships could affect the length of the passage and the conditions of the people onboard. The conditions of the Middle Passage are best described by contemporary accounts, including the testimonies for the British Parliamentary Enquiry into the conditions of the slave trade in 1789—see the various testimonies in the *House of Commons Sessional Papers of the Eighteenth Century* (Lambert, 1975). Of the surviving memories, those of Olaudah Equiano (Equiano, 1789/1995) who was enslaved when he was 11 and shipped from the Bight of Biafra in 1754, and Mahommah Gardo Baquaqua (Law and Lovejoy, 2001), who left the Bight of Benin in 1845, are particularly graphic; the fictionalized rendition of the journey by Barry Unsworth in his award-winning novel, *Sacred Hunger*, is also included here (Unsworth, 1992).

Statistics on mortality during the crossing of the Atlantic demonstrate that death rates were very high.

Table V: Mortality Among the Enslaved Population of the Middle Passage (Percent)

Region	1601–1650	1651–1675	1676–1700	1701–1725	1726–1750	1751–1775	1776–1800	1801–1825	1826–1850	1851–1867
Senegambia	—	—	11.7	10.5	9.6	14.7	12.2	8.4	9.5	—
Sierra Leone	—	—	14.5	10.0	—	15.9	5.7	6.0	6.3	—
Windward Coast	—	—	—	—	6.0	13.0	4.4	2.5	7.1	—
Gold Coast	—	6.0	22.4	14.1	16.0	14.2	8.0	6.1	11.1	—
Bight of Benin	—	22.8	23.4	16.3	15.3	15.3	8.8	5.8	7.3	10.1
Bight of Biafra	—	—	32.9	35.3	42.1	22.8	14.5	16.0	15.8	—
West Central	29.2	—	13.3	13.6	10.7	9.3	7.0	7.6	6.9	13.1
South East Africa	—	—	—	26.0	—	—	27.5	21.0	13.9	30.4
Origin Unknown	16.4	17.7	27.2	13.6	18.5	14.1	15.7	16.5	22.8	20.6
Average	26.2	20.3	21.7	15.8	14.5	14.2	9.9	10.0	9.4	16.1

Data derived from: David Eltis, Stephen Behrendt, David Richardson, and Herbert Klein, *The Atlantic Slave Trade: A Database on CD-Rom (Eltis et al., 1999)*.

As revealed in Table V, the percentage of slaves onboard ship who died fluctuated considerably, depending upon the fortunes of individual ships, the part of the African coast from which the enslaved came, and the period under consideration. In general, death rates declined over time, as European slaving firms introduced some measures to lower the incidence of death—in the interest of profits, of course, because dead slaves were worth nothing. Death rates declined from approximately 26 percent of the people on the ships in the first half of the seventeenth century to 15 percent or so for much of the eighteenth century, declining to 10 percent or less at the height of the trade in the late eighteenth and early nineteenth centuries. Death rates increased again at the end of the slave trade because of efforts to stop the trade and the extra pressure that was put on slave merchants to get their human cargoes to the Americas. The Bight of Biafra and southeastern Africa sustained the highest death rates, in part because of the much longer voyages that were necessary to take slaves from these regions to the Americas. As can be seen from Table VI, the length of voyages varied considerably, but again, trips became shorter as time passed, and there were improvements in ship design and construction that made for faster sailing times.

Table VI: Length of the "Middle Passage" (Days and Half Days)

Region	1651–1675	1676–1700	1701–1725	1726–1750	1751–1775	1776–1800	1801–1825	1826–1850	1851–1867
Senegambia	—	43.5	47.5	41.5	54.5	42.5	52.5	36.5	—
Sierra Leone	—	55.5	45.5	74.5	58	43	45.5	40.5	—
Windward Coast	—	—	54.5	87	65	49.5	44	47	—
Gold Coast	—	82	68.5	94	85	67.5	48.5	30.5	—
Bight of Benin	100.5	91	84	107	120	89	42	36	45
Bight of Biafra	166	89	87	117.5	83.5	66	48	42	—
West Central	165	82	69	70.5	68	58	39	34	46
South East Africa	—	—	—	—	146	121	78.5	62	75
Origin Unknown	—	65.5	82	91.5	85	66	52	46	64
Average	133	78	74.5	87	80.5	64	51	39.5	49

Data derived from: David Eltis, Stephen Behrendt, David Richardson, and Herbert Klein, The Atlantic Slave Trade: A Database on CD-Rom *(Eltis et al., 1999).*

In the second half of the seventeenth century, it took an average of 133 days to cross the Atlantic from Africa, while in the first half of the eighteenth century it usually took 75–80 days, and then only 50–65 days in the last part of the century. In the period 1820–1850, the time was reduced to 40–50 days. The voyages from the Bight of Biafra in the period 1730s–1750s took almost 120 days, while traveling from southeastern Africa in the second half of the eighteenth century could take up to 146 days. The longer individuals were on the slave ships, in the terrible conditions that prevailed, the more likely they would die (for a discussion of mortality, see Klein and Engerman, 1997; Cohn, 1985; Curtin, 1968; Miller, 1980; Miller, 1988a; Miller, 1988b; Sheridan, 1981; Behrendt, 1993; Morgan, 1997).

Because many more female Africans crossed the Atlantic than European women, the "new" societies of the Americas, sometimes called "creole," were largely African in demographic structure. Even when the African component was not dominant, it was usually strong. In North America, the settlement of Europeans and Africans overlapped and were complementary with each other, but even so, the number of African women was still significant in terms of the impact on how they gave birth to the new generations. And it must be remembered that the Native American population, although suffering demographic loss of enormous proportions, nonetheless also contributed to the "new" societies of the Americas. Furthermore, people of African and Native American origins intermingled, generating composite and dynamic communities that owed little if anything to European influence. Most important, these migrations and the intermingling of populations involved individuals; they were people whose history, sometimes even on the individual level, can be known. The scale of the migration, and the tremendous suffering and the terrible destruction it entailed, should not disguise the importance of the individual experiences that went into the construction of the African diaspora and hence the development of the countries and societies of the Americas.

Enslaved Africans, therefore, were essential in the settling of the Americas after the demographic upheaval caused by the European conquest of the Americas. The movement of people of African descent to the Americas was a central dynamic of the resettlement of the Americas after the disastrous decline in the Native American population. As a slave migration, the African exodus was based on coercion and was not voluntary. The reliance on coercion and the perpetual threat of violence defined the African American experience within a colonial, exploitive setting. Africans, and their descendants, were subjected to layers of colonialism and victimization, being forcibly moved from Africa to the Americas and required to remain in the Americas as slaves for generations. Despite this oppression, the enslaved population managed to resist and otherwise survive bondage in numerous ways, from open revolt to sabotage to apparent collaboration. Individuals found ways to express themselves, and despite the oppressive conditions, Africans and their descendants reestablished old practices and formulated new communities in which religious expression, music, and folklore had a prominent role, prompting a series of cultural renaissances in Brazil, Cuba, and elsewhere.

Effects of Migration on the Americas

Based on coercion, the slave trade was a dynamic force in the development of colonialism in the Americas. The migration of Europeans, especially from England, France, Spain, and Portugal, and involving Catholics and Protestants, Christians and Jews, determined who would be sent to the Americas and therefore set the parameters of the African migration. At the time, people of European stock controlled all of the Americas but almost no parts of Africa, except in coastal Angola and Cape Town, South Africa. The principal population movements were across the Atlantic, and the settlement of the colonial territories in the Americas was by immigrants from the Old World, both Europe and Africa. The colonialism that emerged as a result of the international slave trade differed from the later colonial period in Africa. In the era of the international slave trade, European countries did not occupy Africa itself but instead purchased enslaved individuals and transported them to the Americas. That is, the slave trade enabled Europeans to take foreign peoples and forcibly resettle them as slaves.

The forced migration of Africans across the Atlantic was part of an important historical development that resulted in the consolidation of a single "world" around the Atlantic, including western Europe, western Africa, the Caribbean islands, and mainland North and South America. In its broadest outline, the emergence of this Atlantic world led to the dominance of Europe and the industrialization of northwestern Europe. Africans provided much of the labor for this emerging world order, especially in the production of tropical and cash crops and also in mining gold and silver, and in the transportation associated with producing these commodities. Slave labor was the mechanism by which those in political power and with access to economic resources could further amass wealth and influence. While some African merchants and political officials benefited from their cooperation in this concentration of wealth, in general wealth ultimately flowed into the hands of the political and economic elites of Europe, and the benefits to African merchants and officials were incidental. Hence the overwhelming impact of involvement in the rise of the modern Atlantic world was negative for Africa—a loss of population, particularly the able-bodied, and relatively marginal commercial gains for a small elite.

The movement of enslaved Africans to North America was part of a broader context of African migration in the Atlantic world and the emergence of what has been called "Atlantic Africa" or the "Black Atlantic"—for the initial conception, see Paul Gilroy's *The Black Atlantic* (Gilroy, 1993). The experiences of African Americans in North America had similarities and differences from the broader history of the "Black Atlantic," notably in relation to the origins of people and the timing of their arrival and therefore the nature of the cultural and social impact of Africans on the development of North America. Although the North American experience of Africans and their descendants was unique in time and place, enslaved

Africans were also common in the Islamic world, including the Sahara, North Africa, and the Middle East. They were found on the islands of the Indian Ocean, as well as in Persia and Muslim India, and they were known throughout Europe, as far as Russia. These markets for enslaved Africans depended upon commercial networks into Africa that enabled the evacuation of the enslaved and the importation of commodities needed for the exchange. The internal political and social conditions within the continent of Africa allowed the enslavement of people and their sale and exploitation, whether locally or through export to distant lands. That the international slave trade to North America was part of the much larger slave trade, therefore, must be kept in mind in assessing the impact of slavery on Africa and Africans. Moreover, the role of Indian textiles, cowrie shells as a currency, and the relationship between Hispanic America and Asia in the flow of silver, raise questions about the extent to which the Atlantic world was part of the whole world.

The first encounters between western Europe and western Africa set the stage for the development of the Atlantic slave trade. We can trace the origins of the Atlantic trade to the fifteenth century, and the movement of Portuguese ships down the Atlantic coast of Africa in an effort to bypass Muslim–dominated North Africa and access gold, spices, and other commodities wanted in Europe. Atlantic trade grew out of the confrontation between Christian Europe and Islamic North Africa and the Middle East, which led to maritime discoveries and technological improvements in shipping that made the Atlantic more easily navigable. For the first 100–150 years of European trade on the Atlantic coast of Africa, the slave trade was marginal, both in terms of the number of enslaved people who were taken to Europe and then, after the middle of the sixteenth century, increasingly to the Americas. Initially, Portuguese shipping was involved in the transport of a variety of trade commodities, and enslaved Africans were only one of these. Other European countries, especially England and the Netherlands, became involved early, but primarily as pirates preying on Portuguese shipping and raiding the mainland of Africa. Early concentration of European activity was confined to Senegambia (in the interior in the regions of Bure and Bambuhu) and also on the Gold Coast because of the presence of gold. The Portuguese also developed commercial and diplomatic relations with the Kingdom of Benin and the Kingdom of Kongo, initially on the basis of equality, and only after considerable time was this relationship transformed. The Kingdom of Kongo, which became Christian, was tied to and eventually undermined by Portugal and the infectious spread of slave trading, while the Kingdom of Benin moved to restrict Portuguese influence and limited the extent of the slave trade.

Organization of the Slave Trade

The organization of the trade changed over the course of time but can be divided into three periods: 1450–1650, 1650–1807, and 1807–1867. The first period was formative and dominated by the Portuguese. The second period, from the middle of the seventeenth century until the abolition of the slave trade in 1807 by Britain and in 1808 by the United States, witnessed the rise of the plantation economies of the Caribbean, and was dominated first by the Dutch and then the French and the British. This was the period of greatest and most extensive exploitation of enslaved African labor. In the final period, after British and American abolition, enslaved Africans went primarily to Cuba, Puerto Rico, and Brazil. The slave trade continued among the islands in the Caribbean, and within the United States, after the ending of the "legal" transatlantic slave trade, and hence the demographic impact of the trade continued well into the nineteenth century, even though direct arrivals of enslaved Africans from Africa was confined almost entirely to Cuba, Puerto Rico, and Brazil.

The Portuguese dominated the first period. Some slaves were moved along the shores of western Africa, for retention and use within Africa, and some were taken to Portugal and Spain. Already by the 1490s, before Columbus reached the Caribbean, one tenth of the population of Lisbon, then one of the largest cities in Europe, was of African origin. Other slaves were taken to islands off the African shore, including the Madeiras, the Cape Verde, and especially the island of São Thomé, where the Portuguese established sugar plantations using enslaved labor on a scale that foreshadowed the development of plantation slavery in the Americas. Enslaved Africans were already being taken to the Americas; they were part of every expedition into the regions that became the Spanish colonies, and after the 1540s they were taken to Portuguese Brazil to grow sugar, as they had been doing on São Thomé. The Spanish used Africans to grow sugar on Hispañola, and to mine for gold as well; and they were forced to drain the shallow lakes of the Mexican plateau, completing the subjugation of the Aztecs.

Sugarcane was introduced into Hispañola and then Brazil in the sixteenth century, thereby jumping the Atlantic as part of an exchange of food crops and commodities that increased demand for tropical goods and therefore the need for labor. In all these activities, enslaved Africans were used as a principal source of labor, as well as sometime military employment. The transfer of sugarcane was the most important development and would lead to the enslavement of millions of Africans, but many other crops, including indigo, rice, tobacco, coffee, cocoa, and cotton were introduced, with varying degrees of success but always with the input of enslaved African labor. However, before the middle of the seventeenth century, the total number of enslaved Africans that were taken away from western Africa was relatively small, especially in comparison with the great expansion in slavery thereafter. Even in this early period, however, the number of enslaved Africans being forced to cross the Atlantic was greater, by far, than the numbers of Europeans voluntarily doing so.

In this early period, before about 1650, the regions in Africa that were affected by the demand for slaves were relatively restricted, and consequently the corresponding impact was limited. Nonetheless, the impact was real, and it was connected with important developments in western Africa. Slaves came from the far-western coast, in the area of the Senegal and Gambia Rivers, often referred to as "Senegambia." Culturally and linguistically unified via Islam and Manding culture and language, the region had an ancient and glorious history, centered on the ancient kingdom of Ghana and the medieval empires of Mali and Songhay. The early history of Atlantic Africa is closely tied with the history of these empires in the interior of Senegambia, because of the gold trade. West African gold was the principal source of gold for the Islamic lands of North Africa and also for western Europe before the exploitation of gold from the Americas after approximately 1500. In West Africa, gold reached the Mediterranean and hence Europe from Songhay, having been obtained in the headwaters of Senegambia, in Bure and Bambuhu, and also in the Volta basin, south of Jenne and Timbuktu. The arrival of the Portuguese on the Gold Coast in the 1470s tapped these inland sources and gave the coast its name, while the other sources of gold were accessible to the Portuguese along the Senegambian coast. Gold, not slaves, was the quest, but any trade was developed, including malaguetta pepper that would not last long as a delicacy of the European market (it was replaced instead by black pepper from Asia).

By the middle of the seventeenth century, the demand for labor in the Americas was expanding rapidly, and this demand increasingly meant enslaved African labor. The corresponding impact on Africa was intensified as more parts of western Africa were brought into the orbit of transatlantic slavery. This second period lasted until 1807–1808, when the British and Americans abolished the slave trade, thereby beginning a period of contraction in the use of slave labor and the eventual emancipation of those in slavery in the Americas. Inevitably, this demand, and the opportunities provided by attempting to supply that demand, resulted in numerous innovations, encouraged opportunists and entrepreneurs, and resulted in deceptions and barbarities, upon which the slave trade ultimately rested.

There were African collaborators in the slave trade, in addition to the elites and thieves who managed to enslave people in wars and through judicial actions and corruption. Merchants made money from slavery, and they invested in slaves, even marrying or taking as concubines women they had bought or otherwise acquired as gifts. These profiteers were collaborators in the international slave trade, relying on enslavement and its threat as mechanisms of social control in hierarchical regimes dominated by Muslim and non–Muslim men. There were religious brotherhoods in the Islamic lands and in diasporic Muslim communities and other secret societies of the most powerful, which were able to interpret their actions and decrees in religious form that related to ancestral rights and the domain of gods. Wherever the transatlantic slave touched western Africa, there were men, and a few women, ready to profit through deception and clever organization. Control of trade was a serious issue, tied to political control.

The final period of the transatlantic trade in humans lasted until the 1860s. In this period, Brazil, Cuba, and Puerto Rico were the principal destinations for enslaved Africans, since slaves could no longer legally be brought into North America, British or French colonies in the Caribbean, or the independent countries of Spanish America. Despite this restricted market, the numbers of enslaved Africans did not decline until the late 1840s. The trade raged on, despite efforts of British anti-slave-trade patrols and the efforts of abolitionists to expose abuses and thereby close the trade down. The dominant issues in Africa related the jihads of West Africa and the resulting turmoil in the affected coastal regions as well as the impact of the demand for slaves on the turbulent polities of Bantu Africa, both inland from Angola and from Mozambique. This later impact affected the distribution of children and youth, with the propulsion of boys into the external trade, largely to Brazil but also to Cuba, and the retention of girls in the rapidly expanding households of specific "ethnic" groups such as the Cokwe and Yao.

As this overview of the three periods of the slave trade suggests, there were distinct national trades, in which specific western European countries dominated or otherwise established a niche. Moreover, within the various European countries one or two ports tended to monopolize the trade, which demonstrates a concentration in insider knowledge about trade, since the principal merchants knew each other. Similarly, on the African side, most slaves were traded in only a few ports. Of these, Luanda in Angola, Ouidah (Whydah) in the Bight of Benin, Bonny in the Bight of Biafra, and the adjacent trade "castles" at Koromatin and Winneba on the Gold Coast, stand out as the points of departure for the greatest number of enslaved Africans bound for the Americas; these points probably accounted for at least one-third of all Africans sent to the Americas. Other major ports included Old Calabar in the Bight of Biafra; Benguela in southern Angola; Cabinda, to the north of the Congo River; and Lagos, important in the Bight of Benin in the nineteenth century. These ports of departure accounted for more than half of all the enslaved Africans who were sent to the Americas.

The trade, and the way in which the transport of enslaved Africans to the Americas was funneled through relatively few ports that were controlled by relatively few merchants, whether in Europe, Africa, or the Americas, has important implications. The experiences of individuals, including what they were exposed to, the types of information to which they had access, and the cultural and personal bonds that were established and recognized even before boarding ships for the Americas must be considered. While enslaved individuals came from widely different backgrounds, and the number of "ethnic groups" and identifying markers were extensive, certain ethnicities and languages, usually in pidgin and creolized forms, as well as religion, were maintained, sometimes exaggerated and manipulated, but always interpreted in the context of adjustments to slave life in the Americas.

Patterns of Cultural Continuity

These patterns of cultural and historical continuity and rupture can be discerned because people reached the Americas as commodities. The records of this trade are extensive and revealing. There were various national companies, sanctioned by royal decree and parliamentary order; there were private companies; and there were merchants who could turn into pirates. A portion of the trade was nominally covered by the Spanish *asiento*, which gave monopoly rights to companies to transport slaves to the Spanish colonies. The trade involved much smuggling, as well as the fulfillment of contracts. The English trade was handled through the Royal African Company, but interlopers undermined the monopoly. Ships from Bristol and especially Liverpool came to dominate the British trade in the eighteenth century; they not only challenged the interests of the Royal African Company and London in the establishments on the Gold Coast and in the Gambia, but the new merchants also opened up markets, especially in the Bight of Biafra and the northern Angola coast. Each country, and each port, experimented in an effort to win a share of the trade. Sometimes this competition required the maintenance of trading depots, often called factories or trading castles, which was the case on the Gold Coast and in the Bight of Benin, as well as in the less important ports along the upper Guinea coast and in Senegambia. The rule of thumb seems to have been the availability or likely access to gold. European establishments were not found in the Niger Delta or the Cross River, both in the Bight of Biafra, where gold was not available.

The credit that ran the trade tended to flow outward from Europe; that is, European merchants came to West Africa, and in order to buy enslaved people, they had to do it by providing credit. This credit was on goods advanced in lieu of payment in slaves. There were considerable risks involved in trade. In the first place, there were risks because the commodity in question was human, and humans had agency that could result in flight, assassination, suicide, or other calamity for the owner. People could disappear with the goods and never produce what was stated in the contract—slaves. There were also risks because trade was across political and cultural frontiers in which recourse to courts and governments in the event of commercial dishonesty and loss was less than perfect. There was no international court or diplomatic system that could handle abuses of trade, let alone the violations of human rights involved in slavery itself.

The trade was important in terms of the development of modern, capitalist institutions and practices, from modern banking to insurance. Lloyd's of London became a major insurance company in the course of doing business with slave traders, as well as anyone else willing to pay/play the rates. One of the best sources for knowledge of the British slave trade is the records kept by Lloyd's. Technical advances and increasingly sophisticated commercial and banking practices were developed in the slave ports of Europe—Lisbon, Amsterdam, London, Nantes, Liverpool, and Bristol. The merchants who were involved were centered at the major European ports, where credit flowed and the commodities of trade were available. These merchants in the European ports came from a variety of backgrounds themselves, featuring upstart entrepreneurs, diasporic Huguenots, Jews, "New Christians" (Jews or Moors recently converted to Christianity), and Scots. Individuals moved into the margins, hoping to survive and make money. There was a fine line between piracy, entrepreneurship, kidnapping, and slave driving.

In order to guarantee that commercial contracts would be honored, European merchants resorted to a variety of measures, some of them experimental and sometimes tied to African institutions and practices that shaped the commercial exchange in ways that were not recognized in other parts of the Atlantic world. There were local taxes and customs that had to be honored. For example, in some places, such as Old Calabar and in the minor ports of the upper Guinea coast, European ship captains accepted human beings, often relatives of local merchants and officials, as collateral for credit; these were human pawns that could be enslaved if debts were not paid (Lovejoy and Richardson, 2001). In other places, such as in Angola and Senegambia, European merchants married or otherwise cohabited with local women, who sometimes amassed considerable fortunes as agents and merchants in their own right. Their offspring, mulatto and sometimes using Portuguese or other European names, became an intermediate class of merchants along the coast, especially concentrated along the upper Guinea coast as far as Senegambia and in Luanda, Benguela, and their commercial outposts in the interior of Angola.

The principal goods of trade sent to Africa in exchange for slaves can be divided into three groups: items used as money, such as cowries, strips of cloth, iron bars, copper bracelets called "manilas," and even silver coins and gold; consumer goods, especially textiles, alcohol, and a great range of items used as jewelry; and military wares. In general, these imports did not replace African production but rather supplemented output. The import of money increased circulation in the market and therefore tended to promote trade in all goods, not just slaves. Since many of the monies were in fact commodities that had other uses as well, their commodity value could also be realized. Hence, cloth strips, imported via Europe from India, were used as currency in Senegambia, along with gold and other mediums, but the cloth could be and was made into clothing. Local textile production was not undermined; people just had more cloth. The demand for textiles seems to have been virtually inexhaustible, and the more variety the better. Similarly, iron was fashioned into small hoe-shaped pieces of money in the interior of Sierra Leone, but the money could be combined and used to make real hoes or any other iron implement. Even cowries could be strung into necklaces and used to adorn hair, costumes, and baskets. But their principal use remained the role as money, which was acquired through the exchange for slaves.

Military wares, especially firearms, were sometimes important, especially in the nineteenth century and in places such as the Gold Coast in the eighteenth century. However, the importance of the guns in enslavement can be exaggerated. Before the nineteenth century, firearms were not always that effective, especially in tropical areas where the problem of keeping powder dry was serious. Firearms were important on the Gold Coast in the crucial wars of the eighteenth century that enslaved many people and eventually resulted in the political ascendancy of Asante. Firearms were not significant in the rise of Oyo as the dominant slaving power in the interior of the neighboring area inland from the Bight of Benin. Oyo relied on its cavalry and the relative military advantage horses gave in a region in which horses had to be imported from further inland via Oyo's commercial partners. The export of slaves enabled the import of money, in the form of cowries, and consumer goods, especially textiles, for reexport inland for horses. Imported textiles did not replace or otherwise undermine local production of textiles, which was a major industry throughout the interior and often used imported fabrics as a source of thread for embroidery on locally produced cloth.

Alcohol was an important item of trade in Angola, and it was a luxury almost everywhere. Although Muslims were not a significant market, and indeed shunned alcohol, the coastal elites wanted Brazilian rum and French brandies. These were even sent into the interior but usually diluted with distance. Nonetheless, as with many textiles, alcohol was an imported item for conspicuous consumption. There were local alternatives, but the issue was not one of substitution, only cumulative effect. As with textiles, where people wore more clothing if they could afford it, other people drank more if they could afford it. The slave trade was demand driven; people who could afford it wanted labor and did not care how the labor was obtained. The trade was also greed driven. Individuals became involved because they could benefit, from theft, plunder, kidnapping, ransoming, and the sale of humans as commodities. Such an approach to acquisition means that people took advantage of political misfortune, religious differences, legal technicalities, economic crisis, and outright callousness to exploit individuals who were helpless. Such a realization returns us to the specific circumstances of enslavement, the events and places where the reduction to slavery was achieved.

The specific events in Africa that resulted in the transportation of Africans to the Americas and the corresponding methods of enslavement fall into different categories. One category involves war, slave raiding, and political struggle, which probably accounted for the great majority of those who were enslaved and taken to the Americas. Among the most important wars that resulted in massive enslavement, including the export of war prisoners to the Americas, the ransoming of prisoners, and the use of captives as slaves within Africa itself, included the Akan wars of the late seventeenth and first half of the eighteenth centuries that grew out of a power struggle among various states in the hinterland of the Gold Coast, including Akwamu, Akyem, Denkyira, Fante, and Asante, with Asante emerging as the dominant state. Similarly, the consolidation of Oyo as an imperial power after 1650 involved wars with the Bariba and Nupe to the north and other Yoruba states to the south (see, for example, van Dantzig, 1975; Law, 1978). War also affected the balance of power among the various Gbe groups, leading to the emergence of Allada as a small kingdom on the lagoons behind the coast, and the rise of Dahomey in the early eighteenth century. Dahomey defeated Allada in 1724, occupied the port of Ouidah in 1727, and was in turn forced to pay tribute to Oyo thereafter. These wars accounted for the deportation of many people along the coast of the Bight of Benin.

The Kongo civil wars that lasted intermittently from about 1680 through 1740 also caused instability that led to the enslavement of many people who were deported to the Americas. One group of victims included the followers of the Antonian martyr, Beatrice of Kongo, who tried to end the civil wars through pacifist protest, but with tragic consequences. Yet another series of wars related to the spread of militant Islam across West Africa began in the Senegambia region in the late seventeenth century. These wars marked the emergence of Futa Jallon as a jihad state in the highlands of modern Guinea and the foundation of Futa Toro on the Senegal River in the late eighteenth century. The jihad movement continued into the nineteenth century, especially with the outbreak of war in 1804 in the Hausa states under the leadership of Sheikh Usman dan Fodio. These wars in turn exacerbated political tensions in Oyo, which resulted in a Muslim uprising and the collapse of the Oyo state between 1817 and 1833. One of the consequences of this collapse was the migration southward of refugees, the founding of new strongholds, and intensified warfare among those attempting to resurrect or otherwise replace the collapsed Oyo state. The most notable of these new centers (Ibadan, Abeokuta, and Ijebu) periodically engaged in hostilities even after the end of the transatlantic trade in slaves in the 1860s.

In addition to these major upheavals, there are many examples of more localized fighting and warfare all along the Atlantic coast, and sometimes European powers intervened on one side or another, often with the aim of obtaining slaves directly in the encounters or indirectly through the political rewards expected for military assistance. In Angola, moreover, Portugal established a permanent colony at Luanda in the 1590s, and later at other points along the Angolan coast, especially at Benguela in the south. The permanent military presence of Portugal was reflected in alliances and joint military ventures with allies in the interior, with the result that Portugal—more than any other European country—was actually directly involved in the enslavement of Africans. Unlike in Angola, the other wars that produced captives for the slave trade almost always involved African rivals, with little if any direct European participation. Nonetheless, the importation of firearms was an important contributing factor to the intensity of many of the wars and therefore must be recognized as a factor in the increased numbers of people who were enslaved, especially after 1700 (Miller, 2001, pp. 21–69; Thornton, 1980).

There were also people enslaved as a result of judicial and religious sanctions and punishment that removed criminals and social misfits, or those deemed to be so, from society through enslavement and banishment. In many places people were used as pawns in credit arrangements, and while those people being held were almost always protected from enslavement by relatives and customary practices that guaranteed the safety of such dependents, there were nonetheless situations in which the arrangements were not honored, and pawned individuals, especially children, were "sold" or otherwise removed from the watchful eyes of relatives and communities. Similarly, there are cases of relatives and other members of communities who for one reason or another were deemed rebellious or uncooperative and were therefore expelled from their homes through enslavement.

Inevitably, there were serious issues of trying to justify enslavement in Africa. People tried to protect their own communities, and various governments and institutions developed means and policies to limit the impact of slavery. Kin were particularly worried about enslavement through kidnapping, which in most places was considered illegal. Also, Muslims were concerned about protecting the freedom of their co-religionists; those who had been born free were supposed to remain so, although that was not always the case. Sometimes captives were ransomed and thereby avoided enslavement, but such actions only encouraged the taking of prisoners in order to obtain the ransom. People, whether Muslims or not, tried to safeguard their own but tragically were not always able to do so.

As a result of these pressures, the slave trade, including the transatlantic trade especially, had a dramatic impact on Africa, which can be seen on the personal, family, communal, and continental levels. Various biographical accounts have survived that demonstrate the trauma of enslavement and the corresponding impact on the families of the enslaved. Mahommah Gardo Baquaqua, who was enslaved in the interior of the Bight of Benin in the early 1840s, was ransomed once by his family, only to be enslaved another time, spirited to the coast, and sold to Brazil. His older brother had earlier been enslaved, but he was more fortunate and was also ransomed by his kin. The impact is clear: it cost this family a lot of money to protect its own, and then not fully successfully. Similarly, in many places in western Africa, the level of insecurity that could lead to enslavement increased in response to the pressures of the transatlantic trade in enslaved Africans. The demographic impact of the slave trade on Africa was severe, especially in those areas most fully drawn into the orbit of transatlantic slavery. The death and destruction from war and kidnapping was extensive, as far as can be deduced from the examples that have survived. The old and the very young were often killed or left to starve in the famines that often followed the destruction of military action. Moreover, among those who were enslaved or held for ransom, mortality rates appear to have been high, because people were force-marched long distances. Since many of those who were enslaved were destined to remain in Africa or to be sent across the Sahara to North Africa rather than to the Americas, the full impact of the slave trade and slavery in Africa was even more severe.

It must be emphasized that slavery intrinsically calls forth resistance. Distinctions can be made between moments of open rebellion and the apparent willingness to acquiesce in servitude to avoid punishment or to obtain minor rewards as inducements for appropriate behavior. Resistance also includes expressions of community and coordinated activity, whether expressed through music, dance, religion, belief, food, or language. Resistance implies agency and identity and therefore highlights the individual and group responses to slavery. In North America, the experiences of enslaved Africans and their descendants manifested resistance through flight, uprising, and murder. The African population coalesced around several religious traditions that had been transferred from Africa and succumbed to the Christian evangelical movements of the late eighteenth century that swept England and North America. The presence of *obeah*, *vodun*, and even Islam reflect the persistence of African traditions in the face of slavery. Musically, there can be no question of the enduring African heritage related to the expressions of the oppressed, their religion, and culture.

Migration

The causes of the migration can be traced to internal African political and social conditions in those parts of western Africa where the enslaved trace their origins. Of course, the European demand for labor for the development of the modern Atlantic world in which European countries, especially Portugal, Spain, Britain, France, and the Netherlands, transported enslaved Africans to their American colonies, was essential. Without that demand, there could not have been a transatlantic slave trade, but there also had to be a willingness to sell, which was related to politics, greed, and power. But that does not explain the willingness of European countries to allow the exploitation of people who were perceived to be different and to allow a racist ideology, nor does it absolve those who participated in the exploitation of people as slaves for any reason and whatever the conditions.

However, to understand how this happened, one must examine the conditions in Africa.

First, let us look at the internal political and social conditions in Atlantic Africa, which requires a brief historical overview of the sections of the African coast from where the enslaved traced their origins, from Senegambia in the northwest, south along the Guinea coast to the Bights of Benin and Biafra, and south further along the Loango coast to Kongo and Angola. The political map reveals a dominant pattern for this broad stretch of coast from the sixteenth to the mid-nineteenth centuries—the whole period of the transatlantic slave trade—and that pattern is one of small, centralized states and local federations that governed through secret societies. Even the largest states, such as Asante and Oyo, were reasonably small by modern standards. The consequence of this political fragmentation was the failure to generate methods of government to resist the slave trade. Personal gain and the interests of a small elite supported the slave trade. It is not surprising that the slave trade was closely associated with the political wars of these states and benefited the commercial elites that dominated the trade routes, ports, and secret societies of the federated regions where centralized state institutions were lacking.

The migrating populations can be identified as having their homes in western Africa, from a broad belt along the Atlantic from Senegambia to Angola. The overwhelming majority of enslaved Africans came from two stretches of coast; about nine out of every ten people came either from the region of modern Ghana through Nigeria, known then as the Gold Coast, the Slave Coast or the Bight of Benin, and the Bight of Biafra, or they came from the coast to the north and south of the Congo River in what is today Congo and Angola. There were some enslaved Africans who came from what are now Sierra Leone, Guinea, Senegal, and the interior regions behind the coast, but they were a small minority of the total migration. The presence of Muslims, often known as Mandingo, is widely known, as is also the presence of Bambara in Louisiana, and rice cultivators from upper Guinea in lowland Carolina, who were brought from the upper Guinea coast and Sierra Leone.

Africans in North America

Hence, the origins of the North American population of Africans can be traced to all the regions of Atlantic Africa. Aside from Mandingos and Bambaras, there were Igbo from the Bight of Biafra who were found in the upper South, while Kongo from the Angola/Congo region were found in all parts of North America. Because of the demographic study of the slave trade, we now have a relatively clear idea of when people came to North America from Africa, from where on the African coast they left, their numbers, the ports of disembarkation, and the relative proportions of men, women, and children and how these figures changed over time. From such information and its correlation with known historical events and contexts in Atlantic Africa, it is possible to impute and sometimes to substantiate through recorded experiences of individuals, the processes and, indeed, the events that account for the actual people who were enslaved and sold to the Americas.

Biographical material exists in many forms and is scattered throughout the diaspora. North America stands out because of the richness of available texts—narratives by and about individuals, some of whom were actually born in Africa, but more often were of the second generation, but who nonetheless continue traditions from their African background.

The principal conditions shaping the forced migration of those who ended up as the black slaves of America related to violence and the threat of violence, from the time of enslavement until death, whether along a trade route, onboard a slave ship, or on a plantation in the Americas. Violence could also, and often did, assume sexual dimensions, rape being common. Sexual violence was extended in Islamic lands to castration, but there was essentially no difference in the ways in which women, and boys onboard ship, were treated—the sexual and personal identity of the individual was denied and only existed for the pleasure of the slave owner or his proxy. Avoidance of violence and resistance to violence were therefore determining characteristics of the responses of the enslaved Africans to the experiences of migration. Individuals attempted to avoid violence through varying degrees of accommodation and co-option that complicates the story of how people resisted bondage.

The types of violence that Africans who were enslaved actually experienced can be classified by context. It appears that a great number of individuals were enslaved in war, either because they were engaged in the actual conflict as soldiers or were civilians captured as the spoils of victory. States and secret societies also organized raids and seizures that resulted in enslavement that suggests degrees and forms of government and hence also can be classified as "political," since such actions may disguise enforcement of law, collection of taxes, or abuse of public office. Manipulation of law, legal procedure, and religious sanction in the form of enslavement also represents a form of public and hence customary, if not constitutional, will. In some cases, those people held as collateral for a loan were sold into slavery to recover the debt, whether or not this was legally acceptable in the local context. Sometimes people seized in wars or raids were already slaves; often military campaigns allowed the ransoming of captives, which was most likely for those who were free and owned property or who had families who could pay the redemption price.

The forced movement of enslaved Africans was a fundamental component to the economic development of the frontier of European settlement in the Americas. In North America and elsewhere in the Americas, the use of terror was basic to this mechanism of labor supply. Africans went to areas that were developing economically, often leaving in their wake areas of economic dislocation and desolation in Africa that were a result of slave wars. North America was typical in this regard, since African slave labor was central to several of the most important colonies, particularly South Carolina, Virginia, and Maryland and, indirectly, through commerce in other colonies, such as Massachusetts, New York, and Pennsylvania. The enforced destination of the migrants was to areas where their labor would produce economic development, most importantly to plantations and farms for work in cash-crop agriculture, but also in mining. Africans found themselves in towns and ports as domestic servants; many Africans were urban residents with skilled or semiskilled occupations. They were essential to commerce, serving as porters and teamsters. In eighteenth-century North America, enslaved Africans were concentrated in the agricultural lowlands of South Carolina and Georgia, especially on the Sea Islands, growing rice, lowland cotton, indigo, and other products. In the Tidewater region of Virginia and Maryland, they were employed on tobacco farms, while in Louisiana they grew sugarcane. Enslaved Africans and their descendants constituted a sizable portion of the population of New York, Philadelphia, Charleston, and New Orleans, and they were found in numerous towns. Indeed, enslaved Africans were almost everywhere that European settlement was found, so that slaves worked farms and plantations in upstate New York, Rhode Island, and New Jersey, not only in the South. Moreover, any reasonably prosperous family had slaves as domestic servants, whether in Quebec, Boston, Virginia, or New Orleans. The two most important concentrations of enslaved Africans in North America, the Tidewater area of Virginia and Maryland and the lowlands of South Carolina and Georgia, accounted for at least two-thirds of the slaves brought into North America before the end of legal imports of enslaved Africans in 1808 (Anstey, 1975). On the basis of data on the voyages of slave ships, it is possible to assess the scale and direction of this migration.

Table VII: Origins of Enslaved Africans Shipped to North America

Region of Origin	Carolinas/ Georgia	Virginia/ Maryland	North America Other	North America
Senegambia	29,139	14,491	7,166	50,786
Sierra Leone	19,899	2,134	720	22,753
Windward Coast	11,029	2,867	401	14,297
Gold Coast	20,263	6,898	1,802	28,963
Bight of Benin	2,971	1,966	1,984	6,921
Bight of Biafra	13,370	28,542	—	41,912
West Central	47,585	11,072	1,629	60,286
South East Africa	1,118	1,347	295	2,760
Origin Unknown	43,921	47,249	8,897	100,067
Total Sample	189,295	116,566	22,894	328,755

Data derived from: David Eltis, Stephen Behrendt, David Richardson, and Herbert Klein, The Atlantic Slave Trade: A Database on CD-Rom *(Eltis et al., 1999).*

The largest number of Africans in the lowlands of the Carolinas and Georgia came from the Bantu–speaking areas of west-central Africa, representing perhaps one-third of the total number of African immigrants arriving there (34 percent). A substantial number, perhaps 20 percent, came from the area of Senegambia, while the Gold Coast and Sierra Leone each accounted for about 14–15 percent of the total number of enslaved immigrants. There were also substantial numbers of people from the Bight of Biafra and the Windward Coast. By contrast, the greatest number of slaves in the Tidewater areas of Virginia and Maryland came from the Bight of Biafra, which accounted for approximately 39 percent of immigrants whose African origins are known. Senegambia accounted for perhaps 21 percent of immigrants to the Tidewater, while another 17 percent came from the Bantu regions of west-central Africa. The Gold Coast was also important, with perhaps 10 percent of immigrants coming from there.

Homelands of Immigrants

An examination of the two major importing regions together reveals that 90 percent of the African immigrants in the two major settlement areas came from only four regions in Africa. The largest number came from west-central Africa, where languages and cultures were closely related. Many more of these Africans ended up in the lowlands of the Carolinas and Georgia than in the Tidewater, but they were prominent in both regions, representing perhaps 29 percent of all immigrants to both regions. The second largest group of immigrants, approximately 18 percent of African arrivals, came from the Bight of Biafra; these people were mostly Igbo and Ibibio in origins, or in the course of the Atlantic crossing became associated with these predominant groups. While people from the Bight of Biafra were found in both the lowcountry and the Tidewater, they were proportionately more numerous in Virginia and Maryland, where they constituted the largest single group. The third largest group, approximately 13 percent, came from the Gold Coast, where Twi was the common language, and most people were identified as Akan. Finally, there was a considerable concentration of people from Sierra Leone, approximately 10 percent of all African immigrants, but they were almost entirely concentrated in the lowlands of the Carolinas and Georgia.

Several distinctive patterns emerge from this demographic profile, although only the broad contours are understood, because the African origins of a substantial number of immigrants, approximately one-third of all immigrants, are not known. Nonetheless, the region of west central Africa stands out; this large region had a population that was closely related in language and culture, often referred to as "Bantu" and incorporating people who spoke Kikongo, Kimbundu, or a similar language. People from west central Africa were heavily represented in the African population of large parts of the Americas, especially Brazil. Hence, North America conformed to this pattern, and it is likely that a significant proportion of arrivals in North America whose origins are not known also came from west central Africa. The predominance of these closely related Bantu–speaking peoples had an important impact on the religion and culture of the enslaved population in North America and elsewhere.

Second, the Senegambia region was prominent in North America, much more so than virtually anywhere else in the Americas, with the possible exception of the small French islands in the Caribbean. Since Senegambia was a region strongly influenced by Islam, more so than any other coastal area of origin for enslaved Africans, there appear to have been more Muslims or people who had been exposed to Islam in North America than anywhere else in the Americas, except for Bahia and other parts of Brazil. The importance of Senegambia was especially pronounced in Louisiana, since many people identified as Bambara and Mandingo went to Louisiana, but they were also clearly present in both the lowcountry of the Carolinas and Georgia and in the tidewater region of Virginia and Maryland. Among those African immigrants who can be identified as coming from Senegambia, adult Muslim males stand out most prominently. Indeed, there are very few references to Muslim women, which reflects what is known about the slave trade in the interior of West Africa, where exports to the coast from the interior were almost entirely males. Third, the upper South had a considerable concentration of people from the Bight of Biafra, although there were substantial numbers of Biafran immigrants in the lowlands of the Carolinas and Georgia too. It is likely, moreover, that a large portion of the immigrants whose African origins are not known actually came from the Bight of Biafra, since British trade grew substantially in the Bight of Biafra in the eighteenth century, and Britain was the biggest supplier of slaves to North America, sometimes indirectly through trans-shipments from Jamaica and Barbados. Nonetheless, the size of the population of Igbo and Ibibio origin was substantial, apparently enough to evolve a distinct subculture among the enslaved population. The Bight of Biafra stands out in the demography of the eighteenth-century slave trade because of the relatively high numbers of women in comparison with all other parts of the African coast. Women from the Bight of Biafra were particularly important in giving birth to a new generation in the Americas, in sharp contrast with the virtual lack of women from Muslim areas. The fourth concentration of peoples included those from Sierra Leone and adjacent parts of the so-called Windward Coast. They were heavily concentrated in the low country and especially in areas of rice cultivation. While there were some people from this stretch of the African coast in the tidewater region, they were relatively few in number and probably not enough to have as strong an impact on culture and change as in the Carolinas and Georgia.

Noticeably absent or of minor importance is the region of the "Slave Coast"—the Bight of Benin—even though this was one of the most important sources of enslaved Africans for the Atlantic crossing. The region included Yoruba, Ewe/Fon/Allada (so-called Gbe languages) and other people brought from the interior, including Muslims, and the fact that almost none of these people were to be found in North America marks an important difference between the origins of Africans in North America and elsewhere. While the Bight of Benin accounts for some immigrants, they are very few by comparison with their substantial importance in Cuba, Trinidad, and Brazil. Although the demographic figures are revealing in many respects, the statistics alone disguise the odyssey undertaken by each individual who was forced to cross the Atlantic on a slave ship. Ethnic and regional categories can provide a setting in which to examine the slave trade, but the personal histories of individuals are essential in examining the impact of the slave trade and slavery on society, both in Africa and in the Americas. Biography reveals the experience of African Americans as they became part of the diaspora in North America. It is fortunate that autobiographical and biographical accounts have been recorded for several thousand individuals, and while most accounts relate the experiences of individuals in the nineteenth century, there are some accounts of individuals born in Africa in the eighteenth century that inform our understanding of the defining period of the African diaspora. Biography presents the voices of the enslaved, whether born in Africa or not, and such information as can be derived from these accounts can be supplemented with information contained in fugitive-slave advertisements, plantation inventories, and probate records. Biographies provide information on the direct impact of the transatlantic slave trade on people. The discussion of Muslims is enhanced by several biographies that have survived. For example, Muhammad Kaba Saghanughu of Jamaica lived on one plantation, Spice Grove, from 1777 until his death in 1845. He was the leader of the Muslim community in Jamaica, at least since the 1820s, and was author of an important treatise on prayer that reaffirms the allegiance of the Jamaican Muslims to the Qadiriyya brotherhood. Similar biographical accounts of Muslims have survived from North America, Trinidad, and Brazil.

Resistance to Slavery

Similarly, there are ethnic components to various rebellions and acts of resistance that have to be put in the context of the African background. See, for example, the acts of slave resistance that had clear "ethnic" dimensions, such as the Stono Rebellion, Gabriel's Rebellion, the Bahia Muslim uprising of 1835, and the St. Domingue revolution, with its Kongo background. Similar "ethnic" connections to resistance existed elsewhere. Therefore, the major characteristics of the international slave trade, and especially the place of North America in that trade, are complex. Because of the scale of the migration, and the complexities of the individual experiences that made up that exodus, it is difficult to summarize. However, with respect to North America, the following points are important:

1. The international slave trade to North America, as between Africa and other parts of the Americas, and indeed including the slave trade in the Indian Ocean and the Islamic world at the same time, treated human beings as commodities, buying and selling individuals

like any other property. Unlike in other slave systems, however, racial distinctions were used to keep the enslaved population in bondage in the Americas, with the corresponding development of racialized attitudes and racism.

2. The enslaved Africans brought to North America, as elsewhere in the Americas, were considered to be first and foremost workers, and the degree of power concentrated in the hands of slave owners meant that the enslaved could be worked harder and longer than other laborers. Such exploitation was decidedly to the disadvantage of the health and welfare of the enslaved Africans, who received no wages, minimal clothing and housing, and often had to work overtime to grow food or earn enough to buy food.

3. The degree of power concentrated in the hands of slave owners in North America, as was the case in all slave-based societies, allowed excessive degrees of corporal punishment, the perpetuation of sexual abuse and exploitation, and disregard for kinship, especially in not recognizing relationships arising from paternity. The status of children followed the slave status of the mother, no matter who the father was.

4. Methods of social control were intrinsically associated with racial perceptions, although how racialism developed and how it differed over time and place are important considerations. In North America, any person of identifiable African descent, no matter the degree of "white" ancestry, was deemed "colored," "Negro," or "black," thereby constituting a racial caste, but in other parts of the Americas, racial distinctions were often more complex.

5. The interests of slave owners were in the maximization of profits, which resulted in treating enslaved people as chattel. This treatment was sometimes further mitigated by psychopathic behavior, social perversity, and political expediency that increased the arbitrariness of master-slave relations.

The most enduring consequence of the migration for the migrants themselves and for the receiving communities was the development of racism, which affected the evolution of a sense of an African American community, with its particular cultural manifestations, attitudes, and expressions. The legacy is apparent in music and art, with considerable impact on religion, cuisine, and language. A literary tradition, which began in song and rhythm, is also noteworthy. There were enduring consequences of the migration on the communities that suffered the loss of population in Africa. Transformations of society and economy were caused by involvement in enslavement, slave trading, and the use of slaves locally within

Africa. Places of refuge for those attempting to escape enslavement were developed on such islands of safety as Ganvie, a community built on stilts in the middle of Lake Noue on the lagoons of the Bight of Benin. An enduring legacy of resistance can be seen in the music and art of African immigrants, and in their identification with ethnicity, religion, and race, reflecting common bonds with the cultures of the people who remained in Africa.

The cultural and religious impact of African immigration during the slavery era affected music and expression. It is known that music patterns and rhythms are old, and while the evolution of new styles and changes in instrumentation have affected music, the interconnection of the transatlantic world shows that migrations involve people but also culture. A perspective that does justice to the African background of the modern world demonstrates that "American" culture is not "European" or "African" but its own form, created in a political and economic context of inequality and oppression in which diverse ethnic and cultural influences can be discerned. Moreover, it is clear that influences were both European and African, and in some contexts, Amerindian. Undoubtedly, the transatlantic slave trade was the defining migration that shaped the African diaspora. It did so through the people it brought, and especially the women who were to give birth to children of the new African American population. In North America, those women include many who can be identified as "Igbo" or "Ibibio" but almost none who were Yoruba, Fon or Hausa, who constituted the slave population leaving the Bight of Benin. There were a considerable number of women in the cargoes leaving west-central Africa, so that "Bantu" women, from matrilineal societies, constituted a considerable portion of the fertile population of slave women. Similarly, the immigrant population from Sierra Leone also appears to have had a relatively high proportion of females, which was reflected in fertility rates. These were the women who gave birth to African American culture and society.

The interpretative issues that need to be discussed in presenting the theme of the transatlantic slave trade to the general public and to educators include responsibility, resistance, and reparations. On issues of responsibility, there have to be considerations of who was responsible for the enslavement of individuals in Africa, and whether this enslavement was done through means that were thought to be legal or illegal, whether during acts of war and the taking of political prisoners, or in kidnapping and arbitrary seizure arising from debt or acts perceived to be witchcraft. Responsibility must also be assessed in terms of the merchants and government officials who knowingly or unwittingly sold individuals as slaves for transport across the Atlantic or the Sahara to distant places and unknown hardships and suffering. Responsibility also rests on the shoulders of the merchants and ship crews who carried enslaved Africans to the Americas under barbaric and cruel conditions onboard ship and to the plantation owners and others whose economic prosperity depended upon the exploitation of slave labor. Ultimately in the period of slavery and the slave trade, the Atlantic world that included North America arose on the shoulders of African labor, and its development, achieved in the context of slavery and its aftermath, had a clear effect on the modern world economy.

Chronology

1441	The explorer Antam Goncalves seizes Moors near Cape Blanc in West Africa and carries them back to Portugal as slaves.
1442	The Portuguese build forts along the western coast of Africa and begin to engage in a slave trade.
c. 1445	The Portuguese introduce slavery to the Madeiras, and by 1501 there are 2,000 slaves working on sugar plantations on the islands.
1490	The Portuguese and Kongolese nobles begin to cultivate sugar on the island of São Tomé, using African slaves from Kongo.
1491	The Castilians begin to grow sugar on the Canary Islands, at first using enslaved natives and later enslaved Africans acquired from the Portuguese.
1501	Nicolás de Ovando, the colonial governor of Hispaniola, receives authorization from the Spanish Crown to import enslaved Africans; the first group arrives the following year.
1506	Using slave labor, the Spanish begin to produce sugar in the Greater Antilles.
1510	The Portuguese ship enslaved Africans to Brazil to labor on sugar plantations.
1521	December: The first recorded incident of a slave insurrection in the Western Hemisphere occurs when enslaved Africans rise up on Hispaniola.
1542	Spain outlaws the enslavement of Amerindians, and as a result, the African slave trade intensifies.
1619	August: The first blacks arrive at the British colony of Jamestown. Although they are not termed "slaves," they are considered to be war captives and thus subject to indefinite servitude.
1621	Willem Usselinx and other Dutch merchants charter the Dutch West India Company to establish colonies and transport slaves to the New World.

1629	The French begin to import enslaved Africans into St. Kitts.
1630	English settlers use enslaved Africans to cultivate sugar on Barbados.
c. 1660	There are approximately 100,000 enslaved Africans in the West Indies but only about 5,000 in the North American mainland colonies.
1672	The Royal African Company is granted a monopoly over the English slave trade.
1700	An estimated 28,000 enslaved Africans are in the British North American colonies.
1750	The British North American colonies have approximately 236,000 slaves.
1778	A special commission established by the British Parliament begins to investigate the conduct of the transatlantic slave trade.
1787	Under Article I, Section 9 of the U.S. Constitution, the transatlantic slave trade was prohibited as of 1808.
1807	British Parliament prohibits the transatlantic slave trade; the ban takes effect on March 1, 1808.
1807–1808	USA Congress bans the transatlantic slave trade to the United States and its territories; the ban takes effect on January 1, 1808.
1814	The Netherlands officially ends its involvement in the transatlantic slave trade.
1817	At the prompting of the British government, Spain and Portugal each agree to end the transatlantic slave trade north of the equator.
1817	The French government officially ends its participation in the transatlantic slave trade.
1820	The Spanish government abolishes the transatlantic slave trade south of the equator.
1829	Mexico abolishes slavery.
1830	Brazil signs a treaty with Great Britain and Portugal ending its participation in the slave trade south of the equator; the treaty is not consistently enforced.
1833	August 1: The British Parliament passes the Emancipation Act, abolishing slavery throughout the British Empire. Within five years all slaves in British colonies—but not British Territories—are freed.
1839	Under the Palmerston Act, the British Royal Navy is given the right of search and seizure of ships suspected of carrying enslaved Africans, and subsequent negotiations with particular countries,

	including Portugal, the United States, and others extended this right of search can search Portuguese vessels and ships of other countries suspected of carrying slaves to the Americas.
1848	The French government abolishes slavery in all its colonies, but slavery continued unabated in French Africa.
1851	The Queiróz Law outlawed the African slave trade to Brazil.
1860	The Netherlands enacts a statute abolishing slavery in all Dutch colonies; the law takes effect in 1863.
1867	The transatlantic slave trade, in operation since 1502, ends when the last shipload of African slaves arrives in Cuba. It is estimated that a total of 12 million Africans were sent to the New World as slaves.
1873	The Spanish government abolishes slavery in Puerto Rico.
1886	The Spanish government abolishes slavery in Cuba.
1888	May 13: Brazil is the last country in the Western Hemisphere to end slavery; the *Lei Aurea* (Golden Law) frees approximately 750,000 Brazilian slaves.

Glossary

Abolition. The movement to abolish slavery that began in various countries in the eighteenth century. Though slave trading was outlawed by Great Britain and the United States in 1807 and abolished in British colonies in 1838, slavery was declared illegal by various states in the U.S., beginning with Vermont in 1777, before it was finally abolished throughout the country in 1865; and slavery was abolished in Brazil in 1888.

Akan. Ethnic term for people in modern Ghana, including Asante (Ashanti), Fante, and others who speak the Twi language.

Baquaqua, Mahommah Gardo. African Muslim slave who converted to Christianity. Baquaqua lived in the area south of the great bend of the Niger River in the early nineteenth century. An attendant to a local king, Baquaqua was seized by rivals and sold into slavery. He arrived in Pernambuco, Brazil, in the 1840s, but later he was taken to New York where he was able to gain his freedom through the efforts of local abolitionists. Baptist missionaries helped educate him. Samuel Moore published his memoirs in 1854.
    Birth: [date unknown]
    Death: [date unknown]
    Law, Robin and Paul E. Lovejoy (eds.) (2001), *The Biography of Mahommah Gardo Baquaqua: His Passage from Slavery to Freedom in Africa and America*, Princeton, NJ: Markus Wiener Publishers.

Bight of Benin. Region of the coast of southwestern Nigeria, Republique du Benin, and Togo; also called the "Mina" Coast and the "Slave Coast."

Bight of Biafra. Region of the Niger River delta and the Cross River basin of southeastern Nigeria and Cameroon.

Cowries. Small sea shells from the Indian Ocean used as money in West Africa, and also used in making jewelry.

Creole. A term often referring to people born in the Americas, of African, European, or mixed background; also, by extension, people born in port towns around the Atlantic, including Africa; also, a linguistic term referring to the mixed languages of such populations.

Curtin, Philip D. Herbert Baxter Adams Professor Emeritus in the Department of History at Johns Hopkins University. Curtin received his PhD from Harvard University (1953) and has been a pioneer in African history and comparative world history. While teaching at the University of Wisconsin, he established a graduate program in African studies and mentored some of the most prominent Africanists of today. Curtin is also a former president of the American Historical Association. Among his many works are *Two Jamaicas: The Role of Ideas in a Tropical Colony, 1830–1865* (1955), *The Atlantic Slave Trade: A Census* (1969), *Cross-Cultural Trade in World History* (1984), *The Rise and Fall of the Plantation Complex: Essays in Atlantic History* (1990), and *The World and the West: The European Challenge and the Overseas Response in the Age of Empire* (2000).
   Birth: 1922
   Curtin, Philip D. (2005), *On the Fringes of History: A Memoir*, Athens: Ohio University Press.

dan Fodio, Sheikh Usman. Fulani religious and political leader. A teacher of Islam, Usman had many followers among the Fulani and Hausa peoples of present-day Nigeria. In the late 1790s the Sultan of Gobir, fearful of Usman's power, revoked many of the concessions granted to his Muslim community at Degel. This event sparked a jihad or holy war (1804–1808) and resulted in the defeat of the Gobir ruling dynasty. Around 1809 Usman established the Sokoto caliphate and devoted his remaining years to teaching and writing. His son Muhammad Bello succeeded him as caliph in 1817.
   Birth: December 1754 in Maratta, Gobir, Hausaland (present-day Nigeria)
   Death: 1817, Sokoto, Fulani empire
   Last, Murray (1967), *The Sokoto Caliphate*, New York: Humanities Press.

de Ovando, Nicolás. The first Spanish governor of the West Indies (1501–1509) and a knight of the military Order of Alcántara. Ovando developed the *encomienda*, a system of forced Indian labor, on Hispaniola, but his brutal exploitation of the native population led to his recall by Crown authorities.
   Birth: ca. 1451 in Brozas, Castile, Spain **Death:** ca. 1511
   Lamb, Ursula S. (1949), "Nicolás de Ovando, Comendador Mayor of Alcántara and Governor of the Indies," PhD dissertation, University of California, Berkeley.

Gbe. A linguistic term referring to several related languages in the Bight of Benin, including Fon (Dahomey), Allada, Ewe, and Mahi.

Gold Coast. The region of modern Ghana, named because of gold available in the interior.

Jihad. Muslim holy war, specifically the wars of the eighteenth and nineteenth centuries in West Africa, including those founding the states of Futa Jallon, Futa Toro, and Sokoto.

Middle Passage. A reference to the transatlantic crossing of enslaved Africans.

Manilas. Bracelets imported into the Bight of Biafra and used as money.

"Mina" Coast. A term referring to the "Slave Coast" or Bight of Benin and the Gold Coast, named after Elmina Castle, built by the Portuguese in 1482 for use in gold trade and later used to warehouse slaves for transport across the Atlantic.

Senegambia. The region incorporating the Senegal and Gambia Rivers in the western Sudan.

Slave Coast. The area of West Africa from what is now Ghana to southwestern Nigeria, which served as the principal trading center for African slaves from about 1550 to about 1750.

Unsworth, Barry. British novelist who is known for his historical themes. Unsworth graduated from the University of Manchester in 1951. During the 1960s he served as British Council lecturer at the Universities of Athens and Istanbul. His *Sacred Hunger* (1992) is the story of two cousins and their involvement in the Atlantic slave trade. Unsworth's graphic description of the Middle Passage in this novel earned him the Booker Prize in 1992. Among his other works are *Mooncranker's Gift* (1973), winner of the Heinemann Fiction Award, and *Pascali's Island* (1980) and *Morality Play* (1995), both Booker Prize nominees. **Birth:** August 10, 1930, in County Durham, England.

Naufftus, William F. (1998), "Barry Unsworth," in *Dictionary of Literary Biography, Volume 194: British Novelists Since 1960, Second Series*, Merritt Moseley (ed.), Columbia, SC: Bruccoli Clark Layman/Detroit: Gale Research.

Usselinx, Willem. Antwerp merchant and entrepreneur. The son of a mercantile family, Usselinx spent time in Spain, Portugal, and the Azores Island for his education. He traveled to Holland in 1591 with the idea of developing a Dutch company to establish overseas colonies and compete with Spain for the control of the rich resources in the Americas and Africa. The result of his efforts was the founding of the Dutch West India Company in 1621.
Birth: [date unknown] **Death:** [date unknown]

REFERENCES

Postma, Johannes (1990), *The Dutch in the Atlantic Slave Trade, 1600-1815*, Cambridge: Cambridge University Press.

Recommended Reading

Adamu, Mahdi (1979), "The Delivery of Slaves from the Bight of Benin in the Eighteenth and Nineteenth Centuries," in *The Uncommon Market: Essays in the Economic History of the Atlantic Slave Trade*, H.A. Gemery and J.S. Hogendorn (eds.), New York: Academic Press, pp. 163–180. ISBN: 0122798503.

Adediran, Biodun (1984), "Yoruba Ethnic Groups or a Yoruba Ethnic Group? A Review of the

Problem of Ethnic Identification," *Africa: Revista do Centro de Estudos Africanos da USP*, vol. 7, pp. 57-70. ISSN: 0100-8153.

Anstey, Roger T. (1975), "The Volume of the North American Slave-Carrying Trade from Africa, 1761-1810," *Revue française d'histoire d'outre-mer*, vol. 62, pp. 47-66. ISSN: 0300-9513.

Behrendt, Stephen D. (1993), "The British slave trade, 1785-1807: Volume, profitability, and mortality," PhD dissertation, University of Wisconsin.

Binder, Wolfgang (ed.) (1993), *Slavery in the Americas*, Würzburg, Germany: Königshausen & Neumann. ISBN: 3884797131.

Bühnen, Stephan (1993), "Ethnic Origins of Peruvian Slaves (1548-1650): Figures for Upper Guinea," *Paiduema*, vol. 39, pp. 57-110. Clarkson, Thomas (1785), "Essay on the Inhumanity of the Slave Trade," Honours Degree, Cambridge University.

Cohn, Raymond L. (1985), "Deaths of Slaves in the Middle Passage," *Journal of Economic History*, vol. 45 (Sep.), pp. 685-92. ISSN: 0022-0507.

Colclanis, Peter A. (ed.) (2005), *The Atlantic Economy during the Seventeenth and Eighteenth Centuries: Organization, Operation, Practice, and Personnel*, Columbia: University of South Carolina Press. ISBN: 1570035547.

Crane, Elaine F. (1980), "'The First Wheel of Commerce': Newport, Rhode Island and the Slave Trade, 1760-1776," *Slavery and Abolition*, vol. 1, pp. 178-198. ISSN: 0144-039X.

Crouzet, Philippe Bonnichon, and Denis Rolland (eds.), Paris, France: L'Harmattan, pp. 397-416.

Curtin, Philip D. (ed.) (1967), *Africa Remembered: Narratives by West Africans from the Era of the Slave Trade*, Madison: University of Wisconsin Press.

Curtin, Philip D. (1968), "Epidemiology and the Slave Trade," *Political Science Quarterly*, vol. 83, no. 2, pp. 190-216. ISSN: 0032-3195 Curtin, Philip D. (1969), "The Slave Trade and the Numbers Game: A Review of the Literature," in his *The Atlantic Slave Trade: A Census*, Madison: University of Wisconsin Press, pp. 3-13. ISBN: 0299054047.

Curto, José C., and Paul E. Lovejoy (eds.) (2004), *Enslaving Connections: Changing Cultures of Africa and Brazil During the Era of Slavery*, Amherst, NY: Humanity Books. ISBN: 1591021537.

Curto, José C., and Paul E. Lovejoy (eds.) (2004), *Enslaving Spirits: The Portuguese-Brazilian Alcohol Trade at Luanda and its Hinterland*, Leiden, Netherlands: Brill. ISBN: 9004131752.

Curto, José C., and Raymond R. Gervais (2001/2002), "The Population History of Luanda during the Late Atlantic Slave Trade, 1781-1844," *African Economic History*, vol. 29, pp. 1-59; vol. 30, pp. 15-162. ISSN: 0145-2258.

Curto, José C., and Renée Soulodre-La France (eds.) (2005), *Africa and the Americas: Interconnections during the Slave Trade*, Trenton, NJ: Africa World Press. ISBN: 1592212719.

Drescher, Seymour (1977), *Econocide: British Slavery in the Era of Abolition*, Pittsburgh: University of Pittsburgh Press. ISBN: 0822933446.

Du Bois, W.E.B. (1895), "The suppression of the African slave trade in the United States of America, 1638-1871," PhD dissertation, Harvard University.

Eltis, David (2000), *The Rise of African Slavery in the Americas*, Cambridge, England: Cambridge University Press. ISBN: 0521652316.

Eltis, David (2001), "The Volume and Structure of the trans-Atlantic Slave Trade: A Reassessment," *William and Mary Quarterly*, vol. 58, no. 1, pp. 17-46. ISSN: 0043-5597.

Eltis, David, and Stanley L. Engerman (1992), "Was the Slave Trade Dominated by Men?" *Journal of Interdisciplinary History*, vol. 23, no. 2, pp. 237-257. ISSN: 0022-1953.

Eltis, David, and Stanley L. Engerman (1993), "Fluctuations in Sex and Age Ratios In the trans Atlantic Slave Trade, 1663-1864," *Economic History Review*, vol. 46, no. 2, pp. 308-323. ISSN: 0013-0117.

Eltis, David, Stephen Behrendt, David Richardson, and Herbert S. Klein (1999), *The Atlantic Slave Trade: A Database on CD-Rom*, Cambridge, England: Cambridge University Press. ISBN: 0521629101.

Equiano, Olaudah (1789/1995), *The Interesting Narrative and Other Writings*, London, England: Printed for and sold by T. Wilkins et al.; New York: Penguin, pp. 46-61. ISBN: 0140434852.

Fage, J.D. (1980), "Slaves and Society in Western Africa, c.1445–c.1700," *Journal of African History*, vol. 21, pp. 289–310. ISSN: 0021-8537.

Florentino, Manolo G. (2000), "About the Slaving Business in Rio de Janeiro, 1790–1830: A Contribution," in *Pour l'histoire du Brésil: hommage à Katia de Queirós Mattoso*, François.

Geggus, David (1989), "Sex Ratio, Age and Ethnicity in the Atlantic Slave Trade: Data from French Shipping and Plantation Records," *Journal of African History*, vol. 30, pp. 23–44. ISSN: 0021-8537.

Gilroy, Paul (1993), *The Black Atlantic: Modernity and Double Consciousness*, Cambridge, MA: Harvard University Press. ISBN: 0674076052.

Gomez, Michael Angelo (1998), *Exchanging Our Country Marks: The Transformation of African Identities in the Colonial and Antebellum South*, Chapel Hill: University of North Carolina Press, pp. 17–37. ISBN: 0807823872

Gomez, Michael (2005), *Black Crescent*, Cambridge, England: Cambridge University Press. ISBN: 0521840953.

Gomez, Michael (ed.) (2005), *Diasporic Africa: A Reader*, New York: New York University Press. ISBN: 0814731651.

Hair, P.E.H. (1967), "Ethnolinguistic Continuity on the Guinea Coast," *Journal of African History*, vol. 8, no. 2, pp. 247–268. ISSN: 0021- 8537.

Hall, Gwendolyn (1992), "Senegambia During the French Slave Trade to Louisiana," *Africans in Colonial Louisiana: The Development of Afro-Creole Culture in the Eighteenth Century*, Baton Rouge: Louisiana State University Press, pp. 28–55. ISBN: 0807119997.

Hall, Gwendolyn (2005), *Slavery and African Ethnicities in the Americas: Restoring the Links*, Chapel Hill: University of North Carolina Press, pp. 39–55. ISBN: 0807829730.

Henige, David P. (1986), "Measuring the Immeasurable: The Atlantic Slave Trade, West African Population and the Pyrrhonian Critic," *Journal of African History*, vol. 27, pp. 295–313. ISSN: 0021-8537.

Herskovits, Melville J. (1933), "On the Provenience of New World Negroes," *Social Forces*, vol. 12, no. 2, pp. 247–262. ISSN: 0037-7732.

Herskovits, Melville J. (1936), "The Significance of West Africa for Negro Research," *Journal of Negro History*, vol. 21, no. 1, pp. 15–30. ISSN: 0022-2992.

Heywood, Linda (ed.) (2002), *Central Africans and Cultural Transformations in the American Diaspora*, Cambridge, England: Cambridge University Press. ISBN: 0521802431.

Hofstee, Erik J.W. (2001), "The great divide: Aspects of the social history of the Middle Passage in the trans-Atlantic slave trade," PhD dissertation, Michigan State University.

Hogendorn, Jan, and Marion Johnson (1986), *The Shell Money of the Slave Trade*, Cambridge, England: Cambridge University Press. ISBN: 0521320860.

Hurston, Zora Neale (1927), "Cudjoe's Own Story of the Last African Slaver," *Journal of Negro History*, vol. 12 (Oct.), pp. 648–663. ISSN: 0022-2992.

Inikori, Joseph E. (ed.) (1981), *Forced Migration: The Impact of the Export Slave Trade on African Societies*, London, England: Hutchinson. ISBN: 0091459001.

Inikori, Joseph E. (2002), *Africans and the Industrial Revolution in England: A Study in International Trade and Economic Development*, Cambridge, England: Cambridge University Press, pp. 216–264. ISBN: 9780521811.

Klein, Herbert S. (1978), *The Middle Passage: Comparative Studies in the Atlantic Slave Trade*, Princeton, NJ: Princeton University Press. ISBN: 0691031193.

Klein, Herbert S. (1999), "The European Organization of the Slave Trade" in *The Atlantic Slave Trade*, Cambridge, England: Cambridge University Press, pp. 74–102. ISBN: 0521460204.

Klein, Herbert S., and Stanley L. Engerman (1997), "Long-Term Trends in African Mortality in the trans-Atlantic Slave Trade," *Slavery and Abolition*, vol. 18, pp. 36–48. ISSN: 0144-039X.

Lambert, Sheila (ed.) (1975), *House of Commons Sessional Papers of the Eighteenth Century*, Wilmington, DE: Scholarly Resources. ISBN:0842019111.

Law, Robin (1977), "Royal monopoly and private enterprise in the Atlantic trade: The Case of Dahomey," *Journal of African History*, vol. 18, pp. 555–577. ISSN: 0021-8537.

Law, Robin (1978), "Slaves, Trade, and Taxes: The Material Basis of Political Power in Precolonial West Africa," *Research in Economic Anthropology*, vol. 1, pp. 37–52. ISSN: 0190-1281.

Law, Robin (1991), *The Slave Coast of West Africa, 1550-1750: The Impact of the Atlantic Slave Trade on an African Society*, Oxford, England: Clarendon Press. ISBN: 0198202288.

Law, Robin (ed.) (1997a), *Source Material for Studying the Slave Trade and the African Diaspora*, Stirling, Scotland: Centre of Commonwealth Studies, University of Stirling.

Law, Robin (1997b), "Ethnicity and the Slave Trade: 'Lucumi' and 'Nago' as Ethnonyms in West Africa," *History in Africa*, vol. 24, pp. 205-219. ISSN: 0361-5413.

Law, Robin (2004), *Ouidah: The Social History of a West African Slaving "Port" 1727-1892*, Athens: Ohio University Press; Oxford, England: James Currey. ISBN: 0821415719.

Law, Robin, and Paul E. Lovejoy (eds.) (2001), *The Biography of Mahommah Gardo Baquaqua: His Passage from Slavery to Freedom in Africa and America*, Princeton, NJ: Markus Wiener Publisher, pp. 136-162. ISBN: 1558762477.

Law, Robin, and Silke Strickrodt (eds.) (1999), *Ports of the Slave Trade (Bights of Benin and Biafra)*, Stirling, Scotland: Centre of Commonwealth Studies, University of Stirling. ISBN: 1857691016.

Lovejoy, Paul E. (2000a), *Transformations in Slavery: A History of Slavery in Africa*, Cambridge, England: Cambridge University Press, pp. 1-22. ISBN: 0521780128.

Lovejoy, Paul E. (ed.) (2000b), *Identity in the Shadow of Slavery*, London, England: Cassell Academic. ISBN: 0826447244.

Lovejoy, Paul E. (2002), "Ethnic Designations of the Slave Trade and the Reconstruction of the History of Trans-Atlantic Slavery," in *Trans-Atlantic Dimensions of the Ethnicity in the African Diaspora*, Paul E. Lovejoy and David Trotman (eds.), London, England: Continuum. ISBN: 0826449085.

Lovejoy, Paul E. (ed.) (2004), *Slavery on the Frontiers of Islam*, Princeton, NJ: Markus Wiener Publisher. ISBN: 1558763295.

Lovejoy, Paul E. (2005), *Ecology and Ethnography of Muslim Trade in West Africa*, Trenton, NJ: Africa World Press. ISBN: 1592214258.

Lovejoy, Paul E. (2005), *Slavery, Commerce and Production in the Sokoto Caliphate of West Africa*, Trenton, NJ: Africa World Press. ISBN:1592212530.

Lovejoy, Paul E., and David Richardson (1995), "The Initial 'Crisis of Adaptation': The Impact of British Abolition on the Atlantic Slave Trade in West Africa, 1808-1820," in *From Slave Trade to Legitimate Commerce: The Commercial Transition in Nineteenth-Century West Africa*, Robin Law (ed.), Cambridge, England: Cambridge University Press. ISBN: 0521481279.

Lovejoy, Paul E., and J.S. Hogendorn (1979), "Slave Marketing in West Africa," in *The Uncommon Market: Essays in the Economic History of the Atlantic Slave Trade*, H.A. Gemery and J.S. Hogendorn (eds.), New York: Academic Press, pp. 213-235. ISBN: 0122798503.

Lovejoy, Paul E., and David Richardson (2001), "The Business of Slaving: Pawnship in Western Africa, c.1600-1810," *Journal of African History*, vol. 42, pp. 67-89. ISSN: 0021-8537.

Lovejoy, Paul E., and David V. Trotman (2002), "Enslaved Africans and Their Expectations of Slave Life in the Americas: Towards a Reconsideration of Models of 'Creolisation,'" in *Questioning Creole: Creolisation Discourses in Caribbean Culture*, Verene A. Shepherd, Kamau Brathwaite, and Glen L. Richards (eds.). Kingston, Jamaica: Ian Randle, pp. 67-91. ISBN: 9766370397.

Manning, Patrick (ed.) (1996), *Slave Trades, 1500-1800: Globalization of Forced Labour*, Aldershot, England: Variorum. ISBN: 0860785122.

Miller, Joseph C. (1980), "Mortality in the Atlantic Slave Trade: Statistical Evidence on Causality," *Journal of Interdisciplinary History*, vol. 11, no. 3, pp. 385-423. ISSN: 0022-1953.

Miller, Joseph C. (1988a), "Overcrowded and Undernourished: The Techniques and Consequences of Tight-Packing in the Portuguese Southern Atlantic Slave Trade," in *De la traite à l'esclavage*, Serge Daget (ed.), Paris, France: L'Harmattan, vol. 2, pp. 395-424. ISBN: 2900486025.

Miller, Joseph C. (1988b), *Way of Death: Merchant Capitalism and the Angolan Slave Trade, 1730-1830*, Madison: University of Wisconsin Press. ISBN: 0299115607.

Miller, Joseph C. (2001), "Central Africa During the Era of the Slave Trade, c. 1490s-1850s," in *Central Africans and Cultural Transformations in the American Diaspora*, Linda Heywood (ed.), Cambridge, England: Cambridge University Press, pp. 21-69. ISBN: 0521802431.

Minchinton, Walter E. (1989), "Characteristics of British Slaving Vessels, 1698–1775," *Journal of Interdisciplinary History*, vol. 20, pp. 53– 82. ISSN: 0022-1953.

Morgan, Philip (1997), "The Cultural Implications of the Atlantic Slave Trade: African Regional Origins, American Destinations and New World Developments," *Slavery and Abolition*, vol. 18, no. 1, pp. 98–121. ISSN: 0144-039X.

Mouser, Bruce L. (1973), "Trade, Coasters, and Conflict in the Rio Pongo from 1790–1808," *Journal of African History*, vol. 14, no. 1, pp. 45–64. ISSN: 0021-8537.

Palmer, Colin A. (1995), "From Africa to the Americas: Ethnicity in the Early Black Communities of the Americas," *Journal of World History*, vol. 6, no. 2, pp. 223–237. ISSN: 1045-6007.

Patterson, Orlando (1982), *Slavery and Social Death: A Comparative Study*, Cambridge, MA: Harvard University Press. ISBN: 0674810821.

Richardson, David (1987), "The Costs of Survival: The Transport of Slaves in the Middle Passage and the Profitability of the 18th-Century British Slave Trade," *Explorations in Economic History*, vol. 24, pp. 178–196. ISSN: 0014-4983.

Richardson, David (2001), "Shipboard Revolts, African Authority, and the Atlantic Slave Trade," *William and Mary Quarterly*, vol. 58, pp. 69–92. ISSN: 0043-5597.

Rodney, Walter (1969), "Slavery and Other Forms of Social Oppression on the Upper Guinea Coast in the Context of the Atlantic Slave Trade," *Journal of African History*, vol. 7, no. 4, pp. 431–443 ISSN: 0021-8537.

Rodney, Walter (1969), "Upper Guinea and the Significance of the Origins of Africans Enslaved in the New World," *The Journal of Negro History*, vol. 54, no. 4, pp. 327–345. ISSN: 0022-2992.

Searing, James F. (1993), *West African Slavery and Atlantic Commerce: The Senegal River Valley, 1700–1860*, Cambridge, England: Cambridge University Press. ISBN: 0521440831.

Sheridan, Richard B. (1981), "The Guinea Surgeons on the Middle Passage: The Provision of Medical Services in the British Slave Trade," *International Journal of African Historical Studies*, vol. 14, pp. 601–625. ISSN: 0361-7882.

Taylor, Eric Robert (2000), "If we must die: A history of shipboard insurrections during the slave trade," PhD dissertation, University of California, Los Angeles.

Thornton, John K. (1980), "The Slave Trade in Eighteenth Century Angola: Effects on Demographic Structures," *Canadian Journal of African Studies/Revue canadienne d'études africaines*, vol. 14, pp. 417–427. ISSN: 0008-3968.

Thornton, John K. (1998), *Africa and Africans in the Making of the Atlantic World, 1400–1800*, Cambridge, England: Cambridge University Press, pp. 13–42. ISBN: 0521392330.

Unsworth, Barry (1992), *Sacred Hunger*, New York: Doubleday, pp. 293–340, 369–384. ISBN: 0385265301.

van Dantzig, Albert (1975), "Effect of the Atlantic Slave Trade on Some West African Societies," *Revue française d'histoire d'outre-mer*, vol. 62, pp. 252–269. ISSN: 0300-9513.

Warner-Lewis, Maureen (1997), "Posited Kikoongo Origins of Some Portuguese and Spanish Words from the Slave Era," *América Negra*, vol. 7, no. 13, pp. 83–97. ISSN: 0121-5914.

Race and Constructions of "the Negro" in Colonial Virginia

Anthony Q. Hazard, Jr.

In 1640 in the Virginia colony, three indentured servants attempted to escape their servitude, running away to Maryland where they were eventually captured. The servants, Victor, a Dutchman, James Gregory, of Scotland, and John Punch, a black man, received punishment from the colonial court that would indicate a staying shift in the legal status of people of African descent, and in constructions of race in North America. While the two indentured servants of European descent received from the court four additional years of servitude, John Punch was sentenced to a lifetime of slavery. In his magisterial study of race and Colonial law, the late historian Leon Higginbotham concluded, "the 1640 imposition of lifetime servitude on the black participant alone was not predicated on any previous legislative enactment or any other colonial judicial precedent. Such differentiation of treatment reflected the legal process's early adoption of social values that saw blacks as inferior" (Higginbotham, 1978, 28).

In what follows I explore the process of racialization in colonial Virginia from the moment of the arrival of 20 captives of African descent at Point Comfort in 1619, following the establishment of the first permanent British settlement at Jamestown in 1607. The chapter highlights ideas of human difference or "race" that British colonizers brought with them to North America in the early seventeenth century, while then tracing the philosophical and legal trajectory of theories of race as articulated by British colonizers throughout the colonial era. I ultimately argue that as a system of chattel slavery emerged in the seventeenth century, so too did constructions of race that began to clearly define relational racialized identities in the Virginia Colony. Not only was labor racialized, the ideas of racial difference constructed by European colonizers sought to undermine the very humanity of people of African descent in the Americas. As significant court rulings and laws appeared differentiating the treatment of indentured servants and enslaved persons according to phenotypic or physical difference, the colonial legal apparatus contributed directly to the making of "the Negro" as a socially and biologically inferior being. Upon the emergence of the United States of America as a democratic republic, political leaders embedded these constructions of race within the founding documents of the nation, therefore institutionalizing racialized oppression.

Race Theory, Exploration and Colonialism (1450–1640)

As the European continent emerged from the medieval period and the Renaissance or modern Europe bloomed in the fifteenth century, maritime exploration began apace. With the backing of the Spanish and Portuguese monarchies, seafaring Europeans began venturing deep along the western coast of the African continent, and westward to the Caribbean, along with North, Central, and South America. The European powers sought both trade, to proselytize, and engage in colonial expansion. Along with the process of expansion came violence and exploitation of the indigenous populations the Europeans encountered across the globe. The European powers soon established economically profitable systems, for example, in sugar cane in the Caribbean, and in mining operations in South America. As Spain, Portugal, England, and the Netherlands solidified colonial holdings and corporate interests increased alongside monetary profits, European powers looked to procure an expendable labor source to be exploited in ways that had never occurred in human history. Beginning with the Portuguese and Dutch, European colonizers and their agents began procuring people from the African continent for the purpose of enslaving them as laborers in the so-called New World to solidify the economic basis of European colonial expansion.

Up to this point, scientific ideas of race had not been in existence, however theories of human difference had been firmly established, mainly relating to geography and supplied by natural philosophy. Ancient medical scholars such as Hippocrates and Aristotle believed that human populations varied in physical appearance in relation to different climates, and climates then determined the superiority or inferiority of a particular group. "The English, for example, were convinced of their superiority because their climate was more temperate than the cold of Scotland or the heat of Spain" (Jackson & Weidman, 2006, p. 9–10). In addition to ideas of human difference stemming from natural philosophy, during the medieval period persecution of Jewish people in Europe was common, with its origins in the early Christian church. Jews had been seen as having a central role in the crucifixion, displacing blame from Rome. Negative stereotypes were then placed upon Jewish peoples that went beyond a simple recognition of religious difference. As evolutionary biologist Joseph Graves explains, "Jews were regarded as having inferior physical, mental, and moral characteristics. They were accused of poisoning the water, engaging in sorcery, ritually murdering children, and desecrating the Host and religious images" (Graves, 2001, 21). A key point to make here is that in medieval anti–Semitism elements of a more modern race theory can be seen in that ideas about human difference were constructed and applied to a population without evidence of innate physical difference. Theories were articulated and applied to oppress a group of people viewed as *other* by European Christians prior to the European colonization of the Americas.

Contemporary scholars have also pointed to a supposedly popularly held belief concerning human difference, or race, that rested on a medieval biblical interpretation of the Great Flood, which only Noah and his three sons survived. As the biblical account goes, after the flood Ham had mocked the slumbering Noah, who had imbibed a copious amount of wine. Shem and Japheth, Noah's other sons, refused to mock him, and therefore escaped his wrath upon his awakening. For his transgression, Ham was cursed, along with his descendants who were branded with black skin. The Curse of Ham theory, however, has been shown to be a rhetorical tool used by enslavers and the planter class in the United States in the eighteenth and nineteenth century to justify enslaving non-white peoples. Evidence of such a biblical interpretation in the medieval period is non-existent, and therefore does not confirm a theory of racial difference extant in the period leading up to the age of European exploration and colonialism.

Moving into the sixteenth century however, increasing growth of the European colonial project in the Americas coincided with new theories of racial difference that refuted the notions of single creation articulated by the natural philosophers. The theory of polygenism arose in the work of Paracelsus, the famous Swiss physician and alchemist. In 1520 he offered another biblical interpretation to make sense of racial difference, arguing that descendants of Adam occupied a certain portion of the earth, while all others were of an entirely separate origin. Paracelsus interpreted the lineages of Cain as the non-white peoples of the earth who were marked by God, and Seth as the white and righteous inhabitants of Europe. Later in the sixteenth century, the Italian philosopher Giordano Bruno offered an additional polygenist theory of racial difference. For Bruno, God had created either multiple Adams, or he surmised, people of African descent were descendants pre–Adamite races. These early polygenist ideas, along with a budding European folklore concerning people of African descent proffered an expanding tapestry of racial thinking that would directly influence European colonists in the Americas. The appearance of African characters in the works of literary giants including William Shakespeare offered white European audiences symbolic encounters with villainous figures of a darker hue, connecting skin color to intrinsic evil. Published accounts and oral tales about trade voyages to west and central Africa also fed the European imagining of blackness, as did the increasing appearance of Africans on the continent as a result of those voyages. Skin color, specifically the blackness of people of African descent had become a key form of social identification in England in particular.

Combined with the increasingly exploitative and violent colonial project in North America in the late sixteenth and early seventeenth century, folk ideas of race persisted as the system of chattel slavery came to the fore. In the first decade following the permanent English settlement of Jamestown, Virginia, people of African descent occupied a tenuous or undefined position in the colonial structure. Some were indentured workers, others were enslaved, but while there were Africans or Atlantic Creoles who had been bought and sold, their actual legal standing was undefined. In fact, court cases in the 1620s made no distinction between white and black servants. The Virginia colony had established its own representative assembly in 1619, the very year the first twenty enslaved Africans arrived at Point Comfort, and had organized county courts by the 1630s to deal with local disputes, and it is by the 1630s that legal authorities began banning black people from serving in the militia. In 1648 black people were altogether barred from carrying firearms in the Virginia colony. It is at this precise moment that the courts begin to define the legal status of the enslaved and solidify the link between race and slavery.

The story of John Punch that opened this chapter is most aptly illustrative of this seismic shift in the legal status of black people in the Virginia colony. That John Punch was punished for a life of servitude for committing the same offense that the Dutchman Victor and Scotsman James Gregory had, reveals "an astonishingly harsh decision" that "exemplifies the court's intent to deliberately exercise partiality in its dealings" with black people in the colony (Higginbotham, 1978, 28). The language of the legal ruling does not reveal a rationale for the discrepancy in the punishments handed down, other than race, as it reads, "and that the third being a Negro names John Punch shall serve his said master or his assigns for the time of his natural Life here or elsewhere" (Catterall, 1968, 77). By the early 1640s black people comprised a very small portion of the Virginia population, three hundred out of fifteen thousand, yet the courts began punishing them in ever increasingly harsh ways (Baskin, 1976, 39).

This downward spiral into chattel slavery would continue in Virginia and throughout the colonies along the Atlantic seaboard in the decades immediately following the John Punch case. However ambiguity in the courts and the broader social fabric remained, as the role of Christianity, the presence of Indigenous peoples, and economic concerns of the English Crown contributed to the complexities of race making in Virginia.

Chattel Slavery and Racialized Labor (1640–1776)

Both Indigenous and African peoples in the early Virginia colony understood the strategic potential of embracing Christianity by conversion. This complicated the efforts of the English to solidify a system of chattel slavery, as they viewed conversion as a literal saving grace for the non–Christian people of color they defined as heathens. Those Indigenous and African peoples who would receive the holy water would be viewed in a different light, not necessarily as equals to white Englishmen and women, but deserving at least of a modicum of legal rights and potentially of freedom. One such case is occurred in 1642, regarding an Indigenous man who spoke "perfectly the English tongue" and "desired baptism" (Baskin, 1976, 41). The man was freed from a lifetime of servitude because of his adoption of English culture and religiosity. This occasionally occurred with enslaved Africans as well, as many brought suits to court in an effort to gain their freedom. "A Mulata named Manuel" who had been sold into a lifetime of slavery, successfully petitioned in 1644 for his eventual release on the grounds that he was a Christian. The court ordered that Manuel serve his owner as an apprentice and be set fully free after a twenty-year period.

The legal savvy of Indigenous and African peoples in the Virginia colony at times afforded them positive results in their quest for freedom, however the broader landscape of the status of laborers continued to diminish "between 1642 and 1660" when additional "laws were passed pertaining to the length of service of colonial servants, as were other laws, generally favorable to the interests of the master, attempting to deal with the most frequent areas of conflict in the master-servant relationship" (Higginbotham, 1978, 32–33). What is also clear is that by the early 1660s the increasing numbers of those held in lifetime bondage were in large part of African descent. What the late historian Ronald Takaki has called the "giddy multitude" of laborers of African, European, and Indigenous descent occupying varying degrees of freedom, began to disappear (Takaki, 1994). This trend was buttressed by the passing of a 1662 law that declared the status of a child born in the colony would be determined by the status of the mother. Colonial authorities were particularly concerned about the undefined legal status of children borne to white fathers and black mothers, and therefore adopted a legal statute to clarify the matter in the following terms:

> Whereas some doubts have arisen whether children got up by an Englishman upon a negro woman should be slave or free, be it therefore enacted and declared by this present grand assembly, that all children borne in this country shall be held bond or free only according to the condition of the mother [Baskin, 1976, 44].

Colonial authorities further solidified the status of enslaved Africans by declaring by law in 1667 that "the conferring of baptisme doth not alter the condition of the person as to his bondage or freedom" (Baskin, 1976, 45). A strategy that was once available to enslaved persons had been removed, and the system of chattel slavery had been legally defined as a perpetual condition for black people through the redefining of the legal status of children according to the free or enslaved status of the mother. This matrilineal organization of chattel slavery helped to define the social condition or status of black people as enslaved, and would remain until emancipation two centuries later. Additional laws and court rulings throughout the 1670s and 1680s further entrenched not only the system of chattel slavery, but the racialized distinctions between servant and slave. Blackness was clearly degraded in the eyes of the law, and whiteness was elevated and equated with freedom. Even the indentured servants coming over from Europe existed in a space in which freedom was on the horizon. After completing their assigned time of servitude, European indentured servants could become full citizens with civil rights equal to any other white male. This prospect did not exist for black people, even those who were legally free. Virginia colonial law also forbade free Africans from bearing arms, serving as witnesses in court proceedings, and voting. These legal developments were once again augmented by newly emerging theories of racial difference offered by European thinkers.

As historian Rebecca Anne Goetz explains in her recent study of the role of Christianity in colonial Virginia's constructions of race, "seventeenth-century Anglo-Virginians developed concepts of heredity and wide-ranging theories about the origins and descent of Indians and Africans. Religious differences were not merely artifacts of culture but rather means of assessing the spiritual capacities of Indians and Africans" (Goetz, 2016, 9). Yet the emergence of scientific ideas about race occurred alongside the tail end of that religious construction of race in the seventeenth century. One such contributor to this emerging thought was French physician

Francois Bernier (b. 1625–d. 1688). In his essay "The New Division of the Earth" published in 1684, Bernier offered one of the earliest known classification schemes of human beings according to race. Bernier had gained renown for the published accounts of his travels to Cairo and Persia, and his twelve years in India, where he worked as a colonial official's physician. Informed by his travels, "The New Division of the Earth" put forth four racial categories, the first broadly including north Africans, Middle easterners, Asian Indians, and American Indians. The second category was comprised of African peoples not of the northern part of the continent, the third included east and northeast Asian populations, and the fourth, Lapps, or peoples originating in northern Scandinavia. Bernier based his classification scheme on observable physical characteristics, but he also postulated value judgments according to physical differences. He particularly rated the aesthetic beauty of various peoples according to their phenotype, and tied levels of rationality to physical appearance. Bernier's scientific intervention in European and American understandings of race refute any subsequent claims that the very practice of racial classification were purely objective. His appeal to readers was based in large part on the fact that he had travelled far beyond Europe, and therefore had first hand knowledge of encountering physical variability and "exotic" cultures (Jackson & Weidman, 2006, 14–15).

Arguably more influential on European and English colonial discourses of race than Francois Bernier, was Swedish scientist Carolus Linnaeus (b. 1707–d. 1778), who came up with the system of naming and organizing plants and animals. In 1735, Linnaeus published the first edition of his *Systema Naturae*, in which he detailed the system of binomial nomenclature, designating genus and species classifications for the plant and animal kingdoms. In a later edition of *Systema Naturae* published in 1758, Linnaeus applied his classification system to humans, noting that the species *Homo sapiens* was comprised of four varieties: europaeus, afer, asiaticus, and americanus. Although Linnaeus put forth his system of organizing and classifying plants, animals, and later humans, as scientific and based on objective observation, he nevertheless applied "a hierarchy of perfection in the physical and intellectual characters of human varieties" with *Homo europaeus* "representing the apex" and *Homo afer* "the abyss" (Graves, 2001, pg. 38–39). For Linnaeus, all humans were members of the same species, created by God, but possessing distinct characteristics that deserve outlining here:

    1. Americanus: Reddish skin, black hair, scanty beard, obstinate, merry, regulated by custom.
    2. Asiaticus: Sallow skin, black hair, dark eyes, severed, greedy, covered with loose garments, ruled by opinions.

3. Africanus: Black skin, black, frizzled hair, indolent, women without shame, governed by caprice.
4. Europaeus: White, long, flowing hair, blue eyes, gentle, inventive, covers himself with close-fitting clothing, governed by laws [Jackson & Weidman, 2006, 16].

Here we see that Linnaeus noted as "racial" differences cultural practices or norms, such as style of dress, but he also incorrectly drew lines around the physical characteristics of Europeans by declaring them as defined by "blue eyes" and long flowing hair. All Europeans neither in the eighteenth century certainly did not possess the recessive phenotype of blue eyes, yet Linnaeus comfortably asserted that limited characterization. Linnaeus's system offered large geographic populations as "varieties" that encompassed entire continents, while also selecting very specific physical characteristics as representative of a fixed type.

Also influential in 18th discourses of race was George-Louis Leclerc de Buffon (b. 1707–d. 1788), the wealthy Frenchman and critic of Linnaeus. Buffon had ties to French nobility, as he worked for King Louis XV supervising the Royal Garden. Buffon put forth his critique of Linnaeus in *Historoire Naturelle* published in 1749. Buffon took issue with Linnaeus's contention that animal and human species were fixed and immutable. Buffon argued that while species change was possible, it was determined by the environment, and for humans specifically, he employed the term "race" in place of Linnaeus's term "variety." Buffon did agree with his predecessors in ranking Europeans as the highest type from which all others were degenerations from, and he believed "that little genius cold be found" among people of African descent (Graves, 2001, 40).

Arguably the most influential thinker in matters of racial classification in the eighteenth century was German medical professor Johann Friedrich Blumenbach (b. 1752–d. 1840). Blumenbach was a critic of many previous efforts to classify humans according to "race," noting the arbitrary methods and definitions of identifying races. For Blumenbach, there were five clearly identifiable racial groups: Caucasian, Mongolian, Ethiopian, American, and Malay. Blumenbach noted however that these five races possessed physical characteristics that overlapped or blended, challenging the notion that physical races were completely distinct and separate (Graves, 2001, pg. 40). Blumenbach also challenged the racial orthodoxy of the day by maintaining that members of the African or "Ethiopian" race had shown intellectual abilities equal to that of members of the Caucasian race. Significantly, Blumenbach did offer an aesthetic evaluation of the five races, noting the particular physical beauty of women from the Caucasus Mountain region, hence the classification of "Caucasian." Blumenbach argued that Caucasians were the original race, and all others descended from them, changing in physical appearance over time due to migration and differences in climate and environment (Jackson & Weidman, 2006, 20). Blumenbach classification scheme, particularly his invocation of Caucasian would have far more impact on future Euro-American thinkers than his conclusions about the intellectual abilities of people of African descent. In fact, within the context of the emerging movement toward American independence from Britain in the late eighteenth century, common notions of black inferiority remained staunchly entrenched in the new republic.

Race and the New Republic (1776–1790)

As states began to form their governments during the American Revolutionary era and early republic, many addressed slavery in their state constitutions. In New England, slavery was abolished by the state of Vermont in 1777, and New Hampshire and Massachusetts in 1783. Rhode Island, New York, Pennsylvania, and New Jersey would carry out gradual emancipation in the final decades of the eighteenth century. But in the southern U.S., the centrality of slavery to the southern economy along with the social norms of race and racism served to further entrench chattel slavery throughout the region. While African Americans everywhere understood the implications of white Americans clamoring for freedom from the British on the basis of "a natural human right to freedom, many black Americans asserted their right to be liberated from slavery." The very philosophical basis of white revolutionary fervor further fueled the resistance of enslaved peoples to the system of chattel slavery. For example, petitioners in Massachusetts in 1777 actually referred to a notion of "natural, God-given rights that could not be taken from them without their consent" (Hine et al., 2018, 90). Six years later, the enslaved in Massachusetts would have their freedom. In other cases, African Americans fought as Patriots in the effort to defeat Britain, while others fought as Loyalists for the British, but many on both sides had their own freedom in mind. Other enslaved African Americans would use the chaos and disorganization wrought by the war to escape to freedom.

Upon the war's end when Britain officially recognized the independence of the United States of America in 1783, chattel slavery as a system was clearly dying in the northern U.S., and seemingly declining in the mid–Atlantic. Slavery in the southern United States, however, would experience expansion in the 1790s. Compared to the northern states in which most

African Americans had gained their freedom by 1800, the state of Virginia in 1790 held 293,427 slaves, and that number exploded to 425,531 by 1820, the largest number of enslaved persons in the country (Hine et al., 2018, 122). While the emergence of the new Republic spelled increased economic freedom and power for a select group of white men, it also spelled increased exploitation and surveillance for those enslaved persons in the south. The U.S. Constitution in some ways legitimized this entrenchment of the system of chattel slavery. As it came into effect in 1789, the nation's Constitution, agreed upon by delegates at the Constitutional Convention, included clauses specifically designed to insure the enslavement of African Americans. Such provisions included guaranteeing an additional twenty years of the transatlantic slave trade, a national military assistance in suppressing revolts, and aiding the return of escaped slaves to their masters in the south.

The Constitution also strengthened the political power of slaveholders, like Thomas Jefferson and other "Founding Fathers," by included a provision called the Three-Fifths Clause. The Three-Fifths Clause provided that an individual slaves be counted as three-fifths of a person in determining a state's representation in both Congress and the Electoral College, thus bolstering the representative power of slave holders. This clause, like others which favored slave owners in the south, was the result of compromise between the white men of the north, mid–Atlantic, and south, in order to form a powerful and stable Union in the face of the contradictions of their revolutionary and enlightenment ideals, with chattel slavery. For Jefferson, he composed his *Notes on the State Virginia* within this late eighteenth century context of revolutionary fervor, the liberal and progressive philosophies that he and others articulated to express their desires of freedom, along with the ongoing enslavement of human beings of African descent. As a wealthy land-owner and enslaver, and statesmen, Jefferson sought to explain slavery in his own state, to white audiences in Europe and the U.S. In *Notes on the State of Virginia*, published in several editions throughout the 1780s, Jefferson argued both against the existence of the institution of slavery and for the natural inferiority of people of African descent. Jefferson's thinking particularly on black people, was in line with well-known European philosophers such as David Hume and Immanuel Kant, who argued that "within distinct biological racial groups," cultural abilities and psychological characteristics were biologically determined or inherited (Zack, 2002, 13). "At a time of crisis in his home state and in the new republic as a whole," historian David Waldstreicher shows, "Jefferson brought the method of late eighteenth-century natural history to bear on Virginian and American problems" (Waldstreicher, 2002, 3).

Jefferson in *Notes on the State of Virginia* veered away from the thinking of other theorists who pointed to differences in climate as determining factors of racial difference, and rather focused squarely on skin color. For Jefferson, skin color was *the* marker of racial (and cultural) superiority or inferiority. "The first difference which strikes us is that of color," the future third President of the United States wrote. "Whether the black of the negro resides in the reticular membrane between the skin and scarf-skin, or in the scarf-skin itself; whether it proceeds from the color of the blood, the color of the bile, or from that of some other secretion, the difference is fixed in nature, and is real as if its seat and cause were better known to us." Jefferson also proffered stereotypes about black people having to do with "less hair on the face and body," and that black people "secrete less by the kidneys, and more by the glands of the skin, which gives them a very strong and disagreeable odor." For Jefferson black people "require less sleep," as "after hard labor through the day, will be induced by the slightest amusements to sit up till midnight, or later." Jefferson backhandedly compliments those enslaved persons he has observed as "at least as brave, and more adventuresome. But" he clarified, "this may perhaps proceed from a want of forethought, which prevents their seeing a danger till it be present." (Jefferson, 2002, 176). Jefferson also mused on the lack of cultural achievement of people of African descent, lauding the comparative potential and achievement of "The Indians," who "with no advantages" will "often carve figures on their pipes not destitute of design and merit. They will crayon out an animal, a plant, or a country, so as to prove the existence of a germ in their minds which only wants cultivation." Jefferson makes clear that while he "never yet could find that a black had uttered a thought above the level of plain narration," indigenous peoples "astonish you with strokes of the most sublime oratory; such prove their reason and sentiment strong" (Jefferson, 2002, 177).

In his *Notes on the State of Virginia* Jefferson sought to address on possible example of black genius in the figure of Phyllis Wheatley. The irony clearly lost on Jefferson, he claimed, "misery is often the parent of the most affecting touches in poetry. Among the blacks is misery enough, God knows, but no poetry." It was not her creativity or sense of humanity that allowed her to write, but rather "religion, indeed, has produced a Phyllis Whately [sic]; but it could not produce a poet." For Jefferson, "The compositions published under her name are below the dignity of criticism" (Jefferson, 2002, 177–178). Jefferson's positions on race generally and about black people in particular are made clear in his broader conclusion: "I advance it therefore as a suspicion only, that the blacks, whether originally a distinct race, or made distinct by time and circumstances, are inferior to the whites in the endowments both of body and mind." And further, the implications of his conclusions on race were devastating. "This unfortunate difference of color, and perhaps of faculty, is a powerful obstacle to the emancipation of these people" (Jefferson, 2002, 180).

Jefferson's authoritative theorizing about race and blackness stand as remarkable evidence of the broader beliefs and sentiments on race that existed as the United States of America emerged as an independent nation, founded on the principles of natural rights, but also in the denial of them due to a belief in innate biological differences. These beliefs, as elucidated by the likes of Jefferson and others, would continue to be utilized in order to justify the growing system of slavery in the southern United States. Within a decade of the publication of Jefferson's *Notes on the State of Virginia*, slavery would further expand and become more deeply entrenched in the state apparatus. As historical chance would have it, both the invention of the cotton gin and Congress passing the Fugitive Slave Act in 1793 would offer additional obstacles to emancipation for the enslaved. Allowing for the speedy removal of cotton seeds from the cotton fiber, Eli Whitney's machine increased the efficiency of harvesting, and contributed heavily to cotton becoming the most lucrative U.S. export in the decades leading up to the U.S. Civil War (Hine et al., 2018, 123–124). The Fugitive Slave Act, which was based on an original Constitutional provision, permitted slave masters to recapture slaves who had reached free territory, with the authority of local courts. With the cotton boom both New England and Europe benefited financially, as did slave owners in the south, and black people found it increasingly difficult to procure their freedom from enslavement.

The expansion of the United States westward and the presidency of Thomas Jefferson coincided in the first decade of the nineteenth century to further intensify the centrality of slavery American life, and the attendant theories used to justify holding millions of black people in bondage. As Thomas Jefferson took office in 1801 and executed the Louisiana Purchase just two years later, the United States would double in size, accelerate the expansion of slavery, and increase the internal or domestic trade in slaves from the Chesapeake region to the deep south and southwest. One indication of that growth is found in Louisiana itself. In 1810 the state had 34,660 slaves, and by 1820 the enslaved population had risen to 149,654 (Hine et al., 2018, 126). Slavery had won out, as had ideas about race that condemned black people as mentally, intellectually, and spiritually inferior.

Further evidence of the centrality of slavery and race to the very existence and functioning of the United States lies in the racial categories used in official government policy, specifically in identifying and counting the country's occupants. The first U.S. Census of 1790 included the following categories only: (1) free white males, (2) free white females, (3) all other free persons, and (4) slaves. The category of "Indian" would not appear on the U.S. Census until 1860, the dawn of the Civil War. By 1860, the U.S. government had completed its conquest of westward expansion to the Pacific Ocean, leaving in its wake death and destruction of Indigenous peoples across the north American continent. Within the federal policy of annihilation and dispossession, the U.S. government did not recognize Indigenous peoples as members of American society, much less respect their humanity. The lack of inclusion in the U.S. Census from 1790 to 1850 is an indication of those policies and sentiments. However, the keen focus on recognizing and categorizing black and white people, and the status of the enslaved, shows how central those antithetical racial categories were to white political leaders and citizens alike. Furthermore, U.S. citizens could not choose their own racial identifications for the federal census until 1960, which means that agents of the U.S. government were literally charged with deciding who was white, black, "Indian," and so on.

Conclusions

People of African descent brought to Virginia in the early seventeenth century entered into an ambiguous status in a society that had no statutes defining their legal status as enslaved or free. Those Atlantic Creoles and Africans who landed at Point Comfort and eventually taken to Jamestown were enslaved in name, but no colonial laws existed that defined exactly what it meant to be enslaved. Enslaved persons in the Virginia colony were able to negotiate for wages, in some cases live on their own, convert to Christianity, and legally marry. In the 1640s as tobacco increasingly became more profitable, legal rulings handed down by the colonial court began to differentiate between African and European indentured servants and slaves. By the 1660s legal statutes were put into place to actually define what it meant to be enslaved in Virginia, establishing the basis of perpetual servitude as determined by the status of the mother as free or slave. Additionally, colonial law established that people of European descent were not to be enslaved, which resulted in slavery becoming equated with blackness.

The philosophical basis of the American Revolution, notions of God given individual rights to freedom and justice, did little to intervene in the feelings of those in the Chesapeake region and the deep south who wholeheartedly supported the system of chattel slavery. The combination of European philosophy, social norms based on notions of racial difference and black inferiority, and the economic incentives of slavery solidified a system that would continue apace until the Civil War and Reconstruction era. The understandings of race and racial difference that animated chattel slavery in the colonial era were not simply folk beliefs, held by the few. European philosophers and naturalists during this time systematically went about constructing concepts that relegated black people to the bottom of humanity, and the system of chattel slavery embodied those beliefs. Men like Thomas Jefferson not only embraced, but consistently articulated the belief that people of European descent were superior to black people in a myriad of ways, and, despite the coming the American Revolution, further entrenched the system of slavery that would remain until 1865.

REFERENCES

Baskin, J. (1976). *Into Slavery: Racial Decisions in the Virginia Colony.* Philadelphia: J.B. Lippincott.

Catterall, H.T. (1968). *Judicial Cases Concerning American Slavery and the Negro.* New York: Octagon Books.

Goetz, R.A. (2016). *The Baptism of Early Virginia: How Christianity Created Race.* Baltimore: Johns Hopkins University Press.

Graves, J.L. Jr. (2001). *The Emperor's New Clothes: Biological Theories of Race at the Millennium.* New Brunswick: Rutgers University Press.

Higginbotham, A.L. (1978). *In the Matter of Color: Race and the American Legal Process, The Colonial Period.* New York: Oxford University Press.

Hine, D. Clark, Hine, W.C. & Harrold, S. (2018). *The African-American Odyssey, Volume 1.* New York: Pearson.

Jackson, J.P. & Weidman, N.M. (2006). *Race, Racism, and Science: Social Impact and Interaction.* New Brunswick: Rutgers University Press.

Jefferson, T. (2002). *Notes on the State of Virginia.* (Ed.) David Waldstreicher. Boston: Bedford/St. Martins.

Takaki, R. (1994). *A Different Mirror: A History of Multicultural America.* Boston: Little, Brown and Company.

Waldstreicher, D. (2002). "Introduction." In Waldstreicher (Ed.), *Notes on the State of Virginia* (pp. 1–39). Boston: Beford/St Martins.

Zack, N. (2002). *Philosophy of Science and Race.* New York: Routledge.

The Other Amazing Grace from a Slave Ship

JAMES A. FORBES, JR.

> How amazing that "20 And odd Negroes" from the Motherland
> Should be bearers of a blessing for every woman and man:
> the humanity to question God without shame or fear,
> Persisting in asking, "Lord, How Come Me Here?"

One of the world's best loved hymns is "Amazing Grace." It is reputed to have been composed by John Newton in the late 1700s following a stormy voyage on a slave ship. This commentary is about another slave ship, the *White Lion*, which nearly one hundred years earlier deposited "20 And odd Negroes" at Point Comfort in Hampton, Virginia. That event in 1619, the first landing of Africans on the shores of Virginia, will be closely studied during the Quadricentennial commemorations of the introduction of slavery into the United States of America. The case advanced here is that upon close theological reflection and sociological analysis more than enslaved black bodies were brought here to be sold. Serious critical examination of four hundred years of the black experience reveals that there was also a kind of amazing grace in the hearts and minds of the chained captives from Mother Africa. It was a humanizing spiritual consciousness which brought to these shores a legacy of meaning, purpose, resiliency and hope. With these slaves came a blessing which has impacted our culture in ways seldom celebrated. The Quadricentennial observance of that moment in history comes at a time when our nation is imperiled from serious assault against the spirit of democracy. What the "20 And odd Negroes" brought four hundred years ago may hold the key to a spiritual revitalization that can help save the soul of our nation. Thus the title: The Other Amazing Grace from a Slave Ship.

As plans develop for commemorating the 1619 arrival of Africans at

Point Comfort in Hampton, Virginia, we ought to remember that the significance of such historic moments have sometimes been trivialized. Frederick Douglass in his speech, "What to the Slave, Is the Fourth of July" was compelled to remind his predominantly white audience that July 4 was a celebration of their independence and not his. Today, we find ourselves in the midst of yet another example of not taking history seriously enough. With only a few months left in the year of the 50th commemoration of the assassination of Dr. Martin Luther King, Jr., that shameful epic making moment, will history record that America allowed that event to pass as if the bloodshed in Memphis and around the nation wasn't still crying from the ground for repentance, reparations and repair?

Thus far, our nation has ignored opportunities to appropriately remember, analyze the deeper causes, repent and re-imagine what a more perfect Union would look like. We have not used the memory of that particular tragic event to reconstruct the social, economic and political infrastructure of the hearts and minds of our citizenry or the fabric of the society itself. No major legislative agenda has been advanced, no restorative justice mandates have captured the spirit of our leaders and no domestic Marshall Plan for race and class amelioration has been proposed to atone for the blood shed during those dark days of moral and spiritual collapse. Yes, there were marches, documentary footage of the riots that followed and seminars about King's legacy. I attended the events at Hotel Lorraine in Memphis on April 4, 2018, and I wrote editorial comments for the local newspaper. But what America should do about what we as a nation are becoming was not widely discussed. We have only a few months left to produce a fitting commemoration—one that demands renewed dedication to high ideals and sacrificial action to demonstrate an openness to being transformed by revelations from the past. What will we eventually do in the remaining months to show that we believe in the causes for which King and countless others shed their blood?

Beyond the usual ceremonies of reverence and respect are we prepared to ask history to remind us of what we were not courageous enough to face before now? There are profound insights to be re-discovered that will deepen our understanding, alter our behavior, fortify us against threats, foreign and domestic, and renew our commitments to values that will safeguard us from both external tyranny and internal malignancy of spirit. Shall we seize this moment of Quadricentennial commemoration to confront the transgressions of the participants in the vile system of chattel slavery and its aftermath of segregation and discrimination, and repent for the ill-gotten benefits that some inherited including those the nation still perpetuates? Deal or no deal? Truth or continued denial? We shall see.

Commemorations of the 1619 arrival could become the occasion for God to bless America by revealing that within the disgraceful forced removal of Africans to these shores, divine providence also deposited a hidden grace … a gracious spiritual perspective—the gift of the people despised and rejected, rebuked and scorned, misused, brutalized and traumatized for four hundred years. To those with ears to hear and eyes to see, the Quadricentennial Commemoration of the Arrival of Africans in America could offer insight into what might just save the soul of the nation as we face serious assaults on the very foundation of our democratic way of life. The slave traders who unloaded their cargo at Point Comfort listed "20 And odd Negroes." It never occurred to them to wonder what was in the hearts and minds of these captive people. They were "Negro cargo"—bodies for sale. White supremacist ideology had trained these merchants never to consider that in those black bodies were souls, minds and hearts. Nor would they have imagined what memories or bonds of family and friendship they carried in their battered, bruised and shackled spirits. Those who trafficked in human flesh were spiritually deaf to the mournful song that developed within the breasts of these captive people.

A Word About the Song They Brought from the Homeland

The seeds of their song were planted by the Hand of God when homo sapiens were distinguished from their ancestral animal forbearers. They germinated at every encounter where their lives were threatened by assaults against their wellbeing as well as their survival:

- while awaiting deportation in holding pens on the coast of Africa
- while stacked like sardines in the hole of the boats
- while standing on slave auction blocks
- while cowering in the dark of plantation cabins
- while picking cotton or harvesting corn
- while being lashed for having answered freedom's call
- while beginning the trek toward freedom without 4 acres or a mule
- while sitting in Reconstruction Congresses convened by armed insistence
- while navigating Jim Crow waters of intimidation and domination
- while being surprised by insulting forms of diminishment after being promoted to CEO of the corporation
- while standing by helpless while black and brown youth are murdered at will

- while being resented for daring to be President of the Nation
- while being called excrement from the oval office

The song lived within the souls of these "20 And odd Negroes" who landed in Virginia in 1619 as well as within the spirit of every black person who dares to face the reality of being black in the Americas. I first heard the song when Kathleen Battle, the world-renowned opera singer included it in her concert of Negro Spiritual at Carnegie Hall in New York City. This is what she sang:

Lord, How Come Me Here

Lord, how come me here?
Lord, how come me here?
Lord, how come me here?
I wish I never was born.
There ain't no freedom here, Lord.
There ain't no freedom here, Lord.
There ain't no freedom here, Lord.
I wish I never was born.
They treat me so mean here, Lord.
They treat me so mean here, Lord.
They treat me so mean here, Lord.
I wish I never was born.
They sold my children away, Lord.
They sold my children away, Lord.
They sold my children away, Lord.
I wish I never was born.
Lord, how come me here?
Lord, how come me here?
Lord, how come me here?

A meaningful commemoration of this Quadricentennial requires theological reflection on the deeper meaning of the sentiments of that song. Where was God during the four hundred years of sojourn in the land of bondage? Where is God today? Is there a positive grace in this requiem for the living dead? Such a meaningful commemoration invites us to consider the various responses to that tragic interrogative lament.

Serious theological reflection demands that we accept that all human beings have had intimations or have grappled with this question: Lord, how come me here? Maya Angelou's declaration that "We are more alike than we are unalike" is prophetic. Black people and white people, despite racist myths and demonic thinking, are one human species. A distinction between humans and animals is the gift that came with the evolution into our full humanity on the continent of Africa. We all possess the innate ability to ponder our mortality and to inquire about the meaning and purpose of our lives. Beyond a mere preoccupation with the why and the what for of our existence is a creative imagination that struggles to discern, invent or construct plausible answers to the question: Lord, how come me here? The song, therefore, becomes a divine/human dialogue. It is not a soliloquy. It is a conversation between Creator and creature. This comes as no surprise to the black community. James Weldon Johnson's poem Creation informs us that God was lonely and for the purpose of communion made humankind. What a powerful first clue to human existence—to be in communion and in conversation with God. Sometimes this conversation is conducted in the indicative mood and at other times in the bitter interrogative tone. The Biblical tradition states that at a point of frustration even God repented that humankind had ever been made. There are those who believe that the cry of dereliction from the Cross—"My God, my God, why hast thou forsaken me?"—is a Father-Son conversation, echoing the sentiments of the same song—Lord, How Come Me Here?

I hear this same tune from Jonah in the belly of the whale, from Israel in the land of bondage, from Job on the trash heap, from Jeremiah in the dungeon and from Daniel in the lion's den. Even from the white man's lion's dens the caged birds were still singing this song—Lord, How Come Me Here? In our post-modern society we have outgrown the natural tendency to have conversations with God about who we are and how we should relate to each other. We are not inclined to inquire about how we fit into the larger narrative of existence or how we should relate to the other orders of creation. Could this account for the growing disorientation we are experiencing in these times? If nothing more results from the commemoration of the Quadricentennial than getting our fellow Americans to pause long enough to resume that conversation with God, that in itself will make the celebration well worth four hundred years of waiting.

It was providential that while writing this paper I had an experience that provided some answers to the question of the first Africans who landed on these shores. I was asked to preach the graveside eulogy for Dr. Olivia Hooker, the last survivor of the 1921 massacre in Tulsa, Oklahoma. She was six years old when the Greenwood section of Tulsa, called the Black Wall Street, was burned to the ground. The event took place after a black man was falsely accused of rape without evidence and without a trial. After her community was burned down and many family members and friends perished, she and her siblings escaped. They never returned to their home or to her parents' business. Dr. Hooker survived the experience and went on to become the first black female member of the Coast Guard after the Navy rejected her. She earned a doctorate in psychology from Rochester University and taught for years at Fordham University. At her memorial service,

I took the liberty of suggesting that in times of honor and disdain from six years old to her death at 103 years old she had either sung, hummed or moaned, "Lord, How Come Me Here?" And in conversation with her spirit as I reviewed the highlights of her life, I came to believe that her experiences capture some of the responses of our forbearers at Point Comfort and countless pilgrims of sorrow over the past 400 years. In her conversations with God the following raison d'etre for her survival was revealed.

Here's Why You Here

1. To be a witness to how low human beings can go in their treatment of other human beings

Olivia Hooker had seen a thing or two in her 103 years. She could be a star witness in the eternal courts of glory offering eyewitness testimony to man's inhumanity to man … men and women treating people like beasts of burden and at times as cannon fodder. No matter what the oppressors say, she will stand her ground on the incontrovertible truth seared in her memory as a videotape of violence, violation and victimization.

Edwin Markham had already addressed the men and women of the jury with his poem inspired by Jean-Francois Millet's painting *The Man with the Hoe.*

> Bowed by the weight of centuries he leans
> Upon his hoe and gazes on the ground,
> The emptiness of ages in his face,
> And on his back the burden of the world.
> Who made him dead to rapture and despair,
> A thing that grieves not and that never hopes,
> Stolid and stunned, a brother to the ox?
> Who loosened and let down this brutal jaw?
> Whose was the hand that slanted back this brow?
> Whose breath blew out the light within this brain?
> Is this the Thing the Lord God made and gave
> To have dominion over sea and land;
> To trace the stars and search the heavens for power;
> To feel the passion of Eternity?
> Is this the Dream He dreamed who shaped the suns
> And marked their ways upon the ancient deep?
> Down all the stretch of Hell to its last gulf
> There is no shape more terrible than this—
> More tongued with censure of the world's blind greed—
> More filled with signs and portents for the soul—
> More fraught with danger to the universe.
> What gulfs between him and the seraphim!
> Slave of the wheel of labor, what to him

The Other Amazing Grace from a Slave Ship (Forbes, Jr.)   75

>Are Plato and the swing of Pleiades?
>What the long reaches of the peaks of song,
>The rift of dawn, the reddening of the rose?
>Through this dread shape the suffering ages look;
>Time's tragedy is in that aching stoop;
>Through this dread shape humanity betrayed,
>Plundered, profaned and disinherited,
>Cries protest to the Judges of the World,
>A protest that is also prophecy.
>O masters, lords and rulers in all lands,
>is this the handiwork you give to God,
>This monstrous thing distorted and soul-quenched?
>How will you ever straighten up this shape;
>Touch it again with immortality;
>Give back the upward looking and the light;
>Rebuild in it the music and the dream;
>Make right the immemorial infamies,
>Perfidious wrongs, immedicable woes?
>O masters, lords and rulers in all lands,
>How will the Future reckon with this Man?
>How answer his brute question in that hour
>When whirlwinds of rebellion shake the world?
>How will it be with kingdoms and with kings—
>With those who shaped him to the thing he is—
>When this dumb Terror shall reply to God
>After the silence of the centuries?

In his novel *Juneteenth*, posthumously published in 1999, Ralph Ellison shares with us a verbatim account of the Reverend Hickman's testimony about how low black people had been negated—nearly to the point of non-being:

>Left eyeless, earless, noseless, throatless, teethless, tongueless, handless, feetless, armless, wrongless, rightless, harmless, drumless, danceless, songless, hornless, soundless, sightless, wrongless, rightless, motherless, fatherless, sisterless, brotherless, plowless, muleless, foodless, mindless—and Godless.

That's about as low as a human being can diminish one of the same species, if indeed they are of the same species and if not, somebody ought to discuss that matter with God who made of one blood all the nations of the earth.

Dr. Hooker and the "20 And odd Negroes" and the Reverend Hickman were all star witnesses as were countless others. They will all speak out of a storehouse of remembrances of being called everything but a child of God—from both the German and the American Holocausts, from Rwanda and Nigeria, from the Soviet death camps and the killing fields of Cambodia and the refugees and slaughtered from all around the world. They will join the chorus of those singing, "Lord, How Come Me Here?"

Here's Why You Are Here.

2. To witness to the power of God's Word to lift the lowly.
Against all odds Olivia kept coming and rising and representing and blazing the trail for countless "firsts" including the first President of color of these United States. That's why you here, Olivia—to bear witness to the power of God's love to turn victims into victors, rejects into honorees and second-class citizens into world class champions of freedom, justice and peace. Langston Hughes and Arna Bontemps also take the witness stand to confirm the spirit and the truth imbedded in the beloved prayer meeting song, Love Lifted Me and in the old Negro folklore about the time, "When All Africans Could Fly."

There was the story of a group of slaves recently brought to a plantation on John's Island, South Carolina. It included a young woman who had just had a baby. She was worked as hard as all the rest. With her baby on her back she was overcome by the rigor of her toil and the heat of the sun. After falling to the ground and being lashed by the slave driver several times she cried out to an old man who was standing by, "Father, is it time?" he said, "No, not yet my daughter." But after she appealed to him again, he said "Yes, now is the time, go." And with the baby on her back she flew off into the ridge of the horizon. The old man turned to the other black people and said the same words to them and they flew away as well. The overseers said, Get that black devil, he's causing us to lose all our slaves. The word the old man was saying was "Koolibah!," "Koolibah!" I first heard this story told by Vincent Harding in 1970 at a Black Theology Conference at Howard University in Washington, D.C. Years later a white woman named Winifred Vass told me the meaning of the word. Her father, a missionary who had translated the Bible for the Tchiluba tribe in the Congo told her that "Koolibah" was a diminutive of a phrase which meant: "Let them go up." How come we here? To bear witness in these United States that there is a word that lifts us up no matter how low we are put down. As Maya Angelou said, "Bringing the gifts that my ancestors gave, I am the dream and the hope of the slave. I rise, I rise, I rise" (Ong, 2014, 47).

How Come We Here? We Ask Again.

3. To know the joy of being a blessing to others in need.
One of Martin Luther King, Jr.'s favorite songs was "If I Can Help Somebody." Helping the fallen children was also a source of deep satisfaction to Olivia Hooker. Those who find themselves in a position to make

a significant difference in the lives of others will tell you that it is one of the most sublime satisfactions of life. It is as if God reserved that level of delight for those who earn it, from unselfish sacrificial care shown to the needy. Both Olivia Hooker and Marian Wright Edelman of the Children Defense Fund found this to be what sustained them through the years. They heard the call:

> Love my children, that's all I ask of you.
> Love my children, that's what we've got to do.
> If you love them as I love them, we shall see them safely through.
> Love yourself, love me too, and whatever else you do, love my children.

The existence of over one hundred Black Colleges and Universities bears witness to legendary acts of kindness of blacks and whites who knew that education was the key that would release the oppressed from bondage. It was like a little bit of heaven just to see young people march across the stage with cap and gown and a diploma or degree in their hands.

It is a "peculiar source of pleasure" for black people to be reminded that we built this nation, made cotton king, exploded the potential of the peanut, discovered blood plasma, gave the world spirituals, blues and jazz, put a special flair in fashion and flavor in food, brought excellence and style to dance, sports and literature, played our part in space exploration and now stand ready to help America reconnect to the God who inspires democracy, meaning, purpose and productivity. We are now ready to release our creativity to help us all to make a quantum leap together to the next phase of human development.

We speak of President Barack Obama as the first black President. In a sense that is true. More significantly, he embodies a prophetic symbol of black and white togetherness. Look what God produced from Black and White ancestry to serve this nation and the world. Can any honest assessment rob God of the praise and adoration for what was manifested in the miracle of Michelle and Barack in the White House. You ask, "Lord, How Come We Here?"—To provide the opportunity to show the world what can happen when we are ready to rise above the monstrous myths of White supremacy and racial bigotry.

"Lord, How Come Me Here?"

4. To live a good life and die a good death.

Olivia Hooker did both. Up to the very end, she felt highly favored by God. She experienced the wear and tear of aging. She felt the inconvenience of declining physical health. She had her share of infirmities but she kept on keeping on. Even at 103 her answering machine thanked people for calling and told them she was a bit slow, please call back perhaps she would have reached the phone by the next time they called. Her last words were, "I am with the Lord!" What a way to die! In the good times and in the hard times to have the God of the universe as a conversation partner—To be able to ask—

> Lord, why come me here and to discover
> in sacred dialogue the why and the what for
> "of the lamentable and the nevertheless"
> "of the hold on and you'll see"
> and finally this blessed assurance:
>
> **I'll be With You 'Til The End of Time**
> I'll be with you 'til the end of time
> I'll be with you 'til the end of time
> Don't you worry about what your future holds
> I'll be with you through eternity
>
> I was there when you were nothing
> But a thought, a wish and a prayer
> In your mother's womb I say you
> When she didn't even know you were there
>
> The day you were born I was present
> You were crying and trembling with fear
> Then I smiled and your eyes were opened
> Amazed at your—new world out here
>
> Through you childhood year I followed close
> While you searched for your purpose and place
> In your struggle to reach your life-long dream
> I offer guidance, forgiveness and grace
>
> So tell me why would I forsake you now
> When I've stood by you through thick and thin
> I have chosen you as a dwelling place
> For my Spirit to abide within
>
> When your song of life has ended
> And the curtains can rise no more
> Close your eyes without fear, I'm with you
> My arms will lift you to a brighter shore
>
> I'll be with you 'til the end of time
> I'll be with you 'til the end of time
> Don't you worry about what your future holds
> I'll be with you through eternity.
> —James A. Forbes, Jr.

May we honor the Quadricentennial of the arrival of Africans on indigenous shores remembering the words of Genesis 15:13 (NRSV). Then the Lord said to Abram, "Know this for certain, that your offspring shall be aliens in a land that is not theirs, and shall be slaves there, and they shall be oppressed for four hundred years; but I will bring judgment on the nation that they serve, and afterward they shall come out with great possessions." Let us explore the deeper theological source and significance of the song "Lord, How Come Me Here?" Is that a question that would normally be raised by all human beings? Is this question more likely to be raised by those who experience the brutality of dehumanization? Is it a possible diminishment of human sensitivity not to raise this question? And in regards to the thought, "I wish I never was born," was it only a fleeting moment of Job-like despair that flashed before them or was it a constant nagging sense of futility?

Let us explore how to address the conditions that can prompt such nihilistic sentiments. Let us find a way to effectively encourage other fellow human beings to join the quest for God's intention for their existence? Will 2020 become a year of divine declaration of liberation for black and white captives of principalities and powers that dominate, diminish and destroy? How might we become members of God's dream team:

- To help others to courageously ask God for themselves—"Lord, How Come me Here?"
- To pray earnestly that others will be able to receive God's forgiving Grace and accept restoration to the human family of justice, equality and compassion.
- To remain ready—even eager—to join hands across barriers of race, religion, class and ideology to sing both Amazing Grace and We Shall Overcome.

Then we will be able to show our fellow citizens that black people are one of God's blessings to America at a time when some are being tempted to seek greatness without humbly asking God "Lord, How Come Me Here?"

Reference

Ong, S. (2014). *En-Lovely: Victory Over Weaknesses*. Bloomington, IN: Balboa Press.

1619

A Conceptual Worldview Marker in Africana Cultural Memory Studies

CHRISTEL N. TEMPLE

In Africana cultural memory studies, August of 1619 is not only an historical moment reflecting the first enslavement sale in English North America, but also it is a conceptual marker for a national origin of the African American worldview. Worldview is a set of philosophical assumptions and designs for living reflecting culturally specific categories, queries, and logic formation drawn from a continuum of in-group historical experiences and developments. Molefi Kete Asante in *Afrocentricity* (1981) defines 1619 as a moment of *beginning again* which is compatible with the broader function of cultural memory, particularly in a crisis of relocation and the process of bravely surviving enslavement's relocation to inevitably to engrave identity on new soil (1981, 20–22, 24). This chapter applies a Black cultural mythology theoretical lens to the 1619 *encounter* to suggest a process for critically mining the culture's remarkable historical encounters for their capacity to reveal points of sacred remembrance and inheritance.

Africana cultural memory studies is inclusive of all knowledge on the broadly conceived memory practices of people of African descent, yet from multiple disciplines, however, Black cultural mythology is an aspect of cultural memory studies that prioritizes how memory *functions* most effectively when used as a tool to consider the identities Africans brought to the Americas and *how* African people heroically survived. Historical and cultural studies often over-prioritize the enslavement experience as an enduring traumatic memory. More in line with subject-agency perspectives, Black cultural mythology liberates us from an over-immersion in the atrocities of enslavement, with a preference for highlighting the heroics and ingenuity of *survival*. To best understand survival, we must first study the 1619 African arrival narrative. Evaluating the moment of 1619 as a marker for critical meditation is essential. This challenges us to speculate, to imagine, and to assess the impact of the 1619–2019 historical moment with greater precision, awareness of data and variables, and respect for the Angolans' African identity and adaptations on North American soil.

The historiography of 1619 is an important measure of how scholars have managed discourses on this pivotal year in the early history of the United States. In isolating 1619 as a *conceptual marker* from an African-centered worldview approach, rather than as a mere historical date, this chapter illuminates different aspects of its meaning. Historical sources such the popular editions on African American history reveal much, but central anthologies and collections on Africana Studies and on African American literary history also provide valuable perspectives on 1619. In the archive, however, as we see in the informative excerpts below that show how scholars conceptualize the 1619 encounter, the problem of giving ahistorical credit to *Jamestown* remains. In a revisionist leap, it is imperative to disengage from the archive's dismissal of Point Comfort (present day Hampton), which is the actual site of Africans' first contact in Virginia, and to self-correct the archive's incorrect over-reference to the Jamestown settlement. While it would be awkward to provide a parenthetical, strikethrough-style correction (i.e., "~~James-town~~") for each improperly used historical reference, this chapter asks readers to self-correct the archive as we revisit the historical record. The fact is that the Virginia colony had many different settlements, and Point Comfort is the first site of contact in spite of the historical record's *addiction* to granting claims to ~~Jamestown~~ (again, a deliberate strikethrough for emphasis).

Virginian, Giles B. Jackson (1853–1924), is among the first to commemorate 1619. He was "a former slave, a Richmond lawyer and entrepreneur" who "was also deeply involved in black commemorations in Virginia, having organized the Negro exhibit at the 1907 Tercentennial and already beginning to plan the three hundredth anniversary of the first landing of Africans in the Virginia colony in 1619" (Kachun 250–51). In contrast to Giles's agency in highlighting the African side of the story, in the eight-hundred-page long 1907 commemorative *Blue Book*, the word "African" appears only twice. It provides a unique starting point for a survey of the 1619 narrative because of its clarity in not over-romanticizing indenture versus enslavement. It reads,

In addition to the introduction of the first legislative assembly in 1619 Yeardley's administration was marked by the introduction of negro slaves into Virginia. A Dutch man-o-war came to Jamestown with twenty slaves, twelve men and eight women, and offered them for sale. The system of private ownership of property had already been introduced, the communal system being abolished with the beginning of Yeardley's administration. Each individual planter was raising his own crops and it was thought that the negro would be serviceable for field hands. The Governor himself bought eight out of the twenty slaves and sent them to his plantation of Flowerdieu Hundred on James River. African slavery was not rapidly introduced. In twenty years the population of African slaves did not reach more than three hundred, but in the next twenty years the population increased by births and importation to about two thousand. With the growth of the tobacco industry slavery became a more important economic institution [Keiley 18].

Historical Views

In historical texts, 1619 is a colonial, Western hemispheric phenomenon that is a significant part of the chronology of American nation-formation from a starting point of English colonialism. One of the most enduring African American textbooks, John Hope Franklin's and Alfred Moss's *From Slavery to Freedom* (1994), narrates the first enslavement sale in an innocuous tone:

> The twenty Africans who were put to shore at Jamestown in 1619 by the captain of a Dutch frigate were not slaves in a legal sense. And at the time Virginians seemed not o appreciate the far-reaching significance of the introduction of Africans to the fledgling colony. These newcomers, who happened to be black, were simply more indentured servants. They were listed as servants in the census counts of 1623 and 1624, and as late as 1651 some blacks whose period of service had expired were being assigned land in much of the same way that it was being assigned to whites who had completed their indenture. During the first half-century of existence Virginia had many black indentured servants, and the records reveal an increasing number of free blacks [1994, 56].

In comparison, Lerone Bennett, Jr.'s *Before the Mayflower* (1987), the more popular narrative history that began as an early 1960s series of articles in *Ebony Magazine,* speculates on the 1619 encounter in line with an Africana cultural memory inquiry. He writes, "We can only imagine the feelings of these seminal African-Americans. The record burns with their presence but is strangely silent on their reactions. The black founding fathers and mothers enter history thus: faceless men and women uprooted from Africa and flung into a maelstrom of history. Nothing in the record indicates that the cultural shock was great for either the black or the whites (35–36)." Bennett is unique because he balances a respect for the predicaments of Africans who were flung into indenture with empathy for their European indentured counterparts whose lot would eventually be elevated above Africans' through legalized white privilege.

Bennett's narrative is ideal for a 1619–2019 commemoration because he frames the arrival of the "Dutch man of War" as a rich and intriguing phenomenon that poses lasting questions:

> A year before the arrival of the celebrated *Mayflower*, 113 years before the birth of George Washington, 244 years before the Emancipation Proclamation, this ship sailed into the harbor of Jamestown, Virginia, and dropped anchor into the muddy waters of history. It was clear to the men who received this "Dutch man of War" that she was no ordinary vessel. What seems unusual today is that no one sensed how extraordinary she really was. For few ships, before or since, have unloaded a more momentous cargo.
> From whence did this ship come?
> From somewhere on the high seas where she robbed a Spanish vessel of a cargo of Africans bound for the West Indies.
> Why did she stop at Jamestown, the first permanent English settlement in America?
> No one knows for sure. The captain "ptended," John Rolfe noted that he was in great need of food and offered to exchange his human cargo for "victualle." The deal was arranged. Antoney, Isabella, Pedro and seventeen other Africans stepped ashore in August, 1619. The history of Black America began [1987, 29].

Bennett's narrative is conversational, alternating between presentations of the harsh realities of the enslavement trade, the harsh reality that 1619 "is a story about the merchandising and marketing of human beings," and another superlative perspective that "This is a story about 'the greatest migration in recorded history'" (1987, 29).

In A. Leon Higginbotham's *In the Matter of Color* (1978) the "pathology of the law" is the context for the 1619 encounter (1978, 14). He does not sugarcoat the emergent pathology, beginning with an unusually blunt archival excerpt of the arrival narrative from John Rolfe's personal travelogue which Higginbotham uses as the section's epigraph: "about the last of August there came to Virginia Dutchman of Warre who sold us twenty Negers" (1978, 20). Higginbotham's rendering presents a narrative of ambiguity that was resolved by White colonial commitments to dehumanization and to sacrificing Africans for the nation's alleged prosperity:

> It survives as the earliest known record dating the arrival of blacks at an American colony. These first "Negers," who arrived in Jamestown a year before the Pilgrims landed at Plymouth rock, had not volunteered for the voyage. Unlike the hopeful Pilgrims, they had been brought to America unwillingly, captives, in fact, of Dutchmen who had apparently seized them from a Spanish ship to sell them to the labor-short colonists.

84 The African Experience in Colonial Virginia

> In 1619, when these first twenty blacks arrived in Jamestown, there was not as yet a statutory process to especially fix the legal standing of blacks. Although the American colonists seemed to have practiced from the very beginning "the same discrimination which white men had practiced against the Negro all along and before any statutes decreed it," [Deglar] these first blacks were not exposed to the systematic degradation to which later blacks would be subjected. Yet they were not free. Where did they stand? After centuries of investigation and discussion scholars are still unable to agree.
>
> Paradoxically, it has been argued that the capture by this Dutch ship of the twenty blacks who arrived in Jamestown in 1619 was a "godsend" to these blacks. Their removal from the Spanish slave ship altered their permanent slave status under Spanish rule to "something indeterminate and transitory, which 'faded out' or merged automatically ... into servitude analogous to that of the indentured white servants when they touched Virginia soil" [Catterall]. In fact, the status of these first blacks in America was made even more nebulous because of a fascinating mixture of Spanish and English law whereby a Spanish subject who had been christened or baptized was by that act enfranchised or set free under English law and admitted to the privileges of a free person. Since English law governed Virginia in 1619, and since most of the twenty blacks captured by the Spanish had been baptized by their captors, there was legal as well as moral force to the argument that they should be freed [1978, 20–21].

In comparison to Higginbotham's excerpt here, Bennett, too, further alerts us to reflect on the meaning of being "seized" in piracy and on the competing European countries' religious practices concerning enslaved Africans. Bennett also teases out the *insulting* and *insensitive* conclusions that some citizens draw to suggest that enslavement was a blessing for the 1619 Angolans and their modern-day descendants. Also, Higginbotham addresses a feature of Black indenture, that eventually, liberated Africans were able to participate in economic processes of the colony, somewhat as equals. He writes,

> In Virginia, then, as in other colonies, the first black settlers fell into a well-established socioeconomic groove which carried with it no implications of racial inferiority. That came later. But in the interim, a period of forty years or more, the first black settlers accumulated land, voted, testified in court and mingled with whites on a basis of equality. They owned other black servants and certain blacks imported and paid for white servants whom they apparently held in servitude [1978, 35].

This narrative reiterates an aspect of early African identity as *settlers*, in addition to being sold, indentured, or enslaved.

Charles M. Christian's *Black Saga* (1999), highlights African American history in a year-by-year timeline narrative. For the year 1619 he describes the encounter as "First African Settlers Reach North America." His view of the Angolans as *settlers* sets his approach apart. He writes,

1619: A Conceptual Worldview Marker (Temple) 85

> On August 20, A Dutch ship arrived in Jamestown, Virginia, carrying Captiani Jope and a cargo of twenty Africans. Theough no one really knows why the ship anchored off Jamestown, it is believed that the captain needed food, in exchange for which he offered his cargo of Africans. When the deal was consummated, Antoney, Isabella, and eighteen other Africans disembarked. Although they were not the first Africans to arrive in North America, they were the first African settlers. Regarded as indentured servants rather than as slaves, fifteen were purchased to serve their redemption time working for Sir George Yardley, the governor of Virginia and proprietor of the thousand acre Flowerdew Hundred Plantation [1999, 6].

Historian St. Claire Drake also notes the distinction of the 1619 Angolans as "part of a permanent English settlement in English-speaking North America" (1993, 500).

Darlene Clark Hine, William C. Hine, and Stanley Harrold in *African Americans: A Concise History* (2006) feature the 1619 moment in a context of comparing European, African, and Native American encounters in North America. Also, their narrative is transparent about a lesser known fact that African people were already in the English colonies at the moment of the first known enslavement sale in English North America. They describe that,

> By the early months of 1619, there were, nevertheless, thirty-two people of African-descent—fifteen men and seventeen women—living in the English colony at Jamestown. Nothing is known concerning when they had arrived or from where they had come. They were all "in the service of sev[er]all planters." The following August 4 a Dutch warship, carrying seventeen African men and three African women, moored at Hampton roads at the mouth of the James River. The Dutch warship, with the help of an English ship, had attacked a Portuguese slaver, taken most of its human cargo, and brought these twenty Angolans to Jamestown. The Dutch captain traded them to local officials in return for provisions.
>
> The Angolans became servants to the Jamestown officials and to favored planters. The colony's inhabitants, for two reasons, regarded the new arrivals and those black people who had been in Jamestown earlier as *unfree*, but not slaves. First, unlike the Portuguese and the Spanish, the English had no law for slavery. Second, at least the Angolans, who bore names such as Pedro, Isabella, Antoney, and Angelo, had been converted by the Portuguese to Christianity. According to English custom and morality in 1619, Christians cold not be enslaved. So, once these individuals had worked off their purchase price, they could regain their freedom [2006, 41].

Shifting gears, there is contemporary history that narrates the 1619 moment in a unique way—with the humor and sarcasm of African American folk wit transmitted in the African American cartooning tradition. Roland Owen Laird, Jr., and Taneshia Nash Laird created the volume *Still I Rise: A Cartoon History of African Americans* (1997) and showcased, in the words of famed writer Charles Johnson who wrote the Introduction, "illustrated history from a black point of view" that "chronicles the often 'invisible' history of Black America in Elihu Bey's energetic and uncompromising drawings" (1993, xiv). Johnson describes the volume as being "faintly Afrocentric" in its presentation of images from a black viewpoint, and he notes how the volume presents "a cornucopia of seldom-reported events, facts, and experiences of African-Americans that enriches our understanding of this nation's past" (1993, xv–xvi). We can only sample the cartoon's text here which I also present in quick-pace conversational form. Laird and Laird offer a compelling description of the 1619 encounter that begins in 1618 with English colonial leaders and English indentured servants' dissatisfaction with the labor predicament in the harsh and undeveloped colonial Virginia landscape:

> 1618: Jamestown, Virginia
> Some were Native Americans, but most were Europeans looking for a way out of poverty and misery in Europe. Instead they found misery and poverty in North America.
> "Come now, work harder."
> "Id've been better off keepin' me arse in London."
> Meanwhile, the colonial masters grew greedy.
> "With more indentured servants, I'll be able to buy more wigs."
> And that was the beginning of a North American nightmare for African people.
>
> 1619: The House of Burgesses a legislative body in the British colony of Jamestown, Virginia.
> "Here ye, here ye the meeting to address our labor problems has now come to order."
> Thunk [a gavel pounds].
> "Gentlemen, as you know the cost of indentured servants is becoming too high for us to grow tobacco profitably. Either we find a way to lower our labor costs or we live out the rest of our days as paupers. What say ye?"
> "We all know of the need for less expensive servants. The true problem is where to find them."
> "I understand that Africans in the West Indies are working out quite well."
> "Africans? But they are an inferior race."
> "Perhaps, but I've heard they've improved sugar production by 300 percent in Jamaica, and they cost much less than Europeans."
> "He makes a strong point."
> "Very well, we shall try the Africans."
> When the Africans arrived in Jamestown, they were strangers in a strange land.
> They struggled with a strange language.
> "This is called a plow!"
> "APLOW!" [The African man merges "a" and "plow" into a single word, misunderstanding the language.]
> A strange climate.
> Strange diseases.
> And strange people with strange clothes.

"Here, try this hat on."
"?" [African man puts his hand, not his *head*, in the hat, not knowing what a hat is.]
We had to adapt to survive.
Not only did we adapt, but we were more creative, innovative, and productive than our European counterparts. They had been poor, disenfranchised, and on the margins of society in their own land, while the Africans had been skilled craftspeople and successful farmers [Laird & Laird, 1997, 1–4].

Laird and Laird's narrative and dialogue, along with Bey's drawings, brilliantly convey the meaning of 1619 from a Black point of view, including a display of the motives of the colonists and the complicity of the white indentured servants.

The next round of cartoons illustrates white arrogance about farming and how, in a disagreement between European and African indentured servants, an African man defended his agricultural skillset, emphatically noting, "But his [referring to his African partner] people were farmers for thousands of seasons" (Laird & Laird, 1997, 4). The authors use the images to recount and celebrate a host of African skills and talents manifested during the colonial era. Similar to Bennett's empathy for white indentured servants, Laird and Laird note, "Some Europeans and Africans became friends … but other European servants resented us," noting "These blasted Africans are making us look bad" (Laird & Laird, 1997, 4–5). The authors and illustrator of *Still I Rise* end their visual and textual narrative of the 1619 encounter with an illustration of the vices of jealousy, envy, and a concerted desire among the colonists and some (not all) of the indentured servants to have a privileged "white" status over Africans. In fact, the text and dialogue are explicit:

Meanwhile, the colonial masters planned ways of making more money from others' toil.
"These Africans may prove to be quite productive."
But the colonial masters had gotten more than they expected. Africans were not only expert farmers but shrewd business people. Some quickly working their way out of indentured servitude.
"They didn't even say goodbye." [White settler cries as his formerly indentured Africans depart from his land] [Laird & Laird, 1997, 5–6].

Like Bennett's *Before the Mayflower*, Laird and Laird's dialogue not only presents but also problematizes racial skin color divisions:

Freedom from indenture did not free the former servants from human weaknesses. A number of them formed their own plantations with their own indentured servants….
That didn't sit too well with a lot of white people.
"When you're finished plowing, Smitty, I'm going to need you to chop some wood. I'd like it finished when I get back." [White colonist eavesdrops on African man giving instructions to his white indentured servant.]

"A white man like you don't need to be takin' orders from a bloody nigger."
"He's me boss, Guvnah. I got no choice. Besides, he's a good man."
"That black bastard's no more a man than my mule. I can see you've got a lot to learn, friend" [Laird & Laird, 1997, 6].

This version of the 1619 moment and its immediate aftermath imaginatively explores differences in the motives, points of view, and insecurities of white English populations, across class and status, to explain the social relationships and negotiations that eventually paved the way for the inhumanity and pathology that Higginbotham describes in legal terms. The 1619 account from the Franklin and Moss chapter on "Colonial Slavery" eventually accounts for a shift from allegedly equal and peaceful indenture to the colonists' view of Africans as threats. He writes, "Although Virginians greatly appreciated the importance of slave labor in the development of the colony, they soon became apprehensive about such large numbers of blacks living among whites," and "There were, moreover, persistent rumors of conspiracies of rebellion, and many whites feared for their lives" (Franklin & Moss, 1994, 57). According to Franklin and Moss, the year 1619 through roughly 1661 were years of peaceful indenture. In 1661, 1662, and 1667, the colony of Virginia instituted laws that began to recognize enslavement of Africans. However, in spite of legal conditions and in a more mature reflection embodied in a commitment to Africana cultural memory, the 1619 Angolans deserve a history that reflects their point-of-view, personhood, and human agency, which Table I solicits in its specificity and its model of better learning the pre-enslavement identities of the 1619 Angolans.

A more wholistic cultural remembrance of 1619 would have us studying the cultures of the Kongo and who Africans were in seventeenth century Kongo. It would have us studying the enslavement history of modern-day Mexico, the destination of the enslavement ship from which British America's commemorated "first" twenty Africans were kidnapped additionally through piracy by the ship *White Lion*. The approach to reflecting and remembering this historical encounter first needs to be managed with greater narrative and accuracy, placing Mexico, piracy, and Angolan worldviews into optimum historical consciousness. The approach can be very Pan-African as we explore the possibilities of critical discourse on the meaning of 1619.

Also, in 1619, the ship *Treasurer* arrived several days after the *White Lion* with an additional number of between twenty-five and twenty-nine Africans. A few more were sold in the Virginia colony, then fifteen more were sold in Bermuda. So now, we have a conceptual Pan-African intervention that compels a reconstruction of narratives and linkages between

1619 Angola, Mexico, Virginia, and Bermuda. At that time in Bermuda, the governor said, "if not for the Africans, he would not have been able 'to rayse one pound of Tobacco this year'" to generate revenue. He added that "Thes[e] Slaves are the most proper and cheape [sic] instruments for this plantation" ("Virginia's First Africans"). This narrative is quite different from the Americanized heroes of the 1619 generation whom, as we learn in textbooks, are Anthony and Isabella who have the first-born African son on English North American soil in the annals of history. The narrative also reminds us to itemize the list of European agents (the Spanish, the Portuguese, the Dutch, the English) who participated in the enslavement system against Africans.

In an Africana cultural memory critique, the interest is in exploring the 1619 encounter to narrate what also came *before* it. This gives another nuance to anteriority (seeking to learn the long historical continuum) similar to what Kadiatu Kanneh in *African Identities* (1998) describes as the problem with our vision of time when we consider the enslavement trade and the Middle Passage. Kanneh writes, "This dreaming of the Middle Passage as the unfixed yet eternal space from which an African-American origin can be traced makes the wide and uncertain journey *away* from shore, rather than to the reality of Africa's shore *itself*, into the founding moment of Black American consciousness" (Kanneh, 1998, 123).

Society views the actors of 1619 in myriad ways based on demographics such as racial identity, age group, educational level, profession, and worldview, and these factors determine the sources on which society relies for information that will inform layers of personal and public discourse during the quadricentennial of 1619–2019. The cyber nation likely will rely on two key sources for quick reference. The first is the *Jamestown Rediscovery* website with a page on "The First Africans," and the second is the scholarly short history entry on "Virginia's First Africans" from *Encyclopedia Virginia*. The brief Virginia colony history is worth quoting at length in order to assess what readers will learn about Africans:

> The first Africans brought to an English colony in North America were forcibly landed in Virginia in late August 1619. Tobacco grower John Rolfe wrote that the "20 and odd" Africans came from a Dutch warship, but modern research has shown a more complicated story.
>
> Portuguese traders captured Angolans in West Central Africa on expeditions in 1618–19. The majority of captives were probably Kimbundu-speaking peoples from the kingdom of Ndongo, specifically from a heavily-populated region between the Lukala and Lutete Rivers that included the royal capital, Kabasa. Many of the captives would have come from urban backgrounds and after capture could have received the basics of Christianity because Portuguese law required all slaves to be baptized Catholics before

arriving in the Americas. Following a march of some 200 miles to the port of Luanda, about 350 slaves were put on the *Sao Joao Bautista*, bound for Vera Cruz in the summer of 1619.

En route, the ship was attacked in the Gulf of Campeche, off the coast of Mexico, by two privateers and robbed of some of their human cargo. One raider was an English warship, *White Lion*, sailing with a letter of marque issued to the English Captain Jope by the Protestant Dutch Prince Maurice, son of William of Orange. A letter of marque legally permitted the *White Lion* to sail as a privateer attacking any Spanish or Portuguese ships it encountered. The other ship, the *Treasurer*, was an English ship owned by the Earl of Warwick and commanded by Daniel Elfrith. Rolfe's report that the *White Lion* was Dutch was a way to transfer blame away from the English for piracy.

The two privateers sailed to the West Indies and then to Virginia's post at Old Point Comfort (now Hampton, VA). Some of the Angolans were traded there, including a Christian woman named "Angelo" who was purchased by Lieutenant William Pierce of Jamestown. Some of the Angolans became the property of the governor. Others may have been treated as indentured servants and earned their freedom after years spent laboring at the hoe on tobacco plantations (because the English colony did not have a legal system of lifetime slavery until decades later). But for most, a change of masters did not allow them to escape the practical reality of enslaved work. There were 32 Africans in the colony in 1620, but then a 1625 census recorded 23 Africans in Virginia. In 1649 there were only about 300. A significant spike in enslaved African labor did not occur until after 1700.

An Africana cultural memory orientation to 1619 is interested in the telling of, certainly, "a more complicated story" as the entry warns, but African Americans and society at-large need to be vigilant in properly narrating the history's cultural meaning.

From the historical accounts, we learn that in 1619 the twenty Africans were sold over and over again. They were exchanged for food. They were objectified by the Spanish Asiento that contracted other nations (in this case Portugal) to supply its colonies with enslaved Africans. This entry is comprehensive, but it needs a conceptual intervention.

The 1619 group initially embarked for a Mexican plantation owned by a Spaniard in Seville. They were on a ship bound to deliver enslaved Africans from the Portuguese colony of Sao Paolo Loanda in Angola to Vera Cruz, New Spain (modern day Mexico). They were part of a group of Africans in Virginia that was twenty (or so) in number in August 1619 but was thirty-two in number several months later in March 1620 (15 male, 17 female). While "a few" more came to the colony with the second pirate ship that also sold Africans in Bermuda, the additional twelve Africans are not explicitly accounted for. The ship left Angola in 1619, so accounting for travel time, women were in the hands of at least five different groups of Europeans (Angolan port, Portuguese vessel, the two separate British "piracy" ships who kidnapped the small group of them from a larger population on the attacked Portuguese vessel, sold at Kecoughtan/Point Comfort then throughout the Virginia colony). It is unbelievable and requires a bit of worldview speculation to process the fact that Africans with a recent memory of such turmoil would have willingly named their firstborn William Tucker "in honor of a Virginia planter." The entry cites the origin of the Africans as being from Angola. Most likely,

> they were captured from the nearby kingdom of Ndongo, where in 1618 and 1619 the governor of Angola, Luis Mendes de Vasconcelos, fighting alongside a ruthless African mercenary group called the Imbangala, led two campaigns against the kingdom's Kimbundu-speaking people. Thousands were captured and likely provided the cargo for six Portuguese slave ships from Angola that arrived in Vera Cruz between June 18, 1619 and June 21, 1620 ["First Africans"].

While Franklin and Moss frame 1619 as a neutral event of African status imitating European indentured status, an Africana cultural memory meditation on the humanity of the Angolans who experienced one-way passage, were stolen and traded like property, and were bid on and sold at Point Comfort before being split up between the Virginia colony and Bermuda yields a different opinion from the neutrality readers encounter in *From Slavery to Freedom*. Even the condition of indenture is not parallel, since the European indentured servants *willingly* entered into a contract of servitude. The contract for indenture was imposed on the 1619 Angolans. The historical narrative is not enough of a memorialization and lamentation. African people arrived on an enslavement vessel from Angola, pirated twice between Mexico and Bahamas. They had been baptized with Portuguese names already in Angola, thus losing their original names, and in traditional American historical narratives, the more cultural and experiential dimensions of their stories are overshadowed by bland versions of an African American indentured servitude myth. An African cultural memory pursuit of enhanced meaning for 1619 makes a conceptual difference.

A more itemized deciphering of the identity and worldview of the 1619 Angolans is reflected in Table I on "CRITICAL VARIABLES OF 1619" below, which represents collected history and data that enhance the baseline historical narrative that society receives in most History textbook sources. Much of the data in the table originates with details found in "Virginia's First Africans" by Martha McCartney in *Encyclopedia Virginia*, a publication of the Virginia Foundation for the Humanities in partnership with the Library of Virginia, formerly the Virginia State Archives, cross-referenced with basic historical data about Angola.

Table I: Critical Variables of 1619 African Origins and Experience in the Colonies

REGIONS	West Central Africa (colonized by Portuguese)	From a Kecoughtan (Kikotan) or Algonquian Nation indigenous point of view, similar variables should also be explored to critically explore the Native American societies' encounters with English colonizers of the region prior to the "first African slave sale" in North America
NATION	Angola (also known as Dongo, of which Kabasa was the capital city)	One of the larger vassal states to the Ancient Kingdom of Kongo, south of the mouth of the Congo (or Zaire) River, in a region just to the south.
KINGDOM	Nyasa	Political disruption in the Mbundu region and Portuguese were taking advantage, even though by 1618–1619 the region was under Spanish rule
CULTURE	Ndongo	Ndongo people lived in largely rural areas where they raised crops such as millet and sorghum and tended cattle. There was one densely populated political center, the city of Angoleme with around 30,000 people.
ROYAL CAPITAL CITY	Kabasa	In the watershed of the Kwanza River.
LANGUAGE	Kimbundu (Bantu language family)	
RELIGION	Matrilineal, genealogy-based ancestral worldview; a kimbanda, or diviner, facilitates communion with the spirit world	Even though the Spanish, Portuguese, and English enslavers and colonizers required Christian baptism and renaming, the Angolans should not be considered wholeheartedly Christian.
WORLDVIEW	Complex ethnic identity	
NAMES	Original Angolan names unknown	What we have instead are references to "Angelo/a," "Anthony," "William," "Anthony," "John," "Edward," "Peter," "Antonio," "Frances," "Margaret," "Anthony," "Isabella," "John Pedro," "William," "Brass," and "Mary."
CONTRIBUTION(S) TO CIVILIZATION	Heavily populated rural and urban society between Lukala and Lutete Rivers	
INVADERS	Spanish invaded Angola and hired Portuguese to convert then sell/deliver Angolans to Vera Cruz, New Spain colony (now Mexico)	• The critical survey is incomplete without considering indigenous cultures that were already in Vera Cruz, New Spain and the history of Spanish (and general European) colonization.

1619: A Conceptual Worldview Marker (Temple) 93

KIDNAPPED TRANSNATIONAL GEOGRAPHY	• Angola to Port of Sao Paulo de Luanda (forcibly marched 200 miles east by foot) • 350 Angolans on Portuguese ship *Sao Joao Bautista* (summer 1619) • Headed to Mexico (attacked by two ships on Mexican coast in Gulf of Campeche) • Both ships went to the West Indies first and presumably sold Angolans there (how many?) • 20 or so Angolans (out of original 350) traded for food to colony at Point Comfort, VA August 1619, most sold again in the Virginia colony • Of the 25 to 29 Angolans taken to Bermuda, 14 were sold to the acting governor Miles Kendall and his successor Nathaniel Butler for 50,000 ears of corn. • The ship the *James* landed in 1621 with at least one recorded African man sold • The ship *Margaret and John* landed in 1622 with at least one African woman sold	• Humans were traded for food (what foods?) • What was the nature of the 200 mile march to the port at Luanda? • Who is Sao Paulo de Luanda (a person? Named after what?) • How many families were in the original 350? Did they know each other? Who was separated from whom? • How many Angolans died in passage? • How many Angolans died or were injured during the joint pirate attack by the ships *White Lion* and *Treasurer*? • What was the nature and impact of this trauma (added to the original trauma of Portuguese colonization in Nyasa, Angola?)
EUROPEAN PERPETRATORS	**Countries**: • *Spain*: colonized Angola and had *asiento* policy to hire other countries to manage the enslavement trade for their colonies. • *Portugal*: ships captured and sold Angolans for Spain and its Mexican colonies. • *Netherlands (Dutch)*: The ship *White Lion* sailed out of the port of Vlissingen (in Flushing). Had Dutch permit to attack Spanish ships. • *England*: English-owned pirate ship *Treasurer*, also sailed from Flushing, Netherlands, sold Angolans to colony at Point Comfort, deliberately described as a "Dutch" ship in order to cover English piracy.	**Citizens/companies involved**: • Manuel Mendes da Cunha (captain of Portuguese ship *Sao Joao Bautista*) what does the ship's name mean? • Investors in Seville, Spain profited from 200/350 of the Angolans on his ship, who were to be sold in Vera Cruz, New Spain • John Colyn Jope (Netherlands captain of *White Lion*) • Daniel Elfirth (English Captain of *Treasurer*) • Charles Emmanual I (Duke of Savoy, granted piracy rights to Daniel Elfirth of *Treasurer* on behalf of the independent duchy of Savory, which is now part of Italy and France) • Samuel Argall, Deputy Governor of Virginia (was part owner of the pirate ship *Treasurer*, which is also the ship that delivered Pocahontas to England. Therefore, Pocahontas traveled on an enslavement vessel)

EUROPEAN PERPETRATORS (cont.)	• *Colony of Virginia*: Angolans arrived at Point Comfort. Some were retained to work in the Fort there and the rest were sold in the colony. • *Colony of Bermuda*: Elfirth of *Treasurer* arrived to Point Comfort three to four days later could not sell his 25–29 Angolans to Virginia. He sold them to Bermuda instead.	• Virginia Company of London owned the colony • Sir Edwin Sandys (Treasurer of the Virginia Company). • John Rolfe, Virginia colony secretary • Sir George Yeardley (succeeded Argall as deputy governor; had Angolans as servants in his household) • Captain William Pierce (Colony resident who had Angolans as servants in his household) • Abraham Peirsey (Cape Merchant who helped broker sale of food for Angolans) • Miles Kendall (Governor of Bermuda) bought 14 Angolans for the price of 50,000 ears of corn • Nathaniel Butler (next Governor of Bermuda) claimed tobacco skills of Angolans saved Bermuda's economy • William Pierce (owned Angolan servants in Virginia colony) • Richard Kingsmill (owned Angolan servants in Virginia colony) • Edward Bennett (owned Angolan servants on lower side of James River in Virginia colony) • Captain William Tucker (owned Angolan servants in Elizabeth City) • Frances West (owned Angolan servants in Elizabeth City) • Captain Nathaniel Bass (court dispute over African names "Brass") • Captain Jones (court dispute) • Lady Temperance Flowerdew Yeardley (court dispute) • Governor Frances Wyatt (court dispute)
TRANSATLANTIC PATH/KINSHIP	Angola, Mexico, Jamaica, Virginia, Bermuda	No data kept on bi-racialism, pregnancies (except one) between 1619 and 1625 among Angolans who were scattered from the mouth of the James River to Flowerdew Hundred Plantation
NUMBERS OF ANGOLANS AND THEIR FATES	350 (but after a joint pirate attack by the two ships, only 147 arrived there in August 1619). 24/147 were Angolan boys who were later sold in *Jamaica*.	• What happened to the other 203 Angolans on the original voyage? (150 likely died on the voyage. 50 were pirated and stolen by Captains Jope and Elfirth.
NUMBER THAT ARRIVED IN OLD POINT COMFORT	• 20 or so in 1619 • 32 in 1620 • 23 in 1625 • Between 1619 and 1625	• In 1628, 100 more Angolans sold to Virginia colony after the Massachusetts Bay ship *Fortune* pirated them from a Portuguese ship • Colony of Virginia was how large? How expansive? (Elizabeth City to shores of James River)

COLONIAL LAW	• 1625 muster (census) listed the years of arrival and ships' names for Europeans, they did not record the data for the Africans • 1670 Virginia law defined all non–Christian servants brought to the colony "by shipping" as slaves-for-life	1682 Virginia law defined all non–Christian servants as slaves-for-life (Native Americans)
CULTURAL MEMORY	• Antonio (owned by the Bennett family) gained his freedom. He married Mary, and they were known as "Anthony and Mary Johnson" of Northampton County on the Eastern Shore. By the 1650s they had four children, owned 250 acres of land, and had two sons with adjoining farms of 450 and 100 acres. They moved to Maryland in the 1660s. A grandson, John Johnson, Jr., bought a 44 acre farm in Maryland in 1677 and named it "Angola." • Prior to Engel Sluiter's 1997 research, historians discredited the assumption that the 1619 Africans had come directly from Africa. This corroboration gives African Americans in Virginia and the Eastern shore a more direct heritage line of descent to the continent	Other Africans appear in 1625 court records in possession squabbles between colonists and merchants. They original Angolan Africans came from the watershed of the Kwanza River, which has symbolic similarity to the Kwanzaa African American cultural holiday, even if only in coincidence

Africana Disciplinary Views

In disciplinary Africana Studies perspectives, 1619 does not retain much chronological value; instead it can be viewed more as symbolic or as a referent. The atrocities of the period including 1619 are inferred as indicators of a shift in worldview and agency and as a U.S. national crisis of early origins reflecting pathologies of injustice against humans of African descent. Scholars have not dealt adequately with the concept of *Njia: The Way*, "the collective expression of the Afrocentric worldview which is grounded in the historical experience of African people" which is centered on survival (Asante, 1988, 20–22). Njia is the conceptual affirmation of reinvented Africanness on American soil, and it reorients African American historical experiences with a revisionist approach to the culture's chronology, or "beginning again" in 1619. It emerges as a central conduit from which we infuse the bland historical narrative with a search for creative heroic agency and autonomous space for original African worldviews and identities locatable from within the tumultuous U.S. history (Asante, 1988, 24). As an alternative to the West's universal timelines of AD or BC, the cultural reference point for Njia offers the acronym ABA to designate *After the Beginning Again* (post 1619), while BBA references history *Before the Beginning Again* (pre-1619). Asante's intervention suggests that European historical timelines do not reflect the culture's chronological worldview.

In *African American History: A Journey of Liberation* (2002), Asante introduces 1619 in a section on "Disclocated and Decentered." He frames the English North American moment of encounter with Angolans noting its costs for African people in terms of lost names, linguistic features, and cultural elements:

> The changes that caused enslaved Africans to experience dislocation began in 1619. Between 1619 and 1719 there was a strong attempt to stamp out any trace of African culture that might have survived the journey across the Atlantic. Among the first things to go were African names. The African who came ashore in 1619 had left Africa with surnames such as Diallo, Nwonko, Awolowo, Obenga, Nyang, Owusu, Asare, Kasavubu, and Amachie. Their African names were changed to European surnames such as Smith, Coleman, Williams, Wilson, Hopkins, Johnson, Taylor, Anderson, Jefferson, Washington, and Simpson [Asante, 2002, 72–73].

This issue of names, as a central indicator of identity and personhood, appears in several Africana Studies narratives that reference 1619. James Stewart's and Talmadge Anderson's introductory textbook situates the meaning of 1619 in a section on "racial identification." They write,

> Africans the New world were denied recognition of their humanity and national origins. Consequently, their identities, designations, and names were arbitrarily decided by their captors and enslavers. In Europe and America, African were called by or given negative and colloquial titles or names such as "nigger," "darkie," "colored," and "negro." The debate concerning a racial/national identity of name for Americans of African descent has not yet been fully resolved [Stewart & Anderson, 2015, 2].

A more detailed reference to 1619 appears later in Stewart & Anderson's exploration of the history of African people in America where he narrates the meaning of 1619 in terms of the colonists' quest to exploit labor for their lucrative tobacco crop. The authors note, "The involuntary arrival of Africans in 1619 was timely and opportune for the settlers. Millions of Africans would follow those initial twenty to America, and their status as slaves and their treatment as such would become more clearly defined by colonial law" (Stewart & Anderson, 2015, 61). This is similar to references that Laird and Laird make in the motives of the Colony Virginia's local leadership to harvest a larger tobacco crop.

1619: A Conceptual Worldview Marker (Temple)

Maulana Karenga, in *Introduction to Black Studies* (2010) addresses the period encompassing 1619 and enslavement origins in the volume's history chapter. His approach is to narrate enslavement as a holocaust (not as an early experience of indenture). He poses an intervention on the bland narratives that deny the humanity of the 1619 Angolans and other Africans. He explains,

> What is intended here is to engage in a discussion using a language that constantly reminds us that we are talking about real people, real lives destroyed and disrupted. Moreover, to use the category "slave" without a cultural, ethnic or national qualifier is to suggest the person had no identity outside of being enslaved, that s/he is a "slave" by nature not by social imposition. But to use the designated "enslaved African" is to affirm cultural identity and indicate that the African was enslaved not simply a slave by birth or being. In a word, it is to begin to resurrect the enslaved Africans from the social death imposed on them [2010, 109].

Karenga's discourse is distinguished by a commitment to conceptual clarity relying on attention to correcting misconceptions. He notes the impact of such an atrocity on Africa and the Americas, and highlights the constant variable of resistance as African people survived the nearly insurmountable. He recalibrates the language society uses to contextualize the historical narrative of enslavement. His narrative references dehumanization, cultural destruction, social violence, holocaust, cultural and physical genocide, exploitative commerce neutralized by referring to it as trade, brutalization, depopulation of Africa, the forced transfer of populations, and underdevelopment (2010, 110–112).

Mario Azevedo's survey textbook considers 1619 in its chapter on "Diaspora Africans and Slavery." He describes the encounter with a focus on a shift in Africans' status from indentured to free that was still unfulfilling:

> In 1619, white Virginians bought twenty slaves from a Dutch ship and gradually moved toward black enslavement. With no law defining a slave status before 1659, masters employed blacks as servants. Indentured whites customarily got freedom dues (clothes, a few acres) after completing their terms. They also assimilated, but his pattern eluded the "black indentured servants." Deemed subhuman, blacks met with harsher discipline and periodically served more years. White racism stigmatized blacks [2016, 93].

He condenses the broader narrative of Africans' emergent seventeenth-century lack of freedom, that A. Leon Higginbotham outlines colony-by-colony in *In the Matter of Color* (1980). Azevedo comparatively emphasizes the white capacity for and interest in assimilation as his contribution to the African arrival narrative. In Claudine Michel's and Jacqueline Bobo's *Black Studies* (2001) the 1619 discussion is nestled in Sethard Fisher's chapter on caste and class in Black American experiences. He identifies five "crucial historical phases, or turning points in Black North American History," and a narrative of the 1619 moment of encounter appears in the first phase of "indenture" (2001, 48). He writes, "This [indenture] is phase one of the oscillation process and it begins around the year 1619, the year of the first arrival of Blacks to the English colonies. This phase ended around 1680, the year of the first major Slave Codes, which originated in Virginia. These repressive codes, applicable only to Blacks, became the model and symbol of Black repression throughout the American South for the next nearly 200 years" (2001, 49).

Views of 1619 in African American Literary Anthologies

In literary history and anthologies, 1619 is a vital part of the experiential timeline in terms of framing the relationship between legal status and literacy. We do not learn of the ideas and personhood of Africans enslaved in the Americas until early African literary voices such as James Albert Ukawsaw Gronniosaw (1705–1775), Jupiter Hammon (1711–1806), Ignatius Sancho (1729–1780), Olaudah Equiano (1745–1796), Phillis Wheatley (1753–1784), and Ottobah Cugoano (1757–1791). Sancho and Wheatley "each produced a single extended portrayal of the continent, and each rooted that portrayal in Western literary conventions of tropical plenty that reached back to the Garden of Eden" (Sidbury 27). He then considers the image they portray of Africa. He notes, "In keeping with these roots in English culture, Africa was a fallen Garden, not a remembered paradise. Sancho noted the continent's natural bounty but quickly turned to a diabolical alliance" between European Christians and Africans who were complicit in the enslavement trade's commerce in human beings (27).

These African voices appear beginning approximately one hundred years after the arrival of the 1619 Angolans, and remind us of the gap in the literary tradition and archive, that does not account for the creative self-expression, identity, personhood, and organic voices of the 1619 Angolans. It is easy to fault the archive for its lapses of capturing a sense of African agency. It was a transnational juncture of European colonial activity, of disregard for African personhood, and a process of British-American nation-building. Narratives and national myths reflect how the colonies and then the nation quickly became enamored of themselves and their late eighteenth-century independence from a colonial status.

In contrast, an Africana cultural memory intervention makes us aware of the absences of the archive, which still must be reconciled. Scholars are attentive to these lapses, such as with Saidiya Hartman's concept of critical fabulation which compels us to be creative and imaginary in reconciling the distance between the archive's inconsistencies and the narratives that do exist. Black cultural mythology's lens demands that while surveying the archive on which we *meditate*, that we develop a greater narrative sensitivity for the dimensions of the culture's broad acts of survival and transformation. The African American literary tradition is not able to address the conditions of creative aesthetics of 1619, and even *The Norton Anthology of African American Literature* (2004) introduces itself in terms on Gronniosaw's "talking book" trope of 1770. Its further clarification is that,

> The text of Western letters refused to speak to the person of African descent; paradoxically, we read about that refusal in a text created by that very person of African descent. In a very real sense, the Anglo-African literary tradition was created two centuries ago in order to demonstrate that persons of African descent possessed the requisite degrees of reason and wit to create literature, that they were, indeed, full and equal members of the community of rational, sentient beings, that they could, indeed, write [Gates and McKay, xxxviii].

However, this does not negate the existence of and the need to recall the rationality and sentiment of the 1619 Angolans who pioneered through the superlative of the first enslavement sale in English North America. Black cultural mythology and Africana cultural memory studies compel us to speculate, and the speculative act of wondering and meditating on the gaps in the first-person experiences of the 1619 Angolans is sacred observation.

Conclusion

This has been a hearty sampling of how pervasive a 1619 narrative is in the African American curriculum. The historical, Africana Studies disciplinary, and literary lenses reveal the richness of chronological and causal variables in narrations of the 1619 moment. Further grounding the historical moment in terms of Black cultural mythology (retelling the encounter in cyclical storytelling that celebrates survival) and Africana cultural memory (negotiating proper commemoration, lamentation, and remembrance) enhances the culture's and the nation's ability to better meditate, *multidirectionally*, about the actual, symbolic, and legacy meaning of 1619. This includes embracing the challenge to connect West Central African history with Point Comfort and Virginia colony experiences, and to then broaden our transcontinental sense of the heroic feat of African survival in the United States. This is a powerful imperative for the relationship between history, worldview, and remembrance.

References

Asante, M.K. (2002). *African American History: A Journey of Liberation, Second Edition.* Saddlebrook, NJ: The People's Publishing Group.

_____. *Afrocentricity.* (1981). Trenton: Africa World Press.

Azevedo, M. (2016). *Africana Studies: A Survey of Africa and the African Diaspora.* Durham, NC: Carolina Academic Press.

Bennett, L. (1987). *Before the Mayflower: A History of Black America.* New York: Penguin.

Christian, C.M. (1999). *Black Saga: The African American Experience: A Chronology.* Washington, D.C.: Civitas/Counterpoint.

Drake, St. C. (1993). "Diaspora Studies and Pan-Africanism," pp. 451–514 in *Global Dimensions of the African Diaspora, Second Edition.* Edited by Joseph E. Harris. Washington, D.C.: Howard UP.

Fisher, S. (2001). "The Democratic Process and Transition from Class to Caste by Oppressed Minorities: Comment on the Case of Black Americans," pp. 47–56. *Black Studies: Current Issues, Enduring Questions,* Edited by Claudine Michel and Jacqueline Bobo. Dubuque, IA: Kendall Hunt.

Franklin, J.H. & Moss, A.A. (1994). *From Slavery to Freedom: A History of African Americans, Seventh Edition.* New York: McGraw-Hill, Inc.

Gates, H.L., and McKay, N.Y. (2004). *The Norton Anthology of African American Literature.* New York: W.W. Norton.

Hentz, E.S. (2018). "An Early Attempt to Build a National Museum for Colored People," Retrieved on September 15, 2018, http://invention.si.edu/early-attempt-build-national-museum-colored-people.

Higginbotham, A.L. (1978). *In the Matter of Color: Race & the American Legal Process: The Colonial Period.* New York: Oxford University Press.

Hine, D.C., Hine, W.C. & Harrold, S. (2006). *African Americans: A Concise History: Combined Volume, Second Edition.* Upper Saddle River, NJ: Pearson/Prentice Hall.

Johnson, C.J. (1997). "Forward." *Still I Rise: A Cartoon History of African Americans,* Edited by Roland Owen Laird, Jr., with Taneshia Nash Laird. New York: Norton.

Kachun, M. (2003). *Festivals of Freedom: Memory and Meaning in African Emancipation Celebrations.* Amherst: University of Massachusetts Press.

Kanneh, K. (1998). *African Identities: Race, Nation, and Culture in Ethnography, Pan-Africanism, and Black Literatures.* New York: Routledge.

Karenga, M. (2010). *Introduction to Black Studies, Fourth Edition.* Los Angeles: University of Sankore Press.

Keiley, C.R. (1909) (ed.). *The Official Book of the Jamestown Tercentennial Exposition, A.D. 1907: The Only Authorized History of the Celebration.* Norfolk, VA: The Colonial Publishing Company.

Laird, R., and Laird, T.N. (1997). *Still I Rise: A Cartoon History of African Americans.* New York: Norton.

Lee, Lauranett. (2018). "Giles B. Jackson," *Encyclopedia Virginia,* https://www.encyclopediavirginia.org/Jackson_Giles_B_1853-1924, Retrieved on September 5, 2018.

No Author. (2017). "The First Africans," *Jamestown Rediscovery.* http://historicjamestowne.org/history/the-first-africans/. Retrieved on October 16, 2017.

Sidbury, J. (2010). "Africa in Early African American Literature." *A Companion to African American Literature,* Edited by Gene Andrew Jarrett. Malden, MA: Wiley-Blackwell.

Stewart, J., and Anderson, T. (2015). *Introduction to African American Studies: Transdisciplinary Approaches and Implications.* Baltimore: Imprint Editions/Black Classic Press.

Twin Events of Summer 1619 in Tidewater Virginia, and the Prospect for Government of, for, and by the American People

A Commentary

PETER WALLENSTEIN

A historian stands on the sidewalk, looks up the street, gathers in the perspective from that site. Then crosses to the other side, again looks up the street, and sees an altered view. Historians do that all the time—working from new sources, or asking different questions, revisiting established sources. The past keeps changing.

Another historian looks up the street, takes in the view. Then turns and looks down the street, and sees something that might be extremely different. The past is transformed before her eyes.

Summer 1619

Events from early Virginia, within a few days of each other in summer 1619—or at most a year or so from each other, so between 1618 and 1620—have long been understood, in one fashion or another, to presage four centuries of development, amplified across time and space to provide the foundations of life in modern America. Which of those events get emphasized, and how they are understood, can have an extraordinary effect in promoting an understanding of how the nation has grown from seeds planted hundreds of years ago. John Rolfe—he who planted commercial tobacco and married Pocahontas, thus fostering peace between English and

Natives for a few years and, at the same time, finding the means by which the English outpost on the James River might find an economic basis—reported the arrival at Point Comfort (at today's city of Hampton) of some 20 or so Africans. Thus can be seen the seeds of a system of racial enslavement that persisted all the way down to the Civil War.

At almost the identical time, just days apart, newly elected delegates met up the river at Jamestown. From that other gathering is generally dated the origins of political democracy in Europe's New World. Therefore at the same time that the fountain of American freedom came into view, so did the worst of American unfreedom. A nominally democratic process of colonial governance emerged; so did a grotesquely uneven distribution of wealth and power. It makes a tremendous difference whose perspective governs any summing up, whether the benefits are emphasized or the costs. What did the meeting of multiple cultures mean for the chances of social justice?

Distinguishing the "by" and "for" People from the "of" People

Was the arrival of the first black Virginians a great exception, an anomaly to be overcome, a contradiction to be reconciled—or might it be viewed instead as a close companion to the convening of that first meeting of the burgesses, a core feature of American social and political development? One leading historian, Edmund S. Morgan, argued some years ago that it was precisely the submergence and suppression of black Virginians in a state of slavery that permitted elite white Virginians to become the statesmen we identify with the American Revolution. Might the history of unfreedom in America be so closely connected to, so intertwined with, the history of freedom that it is scarcely possible to separate them? The past has supplied evidence of formally democratic politics, a politics that benefited a great many people, or certainly has brought forth soaring language, and ideals to be cherished and promoted, at the same time that those ideals offer a darker perspective on the American past and present.

One place to begin an analysis of these twin developments can come from an observation that President Abraham Lincoln made at Gettysburg, Pennsylvania, when he spoke after a horrific three-days battle in what turned out to be the middle year of the American Civil War. On the outcome of the war, as he put it, hinged the future of "government of the people, for the people, by the people." Those three prepositional phrases, to carry out their work in this essay—and in all Americans' understanding of the significance of the events of 1619—must be pulled asunder, rather than being treated as saying much the same poetic thing in three different ways.

New Social and Political Patterns

Beginning in 1619, the House of Burgesses made laws that governed the colony of Virginia—all the people living within the colony's jurisdiction. They made laws, to which they consented, to govern themselves—and, to that extent, they exhibited government of the people, by the people, and for the people. Far more, they made laws that governed others—by class, by race, by gender, by age—and with no gesture toward gaining the assent of any among those others. Thus began a pattern of government "by" and "for" a small fraction of all inhabitants—and "of" everyone else. The proportions might change, and the identities of the various groups to some extent as well, but the sharp distinction long persisted.

By 1620 many hundreds of young English women had landed in the new colony, so the sex ratio among pale-faced newcomers began a halting move from extremely skewed to some point more closely balanced. They arrived as prospective brides of the men who were undertaking to extract a living, perhaps far more than that, from the colony's abundant land. The transplanted English society increasingly displayed white married couples, who comprised the basis for rapid population growth through natural increase rather than heavily reliant on immigration from across the ocean.

The new dispensation taking shape in Virginia toward the close of the 1610s included a means of promoting population growth and economic growth alike. Each current free Virginian could claim a parcel of land all his own, on which he might work intentionally to benefit directly from his own labor. In addition, each subsequent new Virginian who paid his own way could obtain a headright of 50 acres of land, a significant enticement to migration and then to hard work upon one's own land.

Land and Labor in Seventeenth-Century Virginia

But the offer of a headright for each newly arrived member of the colony attached, too, to workers whose means of transportation a would-be tobacco planter paid. The emergent planter thereby gained both the land to be worked and the labor force to work it. The terms of exchange had the new arrivals working someone else's land, then, as an indentured servant, for a period of years. This was no "40 acres and a mule" of 1860s vintage, the brief promise made to former slaves as the Civil War (or at least its organized form, with massive opposing armies) was coming to an end. This was "50 acres and a servant." The 20 or so Africans—about half men, half women—were hardly numerous in the colony. But the foundation of a society based on class, with unfree white workers laboring land acquired by a much smaller number of white owners, together with the headright system, pointed toward a very different social structure a generation or two or three later. What for a time was a triracial workforce became increasingly African rather than white or Native. Planters obtained enslaved labor, unfree on a permanent basis, with enslavement inherited from one generation to the next and on to the next. Virginia became a slave society, something of a transplanted Igbo world but with a configuration and in a context vastly different from its African origins. At the same time, it was becoming a European outpost of ever greater size and power. The settler society that the "maidens" of 1619 and 1620 fostered required ever greater territory to develop, which in turn meant the expulsion of more and more Natives. Events of the months surrounding summer 1619 turned out to be parts of a perpetual motion machine that grew ever bigger and stronger.

Fifty and Then One Hundred Years After 1619

During the second half of the seventeenth century, the patterns begun back in 1619 took an ever more robust and destructive shape. The House of Burgesses made more and more rules to govern a race-based tobacco-producing society. Among their early actions on this front, in 1662 these legislators passed a law that specified the status of people born in the colony—if the mother was a slave, the child was as well. Thus slavery officially became an intergenerational phenomenon, not applied solely to the person first sold into that status. But the labor force must be secured in other ways, too. If unfree workers tried to steal themselves, as men in particular sometimes did, upon recapture they suffered penalties that included far more time in servitude than they had faced before. If a slave ran off with a servant, the burgesses knew that more time could scarcely be added to the slave's unfreedom. So a new law stipulated that, in a case like that, the servant would have additional time tacked on both for his own misbehavior and stolen time and for the slave's as well. What had been a big gamble became, for the servant, an even more dangerous ploy. So the two would be far less likely to band together and seek freedom. And if they tried and failed, the owner benefited anyway.

The power to make laws that governed other people showed up in other contexts. The burgesses knew that women, from their perspective white women in particular, were in short supply. As men they needed to marry to safeguard their estates and leave them to a next generation, their legitimate male progeny. They also knew that they could use their power to coerce sex, outside of marriage, from their social inferiors, whether white or not. So they passed laws to look after these concerns as well. By 1691, they had banned marriage between a white person and a nonwhite; they specified people who were black, Indian, or mixed-race as illegitimate partners in marriage for a white person, whether a man or a woman. A white partner to a banned marriage was liable to be expelled from the colony.

But what if a white woman gave birth to a mixed-race child outside of marriage? The mother paid a hefty fine or, if unable to do that, was sold for a period of years. And the child? He or she would be very long-term servant, not just for five years or seven, not just until adulthood, but all the way to the age of thirty. Later, the burgesses addressed a next-generation question, so that if a woman still in that very long-term state of unfreedom had a child, her child too would be a servant for three decades. In this legislation by and for white male planters, their kind would have access to white women and black women alike. Black women could be shared—black men could have sexual access to black women, but not to white women. Marrying across a line separating white from nonwhite was forever banned—a law that, in one form or another, persisted for most of three centuries, all the way down to the year 1967.

Of the People, for the People, and by the People

In the twenty-first century, few Virginians continue to make a living from growing tobacco. But that is a very recent development, and, in other ways, too, patterns first seen in 1619 reverberated down through the centuries. In 1994, in the face of tremendous numbers of deaths from lung cancer, executives of the nation's top tobacco companies, intent on preserving their economic dominance, swore on oath to Congress that they did not believe tobacco to be addictive. As for racial targeting by the so-called justice system, a 2015 report by the U.S. Department of Justice, in the aftermath of extreme racial unrest in Ferguson, Missouri, made it clear that—in one sample jurisdiction, one that might be extreme but not necessarily anomalous—black Americans were still subject to having their limited wealth systematically extracted, plundered. Voter suppression, in all manner of forms, continued to keep many Americans from participating in the selection of the people who purported to represent them in formulating public policy.

Lincoln spoke in 1863 of something that, according to his language, must be preserved—must not be permitted to "perish from the earth." Viewed another way, government "of the people, for the people, by the people" had yet to come into place; its arrival would require, again in Lincoln's words that day, "a new birth of freedom." In fact, the extreme denial of the formula—the insistence on separating "by" people and "for" people from "of" people—had characterized the war in a wide range of ways, from spurring the secession of so many states after Lincoln's election to the presidency, to the Emancipation Proclamation that preceded the Gettysburg Address by a matter of months, and on to the great struggle that came after the war and has continued down to our own times to end the separation of the "by" and "for" people from the "of" people, so that all people would be equally subject to the rules that they jointly established and consented to.

The Africans who were brought to coastal Virginia in 1619—they and those who arrived in other ports, both before and after 1619—and their progeny across the generations proved to be a central part of the American story. Their quest to break free of their "of" condition and join those in the ranks of the "by" and "for" people continues. From 1619 to the present, those already in the "by" and "for" groups did not prove eager to see the "of" groups join them in the ranks of those who got to do the governing. The power to govern "of" people for the benefit of the "by" and "for" people must, those doing the governing insisted, never be relinquished. In this fashion, the implications and consequences of those foundational twin developments of summer 1619 continue to unfold.

Engendering Slavery in Virginia
An Examination of Blacks' First Century in the Old Dominion

Maureen Elgersman Lee

Late August 1619 has been heralded as a seminal moment in the history of Virginia and the larger United States. In that month and year, twelve years after England established its first permanent settlement in North America, some twenty Africans were brought ashore at Point Comfort, in Hampton, and traded by their captors for much needed food and supplies. Research contends that the ship carrying these African women and men was the *White Lion*. The scholarly narrative continues that the *White Lion*'s arrival was followed a few days later by that of the *Treasurer*, another vessel which also likely sold a modest, but somewhat undermined number of Africans to early Virginians (Sluiter 1997; Thornton 1998a, 1998b; Heywood and Thornton 2007; McCartney 2018). Africans on the *White Lion* and the *Treasurer* were likely captured from the Portuguese slaver *São João Bautista* which had left Portuguese-controlled Angola, West Africa, from its capital, the port city of Luanda (Thornton 1998a, 1998b; Sluiter 1997). This series of African and transatlantic "exchanges" ultimately introduced Black women and men to colonial Virginia and Virginians. It also introduced colonial Virginia and Virginians to Black male bodies with a capacity to labor, as well as to Black female bodies that had the twin capacities to labor like men and produce children. The importance of 1619 is not to be diminished, for the presence of other African and African descended peoples in Virginia stems from this moment—whether it be via growth from within (natural increase) or growth from without (importation).

But another date looms large in the 1600s as one that further changed the trajectories of Black lives in Virginia for generations thereafter. In 1662, the Virginia House of Burgesses passed a statute decreeing that henceforth the status of children born in the colony would be determined by the status of their mothers, when previously children's status was determined by, among other things, the status of their fathers. The 1662 decision constituted a transformative colonial moment that divided Blacks' first century in Virginia into two discernable periods—those preceding the decision and those that followed. Examining the experience of Black women in Virginia before the 1662 decision and thereafter engenders the study of early Blacks in ways necessary to understand the complexity of the Black experience in early Virginia. This can be best understood through a critical lens that not only considers issues of race and class, but makes considerations of gender central to understanding Virginia's transformation into a slave society. "Engendering Slavery in Virginia" explores how using a gendered lens enables a deeper understanding of Black women's first century and, therefore, the significance of 1619.

Virginia's Black Population During the First Century

In 1620, the year after the arrival of the *White Lion* and the *Treasurer*, Virginia's first census determined that there were 32 Africans—15 females and 17 males—living in the midst of nearly 900 European colonists (McCartney 2018). As the objects of trade, they were not free people; at the same time, they were not yet slaves for life as would be the fate of most Blacks born or arriving thereafter. Whatever their official status at that seminal moment in August 1619, these Black men and women symbolized the complicated social, economic, and political intersections that defined the Atlantic slave trade and the larger Atlantic world of the seventeenth century.

To the question of whether or not slavery in colonial Virginia expanded exponentially overnight, statistics on Virginia's Black population would suggest that the population growth was initially gradual. More than twenty-five years after the first documented Africans landed in the colony, Blacks accounted for a few hundred persons out of the total population. Africans were not immune to the challenges of life on the frontier, to include exposure to harsh elements, disease, starvation, and Native American attacks, so an ebb and flow in their early numbers is understandable. By the mid seventeenth century, Blacks were in numbers almost 10 times that of 1620, and by 1680 they were found in numbers 100 hundred times that of 1620. By the turn of the century, they were more than 500 times the original number; and by the first 100 years after arrival, their numbers were more than 800 times that of their 1620 levels.

Table 1: Black Population in Virginia, 1620–1720

Year	Estimated Population
1620	32
1625	23
1648	300
1680	3,000
1700	16,390
1720	26,559

Source: McCartney, M. (2018). Virginia's First Africans. Encyclopedia Virginia. Retrieved September 29, 2018, from http://www.EncyclopediaVirginia.org/Virginia_s_First_Africans; Slavery and the Law in Virginia: The Growth of the Black Population (2018). Colonial Williamsburg Foundation. Retrieved September 8, 2018, from http://www.history.org/history/teaching/slavelaw.cfm.

Blacks—free, freed, and enslaved—were not relegated to any particular area of the colony, and were represented among populations around Jamestown, Richmond, Williamsburg, and on the Eastern Shore (Tate 1965; Walsh 1997). Surviving documents allow us to lend names to at least some of early African women in Virginia. In 1624 and 1625, a woman known in the records as Angela lived in the Jamestown household of Captain William Pierce, one among his seventeen servants (Morgan 1975). Believed to have been from Angola, Angela arrived in 1619 on the *Treasurer* (Heywood and Thornton 2007; McCartney 2018). A woman by the name of Mary, who would later become (free) Mary Johnson, arrived in the early 1620s on the ship *Margaret and John*, and a woman named Margaret resided on the lower side of the James River (McCartney 2018; Berlin 1998), likely near what is now Isle of Wight. Perhaps the most famous African woman in early 1620s Virginia was Isabell(a), who in the 1624 census is listed in the Elizabeth City household of Captain William Tucker. Like Captain Pierce, Tucker would have been a man of means, having also some seventeen servants (Morgan 1975). By the time of the 1625 muster, Isabell(a) had given birth to son, William, with Anthony, a fellow African bondsman of Captain Tucker's—and her husband. The first African American in Virginia was born (McCartney 2018).

Virginia's Black population grew amidst an expanding European population. Although they numbered little more than two hundred in the decade prior to African arrival, Europeans maintained a majority over Africans in the population.

Table 2. Total Estimated Population of Virginia, 1610–1720

Year	Estimated Population
1610	210
1620	2,400
1630	3,000
1640	7,647
1650	17,000
1660	33,000
1670	40,000
1680	49,000
1690	58,000
1700	72,000
1710	87,000
1720	116,000

Source: United States Bureau of the Census, Estimated Population during the Colonial and Continental Periods: 1610–1790, in Population in the Colonial and Continental Periods, 9–10, Retrieved September 21, 2018, from https://www.census.gov/history/pdf/colonialbostonpops.pdf.

Based on reported U.S. census data, the total population of Virginia in 1720 was more than 550 times what it was in 1610. This was the result of European migration and domestic births. The Black population, which started out only in double digits, grew in 1720 to be more than 800 times what is was in 1620. This total population was a combination of African imports and births among those who were bonded and free.

1619–1655: Prelude to a Law

The Virginia of the early 1600s constituted what scholars (Cooper 2000; Smardz Frost and Tucker 2016) term a fluid frontier. It was a multilayered, multidimensional borderland between land and ocean, Europe and America, Africa and America, Black and White, female and male, rich and poor. In her lead essay in "*A Share of Honour*": *Virginia Women 1600–1945* (1984), Suzanne Lebsock contends "[T]here was a time in Virginia's early history when race relations were fluid, possibilities were open, and blacks and whites of the same class could expect roughly similar treatment" (1984, 27), and non-racialized punishments for the Christian sins of fornication and adultery, and latitude in interracial marriages as evidence. However, historian John Thornton contents that it was not that simple: "Whatever the case, the earliest settlers certainly understood that the Africans they purchased were legally different from the indentured servants they brought from Europe, long before the first slave codes were promulgated in Virginia or the West Indies" (1998a, 147). These two quotes speak to the ongoing tensions in the scholarly narrative about the exact nature of Africans' condition—and race relations—in the years immediately following 1619.

Just as the slave population saw a slow but then accelerated increase in Virginia, so did the racialization of life in the colony. The General Assembly passed a series of laws that addressed various aspects of life along lines that were increasingly racial in nature. In 1630, Hugh Davis was sentenced "to be soundly whipped, before an assembly of Negroes and others for abusing himself to the dishonor of God and shame of Christians, by defiling his body in lying with a Negro" (Hening 1823, 146). The black body, in this case a Black female body, is clearly constructed in the political and social records of early Virginia as being a contaminant. The record's wording suggests that Davis' sin was not simply or even primarily fornication (sex before marriage), as the term itself is not even invoked in the notation. It was the defiling—soiling—of his body by having intercourse with a Black female body that is highlighted here.

A few years later, the General Assembly added Black women to the list of taxable persons, a list that already included men, both Black and white. According to historian Julie Richter, "This distinction may reflect lawmakers' expectation that African women would be field laborers, thus contributing to the colony's wealth" (2013). European women, who were excluded from the tithable list, "would remain in the domestic sphere. The legislators hoped their decision to limit white women to domestic work would further stabilize the colony's social order and give husbands more authority and control over their wives" (Richter 2013).

1655–1662: The Case of Elizabeth Key and the Condition of the Mother

While a number of freedom suits came before the courts in seventeenth-century Virginia, the case of Elizabeth Key (also Kaye) was one of the century's most engaging and significant as it would challenge the definition of freedom and change the legal trajectory of Black women and their offspring for generations and centuries to come (Slavery and Remembrance). Elizabeth Key was biracial, born of a white planter father, Thomas Key, and an enslaved Black mother, possibly by the name of Martha. Said to have been born in Warwick County, Virginia, sometime around 1630, a young Elizabeth was a mere child of six years of age when, in 1636, her father decided to hire her out to fellow Virginian Humphrey Higginson. Key's period of indenture was to have lasted nine years, until she reached fifteen years of age (Robinson 2017; Billings 1973, 468).

Historical accounts suggest that what happened next was a perfect storm of death and betrayal. Thomas Key returned to England while Elizabeth was in Higginson's charge. With Key gone, Higginson may have sought to capitalize on Elizabeth Key's race by selling her to Colonel John Mottrom (also Mottram), a Northumberland County justice of the peace and planter. When Mottrom died in 1655, Key was a twenty-five-year-old woman and the mother of a young son, John. Elizabeth Key and her son were claimed as part of the Mottrom estate; it is this claim as part of the Mottrom that spurred Elizabeth, through a young indentured lawyer William Greensted (also Grinsted, Grinstead), to initiate the freedom suit (Billings 1973, 468; Banks 2008, 809–10; Robinson 2017).

According to the scholarship, the local Northumberland County jury supported Key's freedom, but the Mottrom estate won on appeal that she was, in fact, a slave. Greensted then petitioned the General Assembly to hear the case; the Assembly investigated the case, sent it back to Northumberland County for retrial, and Northumberland confirmed reaffirmed its original decision recognizing Elizabeth Key as a free woman (Billings 1975, 167; Billings 1973, 468).

Elizabeth Key's case was far more complicated than this brief sketch suggests, and Key's position as a biracial woman in early Virginia is essential to the basis, outcome, and significance of the case. Born out of wedlock, the "bastard" child of Thomas Key and an anonymous slave woman, Elizabeth Key seems to have been given her father's name, but not his free status. Thomas Key commodified his daughter by selling or hiring her out to another man for a determined length of time, only to apparently sell her again, in a more definitive manner, to Northumberland planter Colonel Mottrom. Elizabeth Key's *de facto* status as a permanent servant or even chattel resonates in the story of her early life. To complicate the matter further, William Greensted was not only Elizabeth Key's lawyer, he was also her paramour and father of son, John. Greensted's motives would seem to have been both personal and professional, as he fought for Elizabeth's freedom and held up Virginia law to real scrutiny (Robinson 2017; Billings 1975, 167).

Elizabeth Key's freedom suit turned on multiple intersecting and complicating conditions. First, the case required Elizabeth Key to establish that she was, indeed, Thomas Key's daughter. The recorded oaths of numerous persons corroborated Key's paternal claim to Thomas Key, citing their own personal knowledge of the father-daughter relationship and the fact that Elizabeth Key's filial relationship with Thomas Key was public knowledge. Thomas Key, himself, had been fined by the colony for impregnating his slave woman, lending further credence to the fact that Elizabeth was his daughter. Thomas Key's social sins were many in this case—for he committed fornication, miscegenation, and begot a child out of wedlock. While Thomas Key was fined by the courts, his offspring did not take slave status automatically. It was Thomas Key's paternal status as a free Englishman that rendered Elizabeth free, but at the same time was able to allow her to be bound to service (Wolfe 2017).

Second, having completed the nine years of service of the Thomas Key–Hugh Higginson agreement, Elizabeth Key argued that she was entitled to her freedom. A review of the rough facts in Key's case, however, shows that Elizabeth Key served an excess of up to ten years of bond, if one considers that the agreement with Higginson would have expired in 1645. Elizabeth would have been somewhere around 15 years of age at that time, but because she was still held in bond service in 1655, she served as many as 16 years in bonded labor—almost twice as long as the original agreement between her father and Higginson (Billings 1973, 467–8).

Finally, Elizabeth's suit included a third condition that loomed larger than the issues of paternity and contract, because it fundamentally argued for her freedom based on the basis that she was baptized and a practicing Christian. Not only did the General Assembly's committee review and reporting of Elizabeth Key's case confirm her baptism, they noted that "shee hath bin long since Christened[,] Col. Higginson being her God father and that by report shee is able to give a very good account of her faith" (Billings 1975, 167). The investigation into the Elizabeth Key petition revealed the warped racial landscape that was emerging in mid-seventeenth-century Virginia, as Key's godfather, would, for all practical purposes, own her while being able to attest to the very Christianity that would ultimately undermine her bonded status.

The General Assembly had before it a Black woman's freedom suit that turned on gender, paternity, race, and religion. Thomas Key, Humphrey Higginson, and John Mottrom were all men of position and influence in early Virginia. Not only were the men of the General Assembly and Northumberland County watching, but so were other planters and slave-owners—anxious patriarchs (Brown, 1996) whose livelihoods could be impacted by the case's legal decision. Greensted argued that Elizabeth Key's freedom was merited on three conditions. First, she was entitled to Thomas Key's status by virtue of her position as his daughter. Second, she had met and exceeded the term of bondage contracted between her father and her godfather, Higginson. Finally, she was not only symbolically Christian by virtue of baptism, but that she was a practicing Christian who could give a good account of her faith.

Not only did the General Assembly confirm Elizabeth Key's freedom on the grounds presented by William Greensted, it found grounds for restitution—for making Elizabeth whole as a consequence of her excessive service. According to records, Elizabeth Key was to receive corn, clothing, and satisfaction for time served beyond that which was contracted. But the story did not end yet. In July 1656, after Elizabeth Key gained her freedom, she and William Greensted published marriage banns and were married that same year. They married after Elizabeth's freedom was granted and after William, who was still indentured, completed his own contracted term of service. By the time of their marriage, they had at least one child, son John (Billings 1975, 168). The fact that the indentured William Greensted, though white, male, and educated, saw his fate more caught up with Elizabeth Key—a biracial woman born of a slave mother and with tenuous legal status—than that of the emerging planter class is noteworthy.

Elizabeth Key was a product of what Ira Berlin had called the "charter generation" (2003, 21–50) of Virginia Blacks. They were primarily African-born and still largely able to benefit from the fluidity of race relations and status between free and bonded (Wallenstein 2007). Although Key was clearly American born, her birth just over a decade since the first documented Africans set foot in the Virginia colony places her in a time where the possibility of freedom was real. The status and story of Elizabeth Key's unnamed mother is tragically anonymous. Was she brought to Virginia by the Portuguese like many before her? Did she come through the West Indies? Did she ever see freedom in her lifetime? At present, these questions only have a rhetorical quality.

The aforementioned case of Elizabeth Key was exceptional, and would not have been possible had it come before the courts a decade later. The zeitgeist that permitted Key and her soon-to-be husband William Greensted to prevail in the bid for freedom did not endure. If the Elizabeth Key case raised the question as to the status of children born in the colony, the General Assembly closed the loop by answering it definitively. In the spring of 1662, the General Assembly entered the following into the political and historical record:

> WHEREAS some doubts have [arisen] where children got by any Englishman upon a negro woman should be slave or free, Be it therefore enacted and declared by this present grand assembly, that all children borne in the country [shall be] held bond or free only according to the condition of the mother, And that if any [C]hristian shall commit

fornication with a negro man or woman [he or she so] offending shall pay double the fines imposed by the former act [Hening 1832, 170].

The 1662 legislation that the child followed the condition of the mother seems to have been dictated by the Elizabeth Key case. English common law still prevailed in Virginia at the time of her case, so it was necessary to change colonial law and codify a clearly articulated formula for determining who was free and who was enslaved from that point on. This shift from paternity to maternity was neither coincidental nor was it isolated to the British-colonized world. Spain, Portugal, France—all major colonizers and slave traders—made the same epochal systemic shift (Morgan 2007). This legislation made fathers increasingly irrelevant and distanced from their offspring, particularly as the property rights in slave children were retained by the mother's slave owner and not by the mother herself (Billings 1975, 172).

The 1662 legislation championed the condition of the mother over that of the father by the insertion of one simply word. Children would be free or unfree based *only*—solely—on the condition of the mother. The free status of Elizabeth Key's father was enough to keep her from being a slave for life, but the slave status of her mother seems to have kept her from being truly free without legal intervention. Elizabeth Key was in an in-between place, a murky purgatory from which she was freed by the courts through the tireless efforts of herself and her soon-to-be husband, William Greensted.

1663–1719: The Double Bind Becomes a Triple Bind

As if to cement the 1660s as the turning point for Black status in the Virginia colony, the General Assembly passed another piece of legislation in 1667, this time to clarify the inability of baptism to alter one's status. The historical record reads:

> WHEREAS some doubts have risen whether children that are slaves by birth, and by the charity and piety of their owners made partakers of the blessed sacrament of [baptism], should by [virtue] of their baptism be made free; It is enacted and declared by this grand assembly, and the authority thereof, that the conferring of [baptism] doth not alter the condition of the person as to his as to his bondage or [freedom]; that diverse masters, freed from this doubt, may more carefully endeavor the propagation of [C]hristianity by permitting children, though slaves, or those of greater growth if capable to be admitted to that sacrament [Hening 1823, 260].

Common across the Atlantic World was the mandate that Africans forced into the slave trade be baptized, as a means of saving their souls while still compelling their bodies to labor. The question of whether the offspring of enslaved Africans who received the sacrament of baptism retained their slave status was a question of significance as the increasing number of Virginia-born slaves were credited for growing the colony's slave population more so than the number of African-born slaves in the colony. As the first colony in the Americas to grow by natural increase, Virginia had much at stake if baptism and a subsequent practice of the Christian faith, as in the case of Elizabeth Key, could continue as legal grounds for emancipation. Just as the 1662 legislation closed the loophole on the question of paternity vs. maternity, the 1667 statute closed the loophole on the question of baptism.

The closing decades of the seventeenth century in Virginia locked Black men and women in chattel status, and this status was performed on their bodies with different public consequences. The passage of an 1680 statute framed as an act to prevent insurrections prohibited Black men and women from taking up any form of arms, be it club, staff, gun, or sword, for purposes offensive or even defensive. Likewise, they were not to absent themselves from the owners without permission verified by a certificate or pass. The punishment was twenty lashes on the bare back, well laid on (Hening 1823, 481). The same statute exacted a punishment of thirty lashes on the back, well laid on, for each instance in which any slave shall "presume to lift up his hand in opposition to any [C]hristian," for which proof was made before a magistrate (Hening 1823, 481). The consequences of a punishment of twenty or thirty lashes on the bare back were different for men and women. Stripping a man to the waist by another man positioned the power of Black masculinity against that of white masculinity. Stripping black women to the waist put their bodies on display in ways that denied them the decorum of female modesty and the propriety of female protection. Unable to cover their breasts from the gaze of the punisher—planter, overseer, or other—as well as the larger public, Black women were further objectified and diminished as they had their chattel status publicly inscribed on their back with each stripe of the lash. Trapped in the triple bind of race, gender, and class, most Black women would never be able to imagine the freedom of Elizabeth Keys—if they ever heard of her at all.

As the seventeenth century drew to a close and the dawn of the eighteenth century rose visible on the horizon, Virginia could no longer be understood simply as a society with slaves. The indices of a slave society had not only emerged, but were crystallizing. The overall population was rising, and enslaved Blacks no longer numbered in the tens or hundreds, but in the thousands. The seat of government shifted from Jamestown (Montgomery 2007) to Williamsburg (Tate 1965), and the ideas and practices around slavery planted at midcentury were further nurtured in new, more comprehensive pieces of legislation. This final portion of Black's first century in Virginia had two striking features: the colony's legal preoccupation with ensuring sexual separation of the races and a concentration of measures intended to completely erode any semblance of power that enslaved Blacks and free Blacks might imagine they could have.

An examination of slave law in the 1690s and early 1700s would suggest that lawmakers were not satisfied with previous measures to keep Blacks and Whites apart, for the early 1700s are filled with the passage and revision of laws vilifying interracial relationships taking place outside or inside of the marriage contract. Ministers faced astronomical fines for marrying persons of different races, persons in interracial marriages were banned from the colony, and interracial children born outside of wedlock could be indentured for thirty or more years. Free black men, who for a brief period of time seem to have had the right to hold public office, lost it. In a similar vein, no Blacks, whether enslaved or free, could offer witness testimony in a court of law (Slavery and the Law).

These legal statutes did not operate in a vacuum, for the aforementioned population figures reveal that they were passed at a time when the Black population of Virginia grew by the tens of thousands over the course of a few decades. Whites benefited from the labor produced by more Black bodies, even as the increase of those same bodies—which in many cases came through the bodies of enslaved Black women—was met with more even regulation and punishment.

Conclusion

When some twenty Africans were removed from the *White Lion* and exchanged for provisions in August 1619, they became part of a fluid frontier. Having crossed the tempestuous Atlantic Ocean, they faced an uncertain future in Virginia. The significance of 1619 cannot be denied. It is best understood not as a destination in itself, but as a seminal moment that put in process other seminal and transformative moments best understood not only by looking at race and class, but also by looking at gender. When the General Assembly passed the statute that the status of children born in the colony would be decided *only* by the condition of their mothers, they effectively created a defining moment in the history of Virginia, Black women, and slavery that serves as a reference point for events that took place prior and for those that took place thereafter.

In a tragic twist of fate, William Greensted died in 1661, just five years after legally marrying Elizabeth Key. Before her husband's death, Elizabeth

Key had another son, William II (Robinson, 2017). Elizabeth Key's status as a free woman had determined the condition of her first son retroactively and determined the condition of her second son at birth. By the early eighteenth-century Virginia society was so transformed that it was difficult to imagine that the case of women like Elizabeth Key would have been possible.

REFERENCES

Banks, T.L. (2008). Dangerous Woman: Elizabeth Key's Freedom Suit—Subjecthood and Racialized Identity in Seventeenth-Century Colonial Virginia. *Faculty Scholarship*, 52, 799-837. Retrieved from https://digitalcommons.law.umaryland.edu/fac_pubs/52/ on October 22, 2018.

Berlin, I. (1998). *Many Thousands Gone: The First Two Centuries of Slavery in North America*. Cambridge, MA: Harvard University Press.

Berlin, I. (2003). *Generations of Captivity: A History of African-American Slaves*. Cambridge, MA: Harvard University Press.

Billings, W.M. (1973). The Cases of Fernando and Elizabeth Key: A Note on the Status of Blacks in Seventeenth-Century Virginia. *William and Mary Quarterly* 30, 1973, 467-474.

Billings, W.M. (2004). *A Little Parliament: The Virginia General Assembly in the Seventeenth Century*. Richmond: Library of Virginia/Jamestown-Yorktown Foundation.

Billings, W.M., ed. (1975). *The Old Dominion in the Seventeenth Century: A Documentary History of Virginia 1606-1689*. Chapel Hill: University of North Carolina.

Brown, K.M. (1996). *Good Wives, Nasty Wenches and Anxious Patriarchs: Gender, Race, and Power in Colonial Virginia*. Chapel Hill: University of North Carolina Press.

Colonial Williamsburg Foundation. (2018). Elizabeth Key (Kaye). Slavery and Remembrance: A Guide to Sites, Museums, and Memory. Retrieved from http://slaveryandremembrance.org/people/person/?id=PP031 on October 22, 2018.

Cooper, A. (2000). "The Fluid Frontier: Blacks in the Detroit Region. A Focus on Henry Bibb," 30, 127-148. DOI: 10.3138/CRAS-s030-02-02.

Craven, W.F. (1977). *White, Red, and Black: The Seventeenth-Century Virginian*. New York, NY: W.W. Norton and Company, Inc.

Hening, W.W., ed. (1823). *The Statutes of At Large, Being a Collection of All the Laws of Virginia from the First Session of the Legislature, in the Year 1619*. Vol II. New York, NY: R & W & G Bartow. Archive.org. Retrieved from https://archive.org on October 21, 2018.

Heywood, L.M. and Thornton, J.K. (2007). *Central Africans, African Creoles, and the Foundation of the Americas, 1585-1660*. Cambridge: Cambridge University Press.

Lebsock, S. (1984). "A Share of Honor": Virginia Women 1600-1945. Richmond: Virginia Women's Cultural History Project.

McCartney, M. (2018). Virginia's First Africans. *Encyclopedia Virginia*. Retrieved from http://www.EncyclopediaVirginia.org/Virginia_s_First_Africans on September 21, 2018.

Montgomery, D. (2007). *1607: Jamestown and the New World*. Williamsburg, VA: Colonial Williamsburg Foundation.

Morgan, E.S. (1975). *American Slavery, American Freedom: The Ordeal of Colonial Virginia*. New York, NY: W.W. Norton and Company, Inc.

Morgan, P.D. (2007). Virginia's Other Prototype: The Caribbean. In P.C. Mancall (Ed.), *The Atlantic World and Virginia, 1550-1624* (pp. 342-380). Chapel Hill: University of North Carolina Press.

Richter, J. (2013). Women in Colonial Virginia. *Encyclopedia Virginia*. Retrieved from https://www.encyclopediavirginia.org/Women_in_Colonial_Virginia on September 18, 2018.

Robinson, Y. (2017). Grinstead, Elizabeth Key (1630-1665). Blackpast.org. Retrieved from https://blackpast.org/aah/grinstead-elizabeth-key-1630 on October 22, 2018.

Slavery and the Law in Virginia. (2018). Colonial Williamsburg Foundation. Retrieved from http://www.history.org/history/teaching/slavelaw.cfm on September 18, 2018.
Sluiter, E. (1997). New Light on the "20. and Odd Negroes" Arriving in Virginia, August 1619. *William and Mary Quarterly*, 54, 395–398.
Smardz Frost, K., and Tucker, V.S., ed. (2016). *A Fluid Frontier: Slavery, Resistance, and the Underground Railroad in the Detroit River Borderland*. Detroit: Wayne State University Press.
Stanard, M.N. (2005). *The Story of Virginia's First Century*. Reprint *A History of the Jamestowne Period 1607-1700—400th Anniversary Edition*. Dexter, Michigan.
Tate, T.W. (1965). *The Negro in Eighteenth-Century Williamsburg*. Williamsburg: Colonial Williamsburg Foundation.
Thornton, J. (1998). *Africa and Africans in the Making of the Atlantic World, 1400–1800*. 2d. ed. Cambridge: Cambridge University Press.
Thornton, J. (1998). The African Experience of the "20. and Odd Negroes" Arriving in Virginia in 1619. *William and Mary Quarterly*, 55, 421–434.
United States Bureau of the Census. Estimated Population during the Colonial and Continental Periods: 1610–1790, in *Population in the Colonial and Continental Periods*. Retrieved from https://www.census.gov/history/pdf/colonialbostonpops.pdf on September 21, 2018.
Wallenstein, P. (2007). *Cradle of America: Four Centuries of Virginia History*. Lawrence: University Press of Kansas.
Walsh, L.S. (1997). *From Calabar to Carter's Grove: The History of a Virginia Slave Community*. Charlottesville: University Press of Virginia.
Wertenbaker, T.J. (1957). *The Government of Virginia in the Seventeenth Century*. Jamestown 350th Anniversary Historical Booklet Number 16. Williamsburg, VA: Clearfield.
Wolfe, B. (2017). Free Blacks in Colonial Virginia. *Encyclopedia Virginia*. Retrieved from https://www.encyclopediavirginia.org/Free_Blacks_in_Colonial_Virginia on September 18, 2018.

"Wash Me and I Shall Be Whiter Than Snow"

A Living Historiography of African Women and Christianity in the Virginia Colony

VALERIE M. JOYCE

In 1649, the Court of Lower Norfolk in the Virginia Colony convicted a woman named Mary of fornication and sentenced her to do penance. The court record reads:

> It hath appeared to the Lower Norfolk Court that William Watts hath Comitted the filth sin of fornication with Mary a Negro belonging to Mr. Cornelius Lloyds. It is therefore ordered that each of them doe penance by standing in a white sheet with a white Rodd in their hands in the Chappell of Elizabeth River in the face of the Congregation on the next Sabbath day that the minister shall make penance service [Billings, 1975, p. 161].

This indelible image of Mary, with her brown skin wrapped in the traditional penitential white sheet, standing with a white rod in her hand, and facing the white Congregation on the Sabbath day, ignited my imagination. I envisioned Mary speaking a language that was not hers, while reciting a prayer in a religion that was not hers, to a god that was not hers, in order to repent for a sin that was almost assuredly not consensual "fornicating," but rape. She could not possibly have stood under the condemning gaze of a sea of white faces and recite the Church of England's Penitential Psalm without raging internally at the relentless injustices heaped upon her.

The juxtaposition of images and emotions that surround Mary's undocumented rage fueled my scholarship and creative activity around African American women before Emancipation by provoking fascinating research questions, including: What was the Lower Norfolk Court and why was the legal court ordering penance in a Christian Church? Who was Mr.

Cornelius Lloyds and what was Mary's state of "belonging" to Mr. Lloyds? What does the white sheet and white rod signify? Did Mary know English? How did she learn it? Was Mary a practicing Christian? How many other Africans were actively a part of the parish? How many Africans were in the Virginia Colony in 1649? How did Mary learn the penitential psalm? What does Mary's voice sound like? What does her English sound like? Who was William Watts and what was his relationship with Mary? These questions eventually led me to write a play, titled *I Will Speak for Myself*, and in turn the play led me to write about the research and live performance that went into creating the Living Historiography of the character Mary.

Through an embodied writing of history, a Living Historiography can begin to breathe life into absence and sound into silence, in order to shape a fuller, more nuanced understanding of women in the past. In this case, with only the court record that remains to attest to Mary's presence in the world, I examined the limited written evidence and imagined the possibilities inherent in Mary's social, cultural, religious, educational, and economic realities, and an outline of the human who inhabited that temporal space began to emerge. I then utilized performance as a way to envision the complexities of an African woman's life as she encountered Virginia Colony in the 1640s. By tracing this outline and filling these imagined experiences with the live performer's body, this historically silenced woman's voice now rings out loud and clear and we are able to share it with new audiences. This chapter will examine aspects of the research as well as the many iterations of the development of Mary's character and monologue, in order to suggest a methodology for future Living Historiographies.

The Given Circumstances of Colonial Life: The Research

When developing a character, either as a playwright or as an actor, one of the first steps is to invest in the character's experience of the world around them, or their "given circumstances." In Mary's case, her journey from West Africa to the Virginia Colony plays a large part in her mindset and linguistic complexities, her position in colonial society informs her state of vulnerability, and her status as an indentured servant gives her both an obstacle in her master and an objective in the form of her eventual freedom. The world around Mary is controlled by larger organizational forces, including the court system and the church. Understanding the ways in which these forces create expectations and pressures within the society at large, and how these pressures impact Mary specifically, informs the behaviors and actions of the characters within the plot of her monologue. Archival material can provide a launching point for the generation of a Living Historiography text and for the collaborative process in rehearsal. Although there are no records of Mary's life, detailed accounts of the social, domestic, and religious life of Virginia Colony exist to support her character's development.

To place Mary's given circumstances in perspective, from the early–1500s European traders uprooted millions of Africans from a three thousand mile stretch of the West Coast and dispersed them across the Atlantic world. These people were from hundreds of tribes that included "many racial stocks ... from the spirited Hausas, the gentle Mandingos, the creative Yorubas, from the Ibos, Efiks and Krus, from the proud Fantins, the courageous Ashantis, the shrewd Dahomeans, the Binis and Senegalese" (Bennett, 1993, p. 47). There was no class structure or status at play in this cultural destruction, as priests and nobles were sold and princesses and warriors were stolen equally and sent to Europe and South America (Bennett, 1993, p. 47). As a result of this trading, Africans were living in England by the mid–1500s and the first Africans were brought to North America on a Dutch ship that landed at Point Comfort, Virginia in 1619 (Bennett, 1993, pp. 36–37).

When imagining Mary's particular journey to America, though it is possible she came directly from England, the data asserts that Dutch or Portuguese traders likely brought Mary against her will from Africa by the early 1640s. As I developed the character in rehearsal with actress Kimberley S. Fairbanks, we needed more specific details in order to establish Mary's history and particularly her first language. While no evidence exists as to Mary's original dialect, it would have been from a West African language with strikingly different vocal placements and muscular structures than used for producing the English language. We chose Twi for her native tongue, and this became the force against which Mary would work to place the English sounds into her mouth. In addition to the language question, Mary's prior life in Africa played a part in our character development work. When working with a short piece and little time for narrative back story, it is important to make strong choices that appeal to the actor's imagination. Therefore, Mary became the daughter of a warrior in her tribe. This history supported her strength and courage in the face of relentless adversity and also fueled her rage at her drastic shift in status and power.

Lighting and sound design also played a large part in creating this Living Historiography. Mary's monologue is broken into several vignettes across *I Will Speak for Myself* and interspersed with fifteen other characters but, each time her character appears, African drums play first in the darkness. In her first appearance, the drums are soon eclipsed by a voice-over of a man reading out the Lower Norfolk Court's ruling against Mary and the declaration of her sentence. Before the audience sees Mary, they have received aural information about the crux of her internal conflict as she navigates the loss of her identity, family, and home in the overgrown forests and marshy swamps of the Virginia Colony.

When she landed, Mary's given circumstances certainly included a fairly strange mix of English social classes in the Virginia Colony. Mary's powerless position in society is magnified by the social realities at play around her. Most prominently, the African population in the Virginia Colony was incredibly small between 1619 and 1649. From the first arrival at Point Comfort to the first detailed census of 1624–25, the African population grew to be "about two percent of the total population of 1,227" and through the 1630s and 1640s approximately 160 men and women were imported into the colony from West Africa (Bennett, 1993, pp. 35–36). Elizabeth City, where Mary lived and was convicted, was "one of the eight original shires into which the Virginia Colony was divided" (Mason, 1938, p. 269). By the time of Mary's sentencing in Lower Norfolk in 1649, the colony officials estimated that in all of the Virginia Colony there were only "about fifteen thousand English, and of Negroes brought thither, three hundred good servants" (Bennett, 1993, p. 36; Billings, 1975, p. 149). This racial imbalance, which continued late into the 1600s, when Africans comprised "less than eight percent of the Chesapeake population," was likely overwhelming to Mary as she tried to survive and defend herself in the disease-riddled, male-dominated wilderness (Morgan, 1993, p. 19).

The vast racial and gendered power imbalance within Mary's given circumstances resulted from the way Virginia developed over the first forty years of English presence into "a place where the ordinary restraints of civility could be abandoned" (Morgan, 1993, p. 26). This chaos occurred as several factors coincided, including the rise of English societal pariahs who attained a bit of redemption and power in America, the fact that white women were outnumbered by white men by six to one, and the reality that Africans and Native Americans "could be reduced to subhuman statuses, worked like animals, and denied the most elemental benefits of law" (Morgan, 1993, pp. 18 & 26). Therefore, Mary's given circumstances in the Virginia Colony were firmly in the extreme minority as both an African and as a woman.

The next important set of choices in developing a Living Historiography include establishing the character's obstacles, objective, and what is at stake in their scenario. In Mary's case, her obstacles were at every turn, including her language skills, her powerlessness, her conviction, and most importantly Cornelius Lloyds, the man to whom she "belongs." Lloyds was one of the most prominent figures in mid-to-late seventeenth century Virginia, having served as a Burgess from 1642 to 1653 and as a military officer for the King (Glover & Standard, 1902). As her obstacle, Lloyds also provides Mary's objective, which is a goal that the character pursues, usually throughout a plot. Mary's objective is to be an obedient servant because her freedom is at stake. This objective becomes complicated and her potential freedom is threatened as she defends her honor and innocence.

Mary is in the position to be free because, in the 1640s, slavery was not yet a common term or practice in the colonies. In fact, in the Virginia Colony the driving social force was survival, since malaria or other diseases killed most of the population and those who "survived to the age of twenty died before reaching forty" (Morgan, 1993, p.18). Since its inception, the men governing the colony sought a continual supply of man-power to keep the colony growing, even begging for "all offenders out of the common gaols condemned to die" (Morgan, 1993, pp. 17 & 31). Records indicate that "most of Virginia's population increase between 1634 and 1674 was the direct result of an influx of men and women who had willingly sold themselves into bondage" (Billings, 1975, p. 129). These immigrants were primarily unmarried men who entered into a contract in exchange for transportation. Once an indentured contract was purchased by a colonist, the servant was bound into full-time labor to four or more years with a promise of sustenance and their "freedom dues," a bushel of corn and a new suit of clothes, at the end of their contract (Morgan, 1993, pp. 18 & 37 & Billings, 1975, p. 129).

I decided that Mary is one of Cornelius Lloyds' indentured servants because this time-bound contractual relationship provided the strongest stakes for the character and was most common in America until the late 1600s when the lifetime bondage and the term "slave" begin to appear more regularly in legal and archival documents (Billings, 1975, p. 149, & Banks, 2008, p. 799 & Hendrick, 2007, pp. 686–687). This position also fit into Mr. Lloyds' given circumstances as one of the wealthiest men in the colony, with a personal estate "valued at 131,041 pounds of tobacco" who consistently transported people to the colony in exchange for land and labor from 1642 to 1648 (Bruce, 1896, p. 157). The precarious nature of Mary's position and her anticipated release give her a set of expectations that motivate her obedience to both Mr. Lloyds and the larger community in order to obtain her freedom. These stakes are crucial for the tension within the plot of the monologue.

The final aspects of Mary's given circumstances that helped shape her

Living Historiography were the values and resulting pressures applied by the larger community through religion and the burgeoning legal system. From its inception, the Virginia Colony's strongest organizing social force was the Church of England, under the guidance of the Bishop of London. When setting out the charter that incorporated the Virginia Company in 1606, King James anticipated his glory "in propagating the Christian religion to such people, as yet live in darkness and miserable ignorance if the true knowledge and worship of God" (Miller, 1964, p.101). Therefore, the church's contingent had many aims in the New World, including converting the Heathen, spreading the gospel, and advancing the cause of Protestantism (Sweet, 1950, pp. 39–41 & Wills, 2005, 9–11).

Over the first year in the colony, the "wholesome" chaplain Robert Hunt oversaw the construction of a "rude, barnlike" church and held regular prayer services as well as two sermons on Sundays and "every three months the sacrament" (Sweet, 1950, p. 39). The next decade was harsh and unforgiving, and reports from the colony complained of the lack of parish churches. (Miller, 1964, p. 103). However, in 1616 the zealous "Apostle to Virginia" Rev. Alexander Whitaker arrived and revitalized religion as the core value of the colony (Sweet, 1950, p. 44).

The years between 1619 and 1624 saw great focus on religion in Virginia, as the population increased by the thousands. The 1619 Assembly decreed that regular Sunday services were mandatory and "attendance was compulsory." The Burgesses also condemned "idleness, gaming, drunkenness" and "excess in apparel" (Miller, 1964, p. 105). However, the growing pains of distance, with some parishes "fifty to a hundred miles in length," and scattered population made ministering to the colony's faithful challenging (Sweet, 1950, pp. 51–56). In 1624, the King ended the Virginia Company's control of the colony, at least in part over "its failure properly to propagate the Christian religion," and installed a royal government until 1630 when Sir John Harvey arrived to govern the colony (Sweet, 1950, p. 52). At this juncture, the legal and religious systems within the colony begin to actively co-mingle.

In the mid–1630s, the Virginia Assembly established the setting for Mary's sentencing and punishment, Lower Norfolk County, "out of the eastern part of New Norfolk." Soon the Lower Norfolk Court and Parish were established as well. Walter Billings, in his thorough assessment of the Virginia's legal records in the 1600s, notes that "instances of capital crimes were fairly rare, so the courts' attention was taken up with prosecuting misdemeanors" (Billings, 1975, p. 80). One of the main points of focus for the courts were violations of the strict sexual and moral codes established for the colonists in England, which Sir Thomas Dale Knight, Marshall and

Deputie Governour, recorded in his "Articles, Lawes, and Orders, Divine, Politique, and Martiall for the Colony in Virginia" from June 22, 1611:

> Know ye that he or shee, that shall commit fornication, and evident proffe made thereof, for their first fault shall be whipt, for their second they shall be whipt, and for their third they shall be whipt three times a week for one month, and aske publique forgiveness in the Assembly of the Congregation [as cited in Ruether and Keller, 1983, p.246].

In England, ecclesiastical courts would prosecute violations of these orders and enact the required penitential punishment. However, in the absence of ecclesiastical courts in Virginia, local courts were empowered regulate private moral lapses with whipping and penance (Billings, 1975, p. 80). To ensure the regulation of these codes, parish ministers were ordered (under threat of losing their weekly stipend) to read the laws and ordinances to the congregation each Sabbath day when services were held (Billings, 1975, p. 80 & Ruether and Keller, 1983, p. 246).

Lower Norfolk Parish developed into two and then three "distinct church bodies" which sectioned off by 1640 into Elizabeth River, Lynnhaven, and Southern Shore Parishes (Mason, 1938, p. 270 & Rawlings, 1963, p. 153). However, across the colony from 1624 to 1640, in the absence of functional leadership by ministers sent from England, local church councils, led by vestrymen, gained more political power and began to appoint local ministers. Sweet argues that the vestry, who would enforce attendance at services, was usually a group of aristocrats who "thought of the church as a necessary institution, [but] were devoid of any religious feeling" (Sweet, 1950, p. 53). Cornelius Lloyds served as a vestryman of the Elizabeth River Parish, where records show that he and two other men agreed to pay "thirty-three pounds Sterling for the inhabitants of the Western Branch and Carney Point" (Stewart, 2017) Lloyds and the other vestrymen appointed John Wilson as the first Minister of Elizabeth River Parish. In 1640, the court appointed the Rev. Thomas Harrison as Minister of Elizabeth River Parish.

As was the practice across the colony, parishioners gathered at the Elizabeth River Chapel on selected Sundays throughout the year to hear their local minister preach, at which time the minister would "examine, catechise, and instruct the youth and ignorant of the parish based on the *Book of Common Prayer*, a collection of prayers for use in Anglican ceremonies" (Shifflett, 1998). Mary's punishment in 1649 sits in a very interesting religious moment, as it bridges the English Civil Wars and the establishment of the Commonwealth, which affected even the workings of the remote Virginia churches (Sweet, 1950, p. 54). During the Commonwealth, many practices in England and America would be abandoned or outlawed as

Presbyterian ecclesiology replaced the episcopate with *The Westminster Confession* and the *Directory of Public Worship* replacing *The Book of Common Prayer*, however, it is probable that in 1649 Mary's penitential prayer came from *The Book of Common Prayer*.

As Mary's circumstances became clear and the monologue developed, the question of how an African woman would learn to say the required penitential prayers became the focus of our rehearsal time. After being ripped from her home, Dutch or Portuguese was likely the first language Mary encountered. However, she would have had to learn some European language as a means of survival and this likely began with her conversion process. Conversion and the "gift" Africans would receive through their "introduction to Christianity" was one of the earliest justifications European traders had for tearing them from their culture (Hendrick, 2007, p. 688). Thousands of men and women like Mary became Christians by being baptized and renamed somewhere along their journey across the Atlantic or in the West Indies (Bennett, 1993, p. 37 & Morgan, 1993, p. 132). The magnitude of African cultural erasure during this period is clearly illustrated in the almost exclusively English or Spanish Christian names for Africans referenced in all English records of the period, such as Mary (Reuther & Keller, 1983, p. 235).

The final piece of background research that was required for Mary's Living Historiography centered on her punishment's requirement that she "do penance in front of the congregation in the Chapel at Elizabeth River." This sentence made it seem probable that Mary had attended, if not participated in, services in the parish. This was certainly possible, as the first colonists mixed more freely in society and many masters of slaves and bonded workers either brought or sent their chattel to religious services when they were offered (Morgan, 1993, p. 184). Also, obediently participating in the conversion process and religious life of the colony had the potential to increase an African's status in Virginia. In fact, in the early years of the colony, being baptized provided leverage for bonded African men when securing their freedom papers (Billings, 1975, p. 149). Armed with the evidence to support Mary's place in her world and the motivations for her actions, we then began to develop her experiences within the colony that led to her conviction and penance.

An Embodied Writing of History: The Performance

The process of writing Mary's monologue in *I Will Speak for Myself* took years and many iterations. At different times it has been one extended monologue, then a series of five vignettes, and then placed in the third person with a narrator. Each iteration helped us to learn something new about the character and led to more questions to be answered. An examination of portions of the text that were re-envisioned, cut, and revised, as well as other character explorations that impacted Mary's character as we developed the live performance, are offered below as examples of different ways a Living Historiography might develop.

Over the course of the first two vignettes, the audience slowly experiences Mary's transition from Twi speaker to English speaker as she encounters new English sounds during Church of England services and in her domestic life with the Lloyds. During Mary's time, the parishioners of Elizabeth River likely met in a very small wooden or brick church which the parish council began constructing at Seawell's Point before 1637. It had "remained unfinished and ruinous until 1638 and was not repaired and completed until 1640" (Mason, 1938, p. 271 & Morgan, 1993, p. 179). To give a sense of size, the neighboring parish of Linhaven erected a church fifty years later in 1692 that was only "forty five foot in length and twenty two foot in breadth Cleare between the walls … thirteen foot in heighth," so I imagined that the space around Mary in the Elizabeth River Chapel was filled with people in close quarters at the rare Sabbath day service (Mason, 1938, p. 274).

At first, the pain of losing her first language is exposed as Mary learns to restructure the way she produces sound and deciphers the meanings of the words in the prayer book. First, through a voiceover, the congregation intones the Penitential Psalm together as she struggles with the inscrutable prayer book. Mary follows along obediently with the congregation, as Mr. Lloyds is ostensibly also in attendance. However, she cannot read, so she scrutinizes the pages by holding it several ways before abandoning the pursuit. As she sits and listens to another voiceover, the Minister proclaims the opening of the Penitential Psalm 51 from the *Geneva Bible*.

The complexities of the allegiance of the Virginia Puritans and Protestant Ministers to the Anglican base of the Church of England allow for a wide range of possibilities as to which Bible might have been used in the Chapel in 1649. While the *King James Bible* of 1611 also includes Psalm 51, the *Geneva Bible* appealed for two reasons. First, the language in the *Geneva Bible* is more elevated and therefore more theatrical. Second, it includes a prelude about David and the Prophet Nathan which beautifully sets up the penitential rite that is about to take place.

Mary listens as the minister finishes the story of David and the Prophet Nathan saying, "He desireth God to forgive his sins, and to renew in him his Holy Spirit with promise that he will not be unmindful of those great graces," and the congregation joins together in recitation of the Psalm (Joyce, 2016). Group repetition of the prayer is likely one of the ways Mary might have learned both English and the rites of penitence. In this scene, though mostly silent, she tries to shape the sounds in her mouth as she catches bits of the phrases the congregation recites:

> Have mercy upon me, o God, according to thy loving kindness: according to the multitude of thy compassions put away mine iniquities. Wash me thoroughly from mine iniquity, and cleanse me from my sin [Joyce, 2016].

It is noteworthy that Mary's "monologue" begins without Mary speaking, which reveals the most challenging part of this Living Historiography: what dialect might effectively capture the rupture of a violent native displacement as Mary reconfigures the way her mouth forms the sounds of the English language? In many ways, her silences both allowed us to avoid that decision and underscored the vast silence that surrounded this woman in the chapel and at home with the Lloyds.

As part of the Elizabeth River vestry, Cornelius Lloyds was also responsible to supplement catechism in his own home. For Mary's monologue it seemed useful, although she does not appear in the records, that Mrs. Lloyds would fulfill the expected civilizing role in society and teach Mary the Church of England's catechism at home. In the late 1640s, the role of the colonial white woman was also transitioning from survival mode to helpmate, and it is most likely that one of the women in the Lloyds family would have taken on this task. Two centuries later, southern plantation mistresses would express "frustrations" about the challenges of teaching their slaves even the most rudimentary aspects of Christianity, such as "who made them, who Redeemed them … the Creed, the ten Commandments, and exhortations against lying and stealing," but there is little documentation of this process in early Virginia (Fountain, 2010, p. 54). The scene with Mrs. Lloyds illustrates the enculturation Mary experienced as she shed her African religion and language in order to assimilate into the Virginia Colony.

As she continues to learn Psalm 51, Mary sits in the Lloyds' home, which was likely a "Virginia House." During the period of 1619 to 1649, homes along the rivers of the Chesapeake region fell into two categories, isolated, ramshackle farm houses or the slightly more refined "Virginia House." Farm houses were usually a "dark, drafty, dirt-floored, insect-ridden" boxlike temporary structure that was built to be "abandoned as soon as the few acres or farmland it adjoined were exhausted by ruthless tobacco cultivation" (Morgan, 1993, pp. 186–188). In contrast, the English gentry built small one-story oak clapboard or brick country "Virginia

Houses" in the 1640s, "which measured in all only sixty feet by sixty" and had one or two ground floor rooms which centered around a hearth (Morgan, 1993, pp. 186–188). Records remain of household goods, equipment, and furniture from these upper-class homes, which illustrate that even this type of living was comparatively primitive (Morgan, 1993, p. 188). In this setting, the Lloyds have some rudimentary furniture, and Mary is seated by candlelight.

Aside from aurally reinforcing Psalm 51's text, which will become important in the climax of the monologue, in this vignette Mary slowly begins to find her voice and the audience is invited to view her struggle with the language, the content, and the obedience this task requires. In a voiceover, Mrs. Lloyds speaks to Mary as if she is a child throughout, pacing each word slowly and stretching the vowels so that Mary can mimic her mouth and sounds. Mary is only marginally successful but, as Mrs. Lloyds concludes, "According to thy loving kindness," Mary is able to fully form the last word and whispers, "*Kindness.*" Although the vignette was a helpful insight into Mary's language development and relationship with the mistress of the house, eventually the Mrs. Lloyds section was cut as part of a re-envisioning of the script.

Another section of script that was eventually cut, depicted the crime of "fornication" for which Mary stood trial. The word "fornication" in the legal record is a vague enough term (then and now) that could possibly indicate voluntary or active participation in the act, so it was important to demystify the actual event by making clear Mary did not consent. In this vignette, Mary encounters her rapist at night as she prepares to sleep in the Lloyds' barn. Mary sleeps on the floor, in keeping with the squatter culture of farm houses in Virginia Colony where people rested "slumped on the floor, or crouched on the boxes and chests that were the only ubiquitous items of furniture" (Morgan, 1993, p. 188). The barn setting, at some distance from the main home, isolated Mary and made her more vulnerable to William Watts' attack.

As the lights rise dimly on the stage, Mary clearly has become a more confident reader and speaker. This time she more fluently reads an abbreviated version of the Penitential Psalm and combines this with intonations in her native language as she prepares for bed. After snuffing the candle, she is terrified as she hears a drunken man enter, muttering parts of the same psalm in anticipation of the rape he is about to commit. As he approaches in shadow, Mary panics in her native language, eventually crying out in clear English, "NO!" as the lights blackout.

In one script iteration, Cornelius Lloyds (and not William Watts) became the aggressor would rape the defenseless Mary in her bed. Although

Lloyds never appeared onstage, we had a good deal of enthusiasm around this notion since, as part of a 1 percent minority in the colony, Mary was almost certainly not in a consensual relationship and many women who "belonged" to men were raped by them in the rural wilds of early Virginia. While this scene was evocative, ultimately it was confusing to audiences without another actor and there is no proof that Cornelius Lloyds was anything other than a successful businessman and community leader.

After several audiences, I cut the vignettes with Mrs. Lloyds and the rape and replaced this action with a narrator figure who shares Mary's backstory throughout *I Will Speak for Myself*. Mary's silence as she absorbed all that was new around her proved more powerful than watching her develop a pidgin form of English. The narrator tells the audience:

> This story begins even before my time, way back in 1649. With Mary, one of my sisters who cannot yet speak for herself. Mary, whose name was not Mary when she lived in Africa, was ripped from her home and carried across the sea, to the wilderness of the British colony of Virginia. Dutch ships first made this passage only thirty years before.
>
> Mary arrived long before generations of slaves were born in America, learning only to speak English. Mary had no family, no friends, no community. Her language and traditions were all she carried with her into the desolate tobacco fields. You and I can only imagine what Mary was thinking, for surely no one cared to record her thoughts or impressions of her new home.
>
> During her time of service, this warrior-daughter, once of strong mind and spirit, became Mary who is silent. Mary who obediently holds the Bible as she attends services with Mr. Lloyds, the vestryman of the parish at Elizabeth River. Mary who diligently shapes the new sounds in her mouth, even as she craves her freedom lying in wait ahead of her [Joyce, 2016].

Replacing Mary's dialogue with a narrator figure facilitates the audience's direct connection to Mary's given circumstances and stakes without forcing Mary, a character who cannot yet speak, to tell her own story.

In the final vignette of Mary's monologue, which has remained the same in each iteration of the production, the Lower Norfolk County Court finds Mary and William Watts guilty. It is important to note that there is no proof that William Watts was a white man but, since the court records tend to indicate race when the accused is of African descent, as it did with Mary, it is likely that this case drew attention for its interracial nature. In terms of labor, laws, and class structure, race was generally not acknowledged as a determining factor in the early colonial period mainly because, as Morgan points out, "it was difficult to treat people more brutally" than the already cruel conditions permitted (Morgan, 1993, p. 132). There is, in fact, little documentation regarding the treatment of Africans in the Virginia Colony between 1619 and 1634, when the Lower Norfolk County Court was established and began recording legal decisions that provide illustrations of everyday life and the problems colonists encountered. In examining the court records after 1634, scholars assert that, for the first fifty years or more, both races intermingled socially (Billings, 1975, p. 149 & Banks, 2008, p. 799 & Hendrick, 2007, pp. 686–687). The easy intermingling of races supports the circumstances in which Mary might encounter William Watts, her co-defendant.

With class as a great equalizer in the colony, Africans and English servants regularly "ignored strictures against what white lawmakers labeled 'shameful' and 'unnatural' acts" and coupled with others "of their own condition regardless of color" (Morgan, 1993, p. 133). Again, "coupling" is a term that indicates free will, but female servants, like Mary, were particularly susceptible to abuse as they had the least power in the new world. Billings reports that women of both races were frequently "subjected to sexual assaults and made pregnant by their masters or other free men" (Billings, 1975, p. 131). One major concern for the courts, as well as the ministers, was the offspring of these illicit unions, as a portion of the children born out of wedlock in the colony were increasingly recorded and labeled as "mulatto" (Morgan, 1993, p. 133). These children held a troublesome status in the colonial class and cultural structure and created a unique pressure on the courts, since a child who was born to an English person who was a Christian could not also be enslaved (Billings, 1975, p. 152). With rapid population growth, the intermixing of races became one of the leading concerns for the English colonists that led to laws based on race.

As interracial fornication gained legal attention in the 1640s, the courts swiftly revealed an imbalance of power in terms of punishment. Several cases between 1640 and 1681 illustrate some of the range of these punishments according to gender and status within the rapidly shifting cultural climate. Henning (1832, p. 552) reports that in 1640, in a case similar to Mary's, the court condemned a white man named Sweet for impregnating a black woman servant, but produced a sentence in which the pregnant woman "was whipped, and he was sentenced to public penance." (as cited in Ruether and Keller, 1983, p. 236). Later in the 1640s, a magistrate "sentenced two white indentured servants to an additional year of service for running away, and a black indentured servant to labor for the remainder of his life for precisely the same offense" (Bennett, 1993, p. 45). And in 1681, the court records show that a wealthy white woman, Mary Williamson, "hath Committed the filthy sin of fornication with William a negro belonging to William Basnett Squire." Rather than publicly shaming or whipping her, the court punished her financially, ordering "that shee bee fined five hundred pounds to tobacco and Caske for the use of Linhaven parish" (Billings, 1975, p. 161). Cases harshly punishing interracial fornication were harbingers of the seeds of racial discord which would eventually blossom into laws regarding slavery.

In 1649, however, when Mary stood accused, the Lower Norfolk Court could only sentence public penance for such a crime. The narrator concludes before Mary takes the stage:

> The only trace that remains to attest to Mary's fuller life is the record documenting her punishment by the Lower Norfolk Court for Committing the "Filth Sin of Fornication" with a white man, William Watts. However, you and I know that Mary was certainly not committing fornication willingly with this man. She had no power, she could not say No. Because she was property. Mary's voice could not be heard in the public courts. She could not speak as I do here with you today. She *never* had the freedom to speak that I have gained. We cannot know what Mary would have said if she had the power to speak her thoughts. But I believe that this warrior-daughter would have been raging inside at the relentless injustices heaped upon her [Joyce, 2016].

And, thus, Cornelius Lloyds' Negro woman Mary finds herself facing the condemning gaze of the very white congregation in the Chapel at Elizabeth River, forced to speak. At this point in the development of the character and monologue, the juxtaposition of Mary's many voices fascinated me. What should her English sound like, with its mixed background of Twi, Portuguese, and British dialects? And what should her silenced, internal voice sound like—fully divested of her oppression and fully engulfed in rage?

In the final vignette, we worked to explore the dichotomy of the many external and internal forces amalgamating within Mary as she stands in the chapel and finally recites the Penitential Psalm she has been taught throughout the monologue. In a cool, narrow shaft of light, Mary appears draped in the traditional penitential white cloth with a white rod in her hand. She begins, "Have mercy upon me, o God, according to thy loving kindness: according to the multitude of thy compassions put away mine iniquities. Wash me thoroughly from mine iniquity, and cleanse me from my sin (Joyce, 2016)."

With the detailed research and supporting evidence and theories, how Mary found the words to the Penitential Psalm in her mouth will still never be known. She was likely taught a simplified catechism and observed formal services that looked nothing like the modes of worship that wove religion into all aspects of life in West Africa (Fountain, 2010, p. 90 & Morgan, 1993, p. 184). Mary's worldview had developed deeply invested in the supernatural "forces that controlled the universe" (Bennett, 1993, p. 42). And, despite her conversion to Christianity, Mary retained the roots of her own culture, which celebrated communal experiences through song, dance, and "mystical events like religious trances and spirit possession" (Fountain, 2010, pp. 68–69 & 90–91). In her only speech, Mary's repressed cultural traditions blast forth as she finally voices her internal thoughts.

Midway through her penance, the lights shift radically to a full stage flooded with red and the African drums thump beneath her words, as Mary careens from a rejection of enforced Christianity to accusations against her rapist. She experiences a spiritual possession as her emotions grow beyond her control. Then, in an instant, she is in the cool light again, rejoining the world of the chapel and the chaste and hollow psalm proclaiming into the void, "Purge me with hyssop, and I shall be clean: wash me, and I shall be whiter than snow." The contrast in the preceding moments make it clear to the audience that Mary's monologue is not screamed at the congregation, but is in fact her internal monologue. Her hollow transitional line, "Wash me, and I shall be whiter than snow," underscores all of the sharp and painful irony of Mary's situation as an African woman wrapped in white, asking for forgiveness from a god she doesn't believe in for a crime she didn't commit.

As the drums and red light glow once again, Mary breaks free of the psalm, shouting directly at her master as she hurtles toward the climax of the monologue:

> Master Cornelius, you made me forsake my gods and baptized me in the Church of England.
> Your wife taught me this psalm of penitence.
> You know William Watts is *not* my lover.
> Our "filth sin" was *not* of my desire.
> You know he comes into the barn at night and forces me to comply.
> With a knife at my throat so I could not make a sound.
> I could tear at this sheet, mangle it as you stare so solemnly praying for my sins.
> But when will this end? When will I have my freedom clothes?
> When will I be free? Will I be free? [Joyce, 2016].

In this moment the freedom Mary craves is truly at stake and this reminder forces her to regain her composure. She realizes that abandoning obedience will place her into more trouble with the court, and she could lose everything.

Mary is not the only penitent to feel this violent rage. Occasionally, there are fascinating shreds of evidence in the records to illustrate the results of these punishments on the unrepentant. In 1641, a woman named Elizabeth was accused in court of behaving "like a most obstinate and graceless person," since she had attempted to "cut and mangle the sheet wherein she did penance" in the chapel. The Lower Norfolk Court decided that, as a further punishment, she "shall receive at present, 20 lashes on the bare back and, on the Sunday come fort night, do penance" (Billings, 1975, p. 102). The threat of this punishment is enough to subdue Mary and, purged of her rage and obedient once again, Mary finishes the psalm through her tears:

> Make me to hear joy and gladness that the bones, which thou hast broken, may rejoice.
> Hide thy face from my sins, and put away all mine iniquities.
> Create in me a clean heart, o God, renew a right spirit within me.
> Restore to me the joy of thy salvation, and establish me with thy free Spirit.
> Then shall I teach thy ways unto the wicked, and sinners shall be converted unto thee.
> Deliver me from blood, o God, which art the God of my salvation, and my tongue shall sing joyfully of thy righteousness.
> Open thou my lips, o Lord, and my mouth shall show forth thy praise.
> The sacrifices of God are a contrite spirit: a contrite and a broken heart, o God, thou wilt not despise [Joyce, 2016].

Mary stands alone, bereft and defeated, as the audience is left to imagine what becomes of Mary and whether she gains her freedom from Mr. Lloyds. This final moment is somewhat crucial to the effectiveness of the Living Historiography, as it allows the audiences' mind to remain engaged and curious and (hopefully) working to fill in the blank spots in history.

Conclusion

A blank spot in history is certainly the inspiration for this project. What began as a set of disparate and wide-ranging historical questions, through a blending of research and performance eventually developed into the vibrant and distinctive character Mary. As Kimberly Fairbanks performs the role, modern audiences are invited to come to a deeper, more nuanced understanding the life of a long-silenced woman as they engage with the cultural, religious, legal, sexual, and gender constructs of early America.

In tracing the research of Mary's given circumstances and the process of exploring her relationships and experiences, this chapter aims to provide a methodology for future Living Historiographies. For, even with scraps of history or whispers of existence, we have the ability to breathe life into the absence and silence of women in American history in order to understand how they shaped America in foundational ways from the very beginning and to appreciate how much we still have in common.

References

Banks, T. (2008). Dangerous woman: Elizabeth Key's freedom suit: Subjecthood and racialized identity in seventeenth century colonial Virginia. *Akron Law Review*, 41(3), 799–837.

Bennett, L., Jr. (1993). *Before the Mayflower: A History of black America* (6th rev. ed). New York: Penguin Books.

Billings, W. (1975). *The old dominion in the seventeenth century: A documentary history of Virginia, 1606-1689* (Documentary problems in early American history). Chapel Hill: Published for the Institute of Early American History and Culture at Williamsburg, Va., by the University of North Carolina Press.

Bruce, P. (1896). *Economic history of Virginia in the seventeenth century: An inquiry into the material condition of the people, based on original and contemporaneous records.* New York: Macmillan and Co. Citing *Records of Lower Norfolk County*, original vol. 1651–1656, Lloyd, f. p. 168. Retrieved from https://babel.hathitrust.org/cgi/pt?id=umn.31951002399351k;view=1up;seq=11.

Fountain, D. (2010). *Slavery, civil war, and salvation: African American slaves and Christianity, 1830–1870* (Conflicting worlds). Baton Rouge: Louisiana State University Press.

Glover, W., & Standard, M. (1902) *The colonial Virginia register: A list of governors, councillors and other higher officials, and also of members of the House of Burgesses, and the revolutionary conventions of the Colony of Virginia.* Albany: Joel Munsell's Sons, Publishers. Retrieved from https://www.newrivernotes.com/topical_books_1902_virginia_colonialvirginiaregister.htm.

Hendrick, V. (2007). Codifying humanity: The legal line between slave and servant. *Texas Wesleyan Law Review* 13(-2), 685–698.

Henning, W. (1819). *The statutes at large: Being a collection of all the laws of Virginia, from the first session of the legislature, in the year 1619: Published pursuant to an act of the general assembly of Virginia, passed on the fifth day of February one thousand eight hundred and eight* (Llmc-digital (series)). New York: Barton.

Joyce, V. (2016). *I will speak for myself.* Unpublished playscript.

Mason, G. (1938). The colonial churches of Lynnhaven Parish, Princess Anne County, Virginia. *The William and Mary Quarterly, 18*(3), 269–269. doi:10.2307/1923433.

Miller, P. (1964). *Errand into the wilderness* (Harper Torchbooks, tb 1139). New York: Harper & Row.

Minute Book A and Patents 2, State of Va., f 113. RootWeb. First generation: Edward Dorsey. Retrieved from http://freepages.rootsweb.com/~ddorsey/genealogy/dorsey1/d612.htm.

Morgan, P. (1993). *Diversity and unity in early North America* (Rewriting histories). London: Routledge.

Rawlings, J. (1963). *Virginia's colonial churches: An architectural guide; together with their surviving books, silver & furnishings.* Richmond: Garrett & Massie.

Ruether, R., & Keller, R. (1983). *Women and religion in America. Volume 2 the colonial and revolutionary periods: A documentary history.* San Francisco, California: Harper & Row.

Shifflett, C. (1998). Laws and documents relating to religion in early Virginia, 1606–1660. *Virtual Jamestown.* Retrieved from http://www.virtualjamestown.org/rlaws.html.

Stewart, W. (2017). History of Norfolk County Virginia and representative citizens. Retrieved from http://nyvagenealogy.homestead.com/VAPARISHRECORDS.html.

Sweet, W. (1950). *The story of religion in America* (Revised and enlarged ed.). New York: Harper & Brothers.

Webb, L. (1983). Black Women and Religion in the Colonial Period, Lillian Ashcraft Webb. In Ruether, R., & Keller, R. *Women and religion in America. Volume 2 the colonial and revolutionary periods: A documentary history* (pp. 235–235). San Francisco, California: Harper & Row.

Wills, D. (2005). *Christianity in the United States: A historical survey and interpretation.* Notre Dame, IN: University of Notre Dame Press.

What Life? Experiences of Enslaved Africans in Virginia

COLITA NICHOLS FAIRFAX

Introduction

There is evidence that Africans were in the South and North Americas for hundreds of years as explorers, navigators, and active players with Spanish and Portuguese expeditions (Guasco, 2014; Sertima, 1976), prior to the English North America context. Year 1619's significance is that it ushers in perpetual racial enslavement that became foundational to the economic and constitutional development of America. Year 1619 is not celebrated as an "arrival" of Africans, but as a commemoration of those Africans from Angola who were traded as commodities, purchased as cattle, forced to labor without any human, religious or citizenship rights for the remainder of their lives. Although the actual voices of those Africans who were aboard ships *White Lion* and *Treasurer* in 1619 do not exist, the voices of those who experienced the violent horror and inhumanity of enslavement in Virginia are available through the Federal Writers' Project (FWP). The FWP was created in 1935 as a part of the Works Progress Administration (WPA), to provide employment to historians, teachers, librarians, and other white-collar workers, who were mostly white (Hill, 1998, 2). One of the products of the FWP were to gather narratives from formerly enslaved persons who were living primarily in southern states. This "folk" history of enslaved persons, also referred to as the WPA Slave Narrative Collection, is used to show how what I theorize as social justice historiography, provides a different context to think differently about socially applicative history. Social justice historiography is the application of historical data to locate themes of justice and the lived experience. Social justice historiography attends to locating contemporary themes of the lives of dispossessed populations in histories. It challenges dominant ideas of justice and its place in the lives of people. It connects historical data to current challenges that people face, with solutions to improve thinking, sensibility, understanding. Given that enslavement provided an economic, political and social system in America, it is imperative that contemporary discussions about the human condition foreshadows with an understanding of the perniciousness of enslavement:

> The slave system in America was unique in human history. Sometimes slaves were treated cruelly; at other times with kindness. They were more often used as a sign of affluence, a way of displaying one's wealth and of enjoying luxury, rather than as the means for the systematic accumulation of wealth. Previously, slavery had existed in hierarchical societies in which the slave was at the bottom of a social ladder, the most inferior in a society of unequals. While each society normally preferred to choose its slaves from alien people, it did not limit its selection exclusively to the members of any one race. Slave inferiority did not lead necessarily to racial inferiority. In contrast to this, slavery in America was set apart by three characteristics: capitalism, individualism, and racism [Coombs, 2013, 30].

These narratives provide the reader with raw guttural lived experiences that African people endured. They are rich narratives that should be included in every academic field in higher education. "The WPA ex-slave narratives, with all their flaws, indeed hold much evidence related to life under slavery in the antebellum South ... and explores family history, labor history, and a general history of southern race relations from the early nineteenth century well into the twentieth" (Shaw, 2003, 655). By using the exact words of formerly enslaved Africans, we uncover the monstrosity of their experiences and absence of quality of life in perpetual bondage under daily terroristic environs. The utterances of people of African-descent included in this chapter keep their voices alive, maintain the focus on them and the descendant-community, and offer curative measures to their descendants. This evidence also showcases the incomprehensible reality that human beings were forced to live in for centuries. "Sociological neglect of the topic is surprising, since instances of profound institutional change, such as emancipation, offer an unusual opportunity for students of stratification to examine the persistence of structured inequality across institutional regimes" (Ruef & Hughes, 2003, 446). Which makes little sense, because the unmitigated violence of enslavement was a founding institution of America, that persisted for hundreds of years, as "slavery has left an indelible mark on the Black psyche and consciousness" (West, 2016, 650). The narratives provided here are just a glimpse into the brutal aspects of the lived experiences that marked people faceless, nondescript, animalistic. The existence of the lived experience as an enslaved person cannot be fully captured in these pages, yet the purpose of including the voices of the enslaved is to sensitize the reader about enslavement. Including the narratives of women

What Life? Experiences of Enslaved Africans in Virginia (Fairfax) 139

is important, because of the valuable role of female storytelling in African culture—"reaching back to the storytelling traditions of West Africa, specifically those that help define the Yoruba culture, we can see the importance of the oral tradition and that of the female role in sustaining it" (Stover, 2003, 151).

The first excerpted interview is of Mr. Fountain Hughes (1848–1957), who was enslaved in Virginia. The spelling and grammar reflect the original interview:

> **FOUNTAIN HUGHES:** My name is Fountain Hughes. I was born in Charlottesville, Virginia. My grandfather belonged to Thomas Jefferson. My grandfather was a hundred and fifteen years old when he died. And now I am one hundred and one year old.
>
> **HERMOND NORWOOD:** Who did you work for Uncle Fountain when…?
>
> **FOUNTAIN HUGHES:** Well, I belonged to Burness [unclear], when I was a slave. My mother belonged to Burness. But … we … was all slave children and … soon after … when we found out that we was free, why then, we was … bound out to different people…[names unclear] and all such people as that. And we would run away, and wouldn't stay with them. Why then, we'd just go and stay anywhere we could. Lay out at night anywhere. We had no home, you know. We was just turned out like a lot of cattle. You know how they turn cattle out in a pasture? Well, after freedom, you know, colored people didn't have nothing. Colored people didn't have no beds when they was slaves. We always slept on the floor, pallet here, and a pallet there just like … a lot of … wild people … we didn't … we didn't know nothing. [The slave owners] didn't allow you to look at no book. And then there was some free-born colored people … why, they had a little education, but there was very few of them where we was. And they all had … what you call…. I might call it now … jail sentence…[it] was just the same as we was in jail. Now, I couldn't go from here across the street, or I couldn't go through nobody's house without I have a note or something from my master. And if I had that pass … that was what we called a pass … if I had that pass, I could go wherever he sent me. And I'd have to be back … you know … when whoever he sent me to, they … they'd give me another pass and I'd bring that back so as to show how long I'd been gone. We couldn't go out and stay a hour or two hours or something like that. They send you [back]. Now, say for instance, I'd go out here to [unclear] place…. I'd have to walk. And I would have to be back … maybe in a hour. Maybe they'd give me an hour…. I don't know just how long they'd give me. But, they'd give me a note so there wouldn't nobody interfere with me, and [it would] tell who I belonged to. And when I come back, why, I carry it to my master and give that to him … that'd be all right. But I couldn't just walk away like the people does now, you know. It was what they call … we were slaves. We belonged to people. They'd sell us like they sell horses and cows and hogs and all like that. Have an auction bench, and they'd put you on … up on the bench and bid on you just same as you bidding on cattle, you know.
>
> **HERMOND NORWOOD:** Was that in Charlotte that you were a slave?
>
> **FOUNTAIN HUGHES:** Hmmm?
>
> **HERMOND NORWOOD:** Was that in Charlotte or Charlottesville?
>
> **FOUNTAIN HUGHES:** That was in Charlottesville.

HERMOND NORWOOD: Charlottesville, Virginia.

FOUNTAIN HUGHES: Selling women, selling men ... all that. Then if they had any bad ones, they'd sell them to the nigga traders, what they called the nigga traders. And they'd ship them down south, and sell them down south. But, otherwise if you was a good ... good person they wouldn't sell you. But if you was bad and mean and they didn't want to beat you and knock you around, they'd sell you ... to the, what was called the nigga trader. They'd have a regular ... have a sale every month, you know, at the courthouse. And then they'd sell you, and get two hundred dollar ... hundred dollar ... five hundred dollar.

FOUNTAIN HUGHES: See, I wasn't old enough during the war to sell, during the Army. And, my father got killed in the Army, you know. So it left us small children just to live on whatever people choose to ... give us. I was bound out [as bonded laborers] for a dollar a month. And my mother used to collect the money. Children wasn't ... couldn't spend money when I come along. In fact when I come along, young men ... young men couldn't spend no money until they was twenty-one years old. And then you was twenty-one, why, then you could spend your money. But if you wasn't twenty-one, you couldn't spend no money. I couldn't take.... I couldn't spend ten cents if somebody give it to me. Because they'd say, "Well, he might have stole it." We all come along,...you might say we had to give an account of what you done. You couldn't just do things and walk off and say, "I didn't do it." You'd have to ... give an account of it. Now ... after we got freed and they turned us out like cattle ... we could ... we didn't have nowhere to go. And we didn't have nobody to boss us and we didn't know nothing. There wasn't no schools. And when they started a little school, why, the people that were slaves, there couldn't many of them go to school except they had a father and a mother. And my father was dead, and my mother was living, but she had three, four other little children, and she had to put them all to work for to help take care of the others. So we had ... we had it what you call, worse than dogs has got it now. Dogs has got it now better than we had it when we come along. I know.... I remember one night, I was out after I was free, and I didn't have nowhere to go. I didn't have nowhere to sleep. I didn't know what to do. My brother and I was together. So we knew a man that had a ... a livery stable. And we crept in that yard, and got into one of the hacks of the automobile and slept in that hack all night long. So next morning, we could get out and go where we belonged. But we was afraid to go at night because we didn't know where to go, and didn't know what time to go. But we had got away from there, and we afraid to go back, so we crept in, slept in that thing all night until the next morning, and we got back where we belong before the people got up. Soon as day commenced ... come [day]break ... we got out and commenced to go where we belonged. But we never done that but the one time. After that we always, if there was a way, we'd try to get back before night come. But then that was on a Sunday too, that we done that. Now, when we were slaves we couldn't do that, see. And after we got free we didn't know nothing to do. And my mother, she, then she hunted places, and bound us out for a dollar a month, and we'd stay there maybe a couple of years. And she'd come over and collect the money every month. And a dollar was worth more then than ten dollars is now. And I...and the men used to work for ten dollars a month, hundred and twenty dollars a year. Used to hire that way. And ... now you can't get a man for fifty dollars a month. You paying a man now fifty dollars a month, he don't want to work for it.

What Life? Experiences of Enslaved Africans in Virginia (Fairfax)   141

> **HERMOND NORWOOD:** More like fifty dollars a week nowadays.
> **FOUNTAIN HUGHES:** That's just it exactly! He wants fifty dollars a week and they ain't got no more now than we had then!. And we [had] no more money, but course they bought more stuff and more property and all like that. We didn't have no property. We didn't have no home. We had nowhere or nothing. We didn't have nothing, only just … like cattle, we were just turned out. And [you'd] get along the best you could. Nobody to look after us. Well, we been slaves all our lives. My mother was a slave, my sister was a slaves, father was a slave. And … my father belong to … Burness and Burness died during the wartime because … he was afraid he'd have to go to war. But, then … and in them days you could hire a substitute to take your place. Well, he couldn't get a substitute to take his place so he run away from home. And he took cold. And when he come back, the war was over but he died. I don't know, to tell you the truth when I think of it today, I don't know how I'm living. None, none of the rest of them that I know of is living. I'm the oldest one that I know that's living. But, still, I'm thankful to the Lord. Now, if … if my master wanted to send me, he'd never say … you couldn't get a horse and ride … you walk, you know, you walk. And you be barefoot and cold. That didn't make no difference. You wasn't no more than a dog to some of them in them days. You wasn't treated as good as they treat dogs now. But still, I didn't like to talk about it. Because it makes, makes people feel bad you know. I could say a whole lot…. I don't like to say. And I won't say a whole lot more. I remember when the Yankees come along and took all the good horses and took all throwed all the meat and flour and sugar and stuff out in the river and let it go down the river. And they knowed the people wouldn't have nothing to live on but they done that. And that's the reason why I don't like to talk about it. Them people … and if you was cooking anything to eat in there for yourself and if they … they was hungry, they would go and eat it all up, and we didn't get nothing. They'd just come in and drink up all your milk … just do as they please. Sometimes they'd be passing by all night long, walking, muddy, raining. Oh, they had a terrible time! Colored people that's free ought to be awful thankful. And some of them is sorry they are free now. Some of them now would rather be slaves.
> **HERMOND NORWOOD:** Which had you rather be, Uncle Fountain?
> **FOUNTAIN HUGHES:** Me? Which I'd rather be? You know what I'd rather do? If I thought … had any idea that I'd ever be a slave again, I'd take a gun and just end it all right away! Because you're nothing but a dog. You're not a thing but a dog! Night never come without you had nothing to do. Time to cut tobacco … if they want you to cut all night long out in the field you cut. And if they want you to hang all night long, you hang … hang tobacco. It didn't matter about your tired … being tired. You're afraid to say you're tired. They just … well….[voice trails off] [Federal Writers' Project: Slave Narrative Project, 1949].

Mr. Hughes' explanation of his lived experience as an enslaved person illustrated the sheer horror of the human experience. The existence of an "owned" person by another, perversion of working/laboring conditions, bestial treatment, perpetual lawlessness, and the absence of an economic and civic protocol afforded to an entire race of people once the Emancipation Proclamation was issued in 1863. Black people might have been emancipated but were not free. Coombs explains that because "slavery has always been an evil institution, and being a slave has always been undesirable" (2013, 32). The undesirable tenant of one's status, of one's life was always tied to his/her race. Racial status that underscores one's quality of life continues into the twenty-first century.

> The slave in America was systematically exploited for the accumulation of wealth. Being a slave in a democracy, he was put outside of the bounds of society. Finally, because his slavery was racially defined, his plight was incurable. Although he might flee from slavery, he could not escape his race [Coombs, 2013, 32].

The experience of enslavement is felt by generations who did not experience this institution, in areas of labor, wages and salary, absence of wealth, access to local services, food insecurity. "The narratives not only indicate what these elders had to eat, how they obtained it, and how often they got it, but they also provide insight on physical living conditions" (Shaw, 2003, 655). Mr. Hughes lived until 1957. There were formerly enslaved people who lived well within the twentieth century, with families and communities inheriting these memories and scars.

Our next interview is of Mrs. Fannie Berry (1842–1940), who lived to be about 98 years old. Mrs. Fannie Berry was interviewed on February 26, 1937, in Petersburg, Virginia, by Susie Byrd. The spelling and grammar reflect the original interview. Ms. Byrd's questions were not included in this transcription, only Mrs. Berry's responses. Mrs. Berry's interviewed is thematically recorded:

INVENTION
My Master tole us dat de niggers started the railroad, an' dat a nigger lookin' at a boilin' coffee pot on a stove one day got the idea dat he could cause it to run by putting wheels on it. Dis nigger being a blacksmith put his thoughts into action by makin' wheels an' put coffee on it, an' by some kinder means he made it run an' the idea wuz stole from him an' dey built de steamengine.

RELATIONSHIP
I wuz one slave dat de poor white man had his match. See Miss Sue? Dese here ol' white men said, "what I can't do by fair means I'll do by foul." One tried to throw me, but he couldn't. We tusseled an' knocked over chairs an' when I got a grin I scratched his face all to pieces; an dar wuz no more bothering Fannie from him; but oh, honey, some slaves would be beat up so, when dey resisted, an' sometimes if you'll 'belled de overseer would kill yo.' Us Colored women had to go through a plenty, I tell you.

MARRIAGE
Elder Williams married me in Miss Delia Mann's (white) parlor on de crater road. The house still stands. The house wuz full of Colored people. Miss Sue Jones an' Miss Molley Clark (white), waited on me. Dey took de lamps an' we walked up to de preacher. One waiter joined my han' an' one my husband's han.' After marriage de white folks give me a 'ception; an,' honey, talkin' 'bout a table—hit was stretched clean 'cross

de dinin' room. We had everythin' to eat you could call for. No, didn't have no common eats. We could sing in dar, an' dance ol' squar' dance all us choosed, ha! ha! ha! Lord! Lord! I can see dem gals now on dat flo'; jes skippin' an' a trottin.' An' honey, dar wuz no white folks to set down an' eat 'fo you.

WAR

Now, Miss Sue, take up. I jes' like to talk to you, honey, 'bout dem days ob slavery; 'cause you look like you wan'ta hear all 'bout 'em. All 'bout de ol' rebels: an' dem niggers who left wid de Yankees an' were sat free, but, poor things, dey had no place to go after dey got freed. Baby, all us wuz helpless an' ain't had nothin.'

I wuz free a long time 'fo' I knew it. My Mistress still hired me out, 'til one day in talkin' to do woman she hired me to, she, "God bless her soul," she told me, "Fannie yo' are free, an' I don't have to pay your Master for you now." You stay with me. She didn't give me no money, but let me stay there an' work for vitals an' clothes 'cause I ain't had no where to go. Jesus, Jesus, God help us! Um, um, um! You Chillun don't know. I didn't say nothin' when she wuz tellin' me, but done 'sided to leave her an' go back to the white folks dat fus own me.

I plan' to 'tend a big dance. Let me see, I think it wuz on a Thursday night. Some how it tooken got out, you know how gals will talk an' it got to ol' Bil Duffeys ears (ol' dog) an,' baby do you know, mind you 'twont slavery time, but de 'oman got so mad cause I runned away from her dat she got a whole passel of 'em out looking for me; Dar wuz a boy, who heard 'em talkin' an' sayin' dey wuz goin' to kill me if I were found. I will never forget dis boy com' up to me while I wuz dancin' wid another man an' sed, "nobody knowes where you ar,' Miss Moore, dey is lookin' fer you, an' is gwine kill you, so yo' come on wid me." Have mercy, have mercy my Lord, honey, you kin jes 'magin' my feelin' fer a minute. I couldn't move. You know de gals an' boys all got 'round me an' told me to go wid Squreball, dat he would show me de way to my old Mistress house. Out we took, an' we ran one straight mile up de road, den through de woods, den we had to go through a straw field. Dat field seem' like three miles.

After den, we met another skit of woods. Miss Sue, baby my eyes, (ha! ha! ha!) wuz bucked an' too if it is setch a thin' as being so scared yo' hair stand on yo' head, I know, mine did. An' dat wasn't all, dat boy an' me puffed an' sweated like bulls. Was feared to stop, cause we might have been tracked. At last we neared de house an' I started throwin' rocks on de porch. Child I look an' heard dat white 'oman when she hit dat floor, bouncin' out dat bed she mus' felt dat I wuz comin' back to her. She called all de men an' had 'em throw a rope to me an' day drawed me up a piece to de window, den I held my arms up an' day dey snatched me in. Honey, Squreball fled to de woods. I ain't never heard nothin' 'bout him. An' do you know, I didn't leave day 'oman's house no more for fifteen years?

SONG

Lord! Lord! honey, Squreball an' I use to sing dis song.
'Twas 1861, the Yankees made de Rebels run
We'll all go stone blin'
When de Johny's come a marchin' home.
Child an' here's another one we use to sing. "Member de war done bin when we could sing dese songs." Listen now:
Ain't no more blowin' of dat fo' day horn
I will sing, brethern, I will sing.
A col' frosty mornin' de nigger's mighty good

Take your ax upon your shoulder.
Nigger talk to de woods,
Ain't no mor' blowin' of dat fo' day horn.
I will sing brethern, I will sing.

SONG
Kimo, Kimo, dar you are
Heh, ho rump to pume did'dle.
Set back pinkey wink,
Come Tom Nippecat
Sing song Kitty cat, can't
You carry me o'er?
Up de darkies head so bold
Sing song, Kitty, can't you
Carry me O'er?
Sing Song, Kitty, can't yo'
Carry me home?

I wuz at Pamplin an' de Yankees an' Rebels were fightin' an' dey were wavin' the bloody flag an' a confederate soldier wuz upon a post an' they were shootin' terribly. Guns were firin' everywhere. All a sudden dey struck up Yankee Doodle Song. A soldier came along and called to me, "How far is it to the Rebels," an I honey, wuz feared to tell him; So, I said, "I don't know," He called me again. Scared to death I was. I recollect gittin' behind the house an' pointed in the direction. You see, ef de Rebels knew dat I told the soldier, they would have killed me. These were the Union men goin' after Lee's army which had don' bin 'fore dem to Appomattox. The Colored regiment came up behind an' when they saw the Colored regiment they put up the white flag. (Yo' 'member 'fo' dis red or bloody flag was up). Now, do you know why dey raised dat white flag? Well, honey, dat white flag wuz a token dat Lee, had surrendered. Glory! Glory! yes, child the Negroes are free, an' when they knew dat dey were free dey, Oh! Baby! began to sing:

Mamy don't yo' cook no mo',
Yo' ar' free, yo' ar' free.
Rooster don't yo' crow no, mo,'
Yo' ar' free, yo' ar' free.
Ol' hen, don't yo' lay no mo' eggs,
Yo' free, yo' free.
Sech rejoicing an' shoutin', you never he'rd in you' life.

Yes, I can recollect de blowin' up of the Crater. We had fled, but I do know 'bout the shellin' of Petersburg. We left Petersburg when de shellin' commenced an' went to Pamplin in box cars, gettin' out of de way. Dem were scared times too, cause you looked to be kilt any minute by stray bullets. Just before the shellin' of Petersburg, dey were sellin' niggers for little nothin' hardly. Junius Broadie, a white man bought some niggers, but dey didn't stay slave long, cause de Yankees came an' set 'em free.

As evidenced with Mr. Hughes, Mrs. Berry's interview illustrated that Black people had little to no recourse to rebuild their lives after Emancipation, "they were doomed to remain a subservient mass of peasants, [as] prewar slave plantation was replaced by sharecropping, tenant farming, and the convict lease system" (Coombs, 2013, 74). Moreover, the complexity of

What Life? Experiences of Enslaved Africans in Virginia (Fairfax)

working under unnatural duress, marriage rights, lack of rights and privileges render a political and economic dynamic that are not studied in school curriculums, benchmark tests and Standards of Learning tests. Students are not exposed to this data for, "these challenges also point to a lack of complexity found in African American historical narratives and an overall focus placed on truncated, non-controversial histories and one-dimensional heroic figures that limit students' knowledge about power and racial inequities" (Brown & Brown, 2010, 142). Such narratives are often posited as relics of the past, with little synthesis into their carryovers institutionally and ideologically. Although it has been posited that these narratives are only for an examination of enslavement and post-enslavement eras "they remain primarily a source for studying the nineteenth century" (Shaw, 2003, 657), there is evidence in these utterances that the lived experiences of formerly enslaved people also provide pause and pain for their twentieth century experiences, and the twenty-first experiences of their progeny.

The next interview features Private Richard Slaughter, who was in the Army. He was born in Hopewell, Virginia, January 9, 1849 (though his death certificate lists his birth year as 1847), and died in Elizabeth City County (Hampton), Virginia on August 20, 1938. Ancestry.com reports that he is buried in the Hampton National Cemetery. Private Slaughter is interviewed by Claude W. Anderson at his home. Although the questions are not recorded, the utterances are verbatim here.

* * *

Come in, son. Have a seat, who are you and how are you? My life? Oh! certainly you don't want to hear that! Well, son, have you been born again? Do you know Christ? Well, that's good. Good for you. Amen. I'm glad to hear it. Always glad to talk to any true Christian liver. God bless you, son. I was born January 9, 1849, on the James at a place called Epps Island, City Point. I was born a slave. How old am I! Well, there's the date. Count it up for yourself. My owner's name was Dr. Richard B. Epps. I stayed there until I was around thirteen or fourteen years old when I came to Hampton. I don't know much about the meanness of slavery. There was so many degrees in slavery, and I belonged to a very nice man. He never sold but one man, fur's I can remember, and that was cousin Ben. Sold him South. Yes. My master was a nice old man. He ain't living now. Dr. Epps died and his son wrote me my age. I got it upstairs in a letter now. It happened this a-way. Hampton was already burnt when I came here. I came to Hampton in June 1862. The Yankees burned Hampton and the fleet went up the James River. My father and mother and cousins went aboard the Meritana with me. You see, my father and three or four men left in the darkness first and got aboard. The gun boats would fire on the towns and plantations and run the white folks off. After that they would carry all the colored folks back down here to Old Point and put 'em behind the Union lines. I know the names of all the gunboats that came up the river. Yessir. There was the Galena, we called her the old cheese box, the Delware, the Yankee, the Mosker, and the Meritana which was the ship I was board of. That same year the Merrimac and

Monitor fought off Newport News Point. No, I didn't see it. I didn't come down all the way on the gunboat. I had the measles on the Meritanza and was put off at Harrison's landing. When McCellan [McClellan] retreated from Richmond through the Peninsula to Washington, I came to Hampton as a government water boy. While I was aboard the gunboat, she captured a rebel gunboat at a place called Drury's Bluff. When I first came to Hampton, there were only barracks where the Institute is; when I returned General Armstrong had done rite smart.

I left Hampton still working as a water boy and went to Quire Creek, Bell Plains, Va., a place near Harper's Ferry. I left the creek aboard a steamer, the General Hooker, and went to Alexandria, Va. Abraham Lincoln came aboard the steamer and we carried him to Mt. Vernon, George Washington's old home. What did he look like? Why, he looked more like an old preacher than anything I know. Heh! Heh! Heh! Have you ever seen any pictures of him? Well, if you seen a picture of him, you seen him. He's just like the picture.

You say you think I speak very good English. Heh! Heh! Heh! Well, son I ought to. I been everywhere. No I never went to what you would call school except to school as a soldier. I went to Baltimore in 1864 and enlisted. I was about 17 years old then. My officers' names were Capt. Joe Reed, Lieutenant Stimson, and Colonel Joseph E. Perkins. I was assigned to the Nineteenth Regiment of Maryland Company B. While I was in training, they fought at Petersburg. I went to the regiment in '64 and stayed in until '67. I was a cook. They taken Richmond the fifth day of April 1865. On that day I walked up the road in Richmond. When we left Richmond, my brigade was ordered to Brownsville, Texas. We went there by way of Old Point Comfort, where we went aboard a transport. When we got to Brownsville, I was detailed to a hospital staff. We arrived in Brownsville in January 1867. The only thing that happened in Brownsville while I was there was the hanging of three Mexicans for the murder of an aide. In September we left Brownsville and came back to Baltimore. Before we left I was sent up the Rio Grande to Ringo Barracks as boss cook. I then returned to Hampton and lived as an oysterman and fisherman for over forty years. I have never been wounded. My clothes have been cut off me by bullets but the Lord kept them off my back, I guess.

I tell you what I did once. My cousin and I went down to the shore once. The river shore, you know, up where I was born. While we were walking along catching tadpoles, mimows, and anything we could catch, I happened to see a big moccasin snake hanging in a sumac bush just a swinging his head back and forth. I swung at 'im with a stick and he swelled his head all up big and rared back. Then I hit 'im and knocked him on the ground flat. His belly was very big so we kept hittin' 'im on it until he opened his mouth and a catfish as long as my arm (forearm), jumped out jest a flopping. Well the catfish had a big belly too, so we beat 'em on his belly until he opened his mouth and out came one of these women's snapper pocketbooks. You know the kind that closes by a snap at the top. Well the pocket book was swelling all out, so we opened it, and guess what was in it? Two big copper pennies. I gave my cousin one and I took one. Now you mayn't believe that, but it's true. I been trying to make people believe that for near fifty years. You can put it in the book or not, jest as you please, but it's true. That fish swallowed some woman's pocketbook and that snake just swallowed him. I have told men that for years and they wouldn't believe me.

While I was away my father died in Hampton. He waited on an officer. My mother lived in Hampton and saw me married in 1874. I bought a lot on Union Street for a hundred dollars cash. I reared a nephew, gave him the lot and the house I built on it an he threw it away. When I moved around here, I paid cash for this house.

Did slaves ever run away! Lord yes. All the time. Where I was born there is a lots of water. Why there used to be as high as ten and twelve Dutch three masters in the harbor at a time. I used to catch little snakes and other things like terrapins and sell 'em to the sailor for to eat roaches on the ships. In those days a good captain would hide a slave way up in the top sail and carry him out of Virginia to New York and Boston.

I never went in the Spanish American War. Too old, but I had some cousins that enlisted. That was during McKinley's time He went down the Texas and some of them other ships they gave Puerto Rico Hail Columbia. They blew up the Maine with a mine. She was blowed up inward. The Maine left Hampton Roads going towards Savannah. When they looked at what was left of her all the steel was bent inward which shows that she was blowed up from the outside in. Understand. During the World War I was sent to Washington and haven't been anyplace since. I'm a little hard of hearing and have high blood pressure. So I have to sit most the time. Got an invitation in there now wantin' me to come to a grand reunion of Yankees and the Rebels this year but I can't go. Getting too old. Well goodbye, son. Glad to have you come again sometime.

Although Private Slaughter exclaims that people ran from enslavement all of the time, he doesn't explain the specific reasons why to the interviewer. He also includes how the waterways were used as escape routes. Enslavement was a controlled police-state institution, which restricted and controlled the movement of African people held by bondage (Newby-Alexander, 2017). Not only were escapes planned daily, water was a route utilized to be near the water to literally be near freedom. It should be noted that Slaughter served admirably in the military during the Civil War. His post-military work as an oysterman and fisherman was how he made his living in Hampton for the remainder of his days, which allowed him to purchase a home for he and his wife. He lived until he was 89 years old.

Our last featured transcribed interview is with Mrs. Elizabeth Sparks, born circa 1842. At age 95, she was interviewed at the Matthews Court House in Matthews, Virginia on January 13, 1937, by Claude Anderson. According to her interview, she was born in York County, Virginia. Mrs. Sparks indicates more than once in the interview that she is not going to reveal everything about her lived experiences. One may interpret this as fear, yet another interpretation is that the agony and torment of her life as an enslaved person is far too throbbing to even speak of it. The utterances are verbatim here:

> Come in boys. Sure am glad ter see ya. You're lookin' so well. That's whut I say. Fight boys/ Hold em. You're doin' all right. Me, I am so mean nothin' can hurt Me. What's that? You want me to tell yer 'bout slavery days? Well I kin tell yer, but I ain't. S'all past now so I say let 'er rest fs too awful to tell anyway, yer're too young to know all that talk anyway. Well I'll tell yer some to put in yer book, but I ain'ta goin' tell yer the worse. My mistress's name was Miss Jgnrie Brown. Nof I guess I'd better not tell yer. Done forgot about dat. Oh well. I'll tell yer. somethin I guess. She died 'bout four years ago. Bless

her. She was a good woman. Course I mean she'd slap an' beat yer once in a while but she warn't no woman fur fighting fussin' an' beat in yer all day. Ask some I know. She was too young when da war ended fur that. Course no while folks perfect. Her parents a little rough. Abut dat? Kin I tell yer about her parents? Lord yes. I wasn't born then but my parents told me. But I ain't a goin' tell yer nuffin. No I ain't. Tain't no sense fur yer ta know 'bout all those mean white folks. Dey all daid now. They meany good I reckon. Leastways most of 'em got salvation on their death beds. Well I'll tell yer some, but I ain'ta goin' tell yer much more. No sir. Shep Miller was my master. His ol' father, he was a tough one. Lord! I've seen 'Im kill em. He'd git the meanest overseers to put over 'em. Why I member time after he was dead when I'd peep in the closet and jes see his old clothes hangin there an' jes' fly. Yessir, I'd run from them clothes an' I was jes' a little girl then. He wus that way with them black folks. Is he in heaven? No, he ain't in heaven! Went past heaven. He was quick an' was he tough. Sometimes he beat 'em until they couldn't work. Give 'em more work than they could do. They'd git beatin' if they didn't get work done.

Bought my mother, a little girl, when he was married. She wus a real Christian an' he respected her a little. Didn't beat her so much. Course he beat her once in a while. Shep Miller was terrible. There was no end to the beatin' I saw it wif my own eyes. Beat women? Why sure he beat women. Beat women jes' lak men. Beat women naked an' wash 'em down in brine. Some times they beat 'em so bad, they jes' couldn't stand it an' they run away to the woods. If yer git in the woods, they couldn't git yer. Yer could hide an' people slip yer somepin' to eat. Then he call yer every day. After while he tell one of colored foreman tell yer come on back. He ain'ta goin' beat yer anymore. They had colored foreman but they always have a white overseer. Foreman git yer to come back an' then he beat yer to death again.

They worked six days fum sun to sun. If they forcin' wheat or other crops, they start to work long fo day. Usual work day began when the horn blew an' stop when the horn blow. They git off jes' long 'nuf to eat at noon. Didn't have much to eat. They git some suet an' slice a bread fo breakfas, well, they give the colored people an allowance every week. Fo' dinner they'd eat ash cake baked on blade of a hoe.

I lived at Seaford then and was roun' fifteen or sixteen when my mistress married. Shep Miller lived at Springdale. I 'member jes' as well when they gave me to Jennie. We wus all in a room helpin' her dress. She was soon to be married, an' she turns 'roun an' sez to us, which of yer niggers think I'm gonna git when I git married? We all say, I doan know. An' she looks right at me an' point her finger at me like this an' sayed yer. I was so glad. I had to make 'er believe I wus cryin,' but I was glad to go with yer. She didn't beat. She wus jes' a young thing. Course she take a whack at me sometime, but that weren't nuffin.' Her mother was a mean ol' thin.' She'd beat yer with a broom or a leather strap or anythin' she'd git her hands on.

She uster make my aunt Caroline knit all day an' when she git so tired aftah dark that she'd git sleepy, she'd make 'er stan' up an knit. She work her so hard that she'd go to sleep standin' up an' every time her haid nod an' her knees sag, the lady'd come down across her held with a switch. That wus Miss Jennie's mother. She'd give the cook jes' so much meal to make bread fum an' effen she burnt it, she'd be scared to death cause they'd whup her. I 'member plenty of times the cook ask say, "Marsa please 'scuse dis bread, hits a little too brown." Yessir! Beat the devil out 'er if she burn dat bread.

I went wiff Miss Jennie an' worked at house. I didn't have to cook. I got permission to git married. Yer always had to git permission. White folks 'ud give yer away. Yer jump

What Life? Experiences of Enslaved Africans in Virginia (Fairfax) 149

cross a broom stick tergather an' yer wus married. My husband lived on another plantation. I slep in my mistress's room but I ain't slep' in any bed. Nosir. I slep' on a carpet, an' ole rug, befo' the fiaplace. I had to git permission to go to church, everybody did. We could set in the gallery at the white folks service in the mornin' an' in the evenin' the folk held baptise service in the gallery wif white present.

   Shep went to war but not for long. We didn't see none of it, but the slaves knew what the war wuz 'bout. After the war they tried to fool the slaves 'bout freedom an' wanted to keep 'em on a workin' but the Yankees told 'em they wus free. They sent some of the slaves to South Carolina. When the Yankees came near to keep the Yankees from gittin' 'em, sent cousin James to South Carolina. I nevah will forgit when the Yankees came through. They wuz takin' all the livestock an' all the men slaves back to Norfolk, wid 'em to break up the system. White folk head wus jes' goin' to keep on havin' slaves. The slaves wanted freedom, but they's scared to tell the white folks so. Anyway the Yankees wus givin' everythin' to the slaves. I kin heah 'am tellln' ole Missy now. Yes! give'er clothes. Let'er take anythin' she wants. They even took some of Miss Jennie's things an' offered 'em to me. I didn't take 'em tho' cause she'd been purty nice to me. Whut tickled me wus my husban', John Sparks. He didn't want to leave me an go cause he didn't know what they's takin' 'em nor what they's gonna do, but he wanted to be free; so he played lame to keep fum goin'. He was jes' a limpin' 'round. It was all I could do to keep fum laffin'. I kin hear Miss Jennie now yellin' at them Yankees. No who are yer to judge. I'll be the judge. If John Sparks wants to stay here, he'll stay. They was gonna take 'im anyhow an' he went inside to pack an' the baby started cryin'. So one of 'em said that as long as he had a wife an' a baby, that young they guess he could stay. They took all the horses, cows, and pigs and chickens an' anything they could use an left. I was about nineteen when I married. I wuz married in 1861, my oldest boy was born in 1862 an' the fallin' of Richmond came in 1865. Before Miss Jennie was married she was born an' lived at her old home right up the river heah. Yer kin see the place fum ou side heah. On the plantation my mother wuz a house woman. She had to wash white folks clothes all day an' huh's after dark. Sometimes she'd be washin' clothes way up 'round midnight. Nosir, couldn't wash any Nigguh's clothes in daytime. My mother lived in a big one room log house wif an' upstairs. Sometimes the white folks give yer 'bout ten cents to spend. A woman with children 'ud git 'bout half bushel of meal a week; a childless woman 'ud git 'bout a peck an' a half of meal a week. If yer wus workin', they'd give yer shoes. Children went barefooted, the yeah round. The men on the road got one cotton shirt an' jacket. I had five sisters an' five brothers. Might as well quit lookin' an me. I ain't gonna tell yer any more. Cain't tell yer all I know. Ole Shep might come back an' git me.

   Why if I was to tell yer the really bad things, some of dem daid white folks would come right up outen dere graves. Well, I'll tell somemore, but I cain't tell all. Once in a while they was free nigguhs come fum somewhah. They could come see yer if yer was their folks. Nigguhs used to go way off in quarters an' slip an' have meeting. They called it stealin' the meetin.' The children used to teach me to read. Schools? Son, there warn't no schools for niggers. Slaves went to bed when they didn't have anything to do. Most time they went to bed when they could. Sometimes the men had to shuck corn till eleven and twelve o'clock at night. If you went out at night, the paddyrols wud catch yer if yer was out aftah time without a pass. Mos' a the slaves was afeared to go out. Plenty of slaves ran away. If they ketch 'em they beat 'em near to death. But yer know dey' good an' bad people everywhere. That's the way the white folks wuz. Some had hearts; some had gizzards 'stead o' hearts.

When my mothers's master died, he called my mother an' brother Major an' got religion an' talked so purty. He say he so sorry that he hedn't found the Lord before an' had nuttin' gainst his colored people. He was sorry an' scared, but confessed. My mother died twenty years since then at the age of seventy-fo'. She wuz very religious an' all wite folks set store to 'er.

Old Massa done so much wrongness I couldn't tell yer all of it. Slave girl Betty Lilly always had good clothes an' all the priviliges. She wuz a favorite of his'n. But cain't tell all! God's got all!" We uster sing a song when he was shlppin' the slaves to sell 'em 'bout "Massa's Gwyne Sell Us Termerrer." No, I cain't sing it for yer. My husban' lived on the plantation nex' to my mistress. He lived with a bachelor master. He tell us say once when he was a pickinnany oi' tearse Williams shot at 'im. He didn't shoot 'em| he jes' shoot in the air an' ol' man wuz so sceered he ran home an' got in his mammy's bed. Massa Williams uster play wif 'em; then dey got so bad that they'ud run an' grab 'is laige so's he couldn't hardly walk so when he sees 'em he Jes' shoots in de air. Ol' Massa, he. jes' come on up ter the cabin an' say "mammy whah dat boy?"* She say. in dah undah the bed. Yer done scared 'im to deaf! Ol' Massa go on in an' say, Boy. Wthat's the mattah wid yer. Boy say. yer shot me master yer shot me! Master say, Aw Gwan!—Git up an' come along. I ain't shot yer. I jes' shot an' scared yer. Heh.' Heh' Heh.' Yeseir my ol' husban' sayed he sure was scared that day.

Now yer take dat an' go. Put that in the book. Yer kin make out wif dat. I ain't a gonna tell yer no more. Nosir. The end a time is at hand anyway. Tain't no use ter write a book. The Bible say when it git so's yer cain't tell one season from t'other the worl's comin' to end; here hit is so warm in winter that it feels like summer. Goodbye. Keep lookin' good an' com again.

As horrific of the experiences that Mrs. Sparks shares in her interview, she indicates on more than one occasion that she has not revealed the worst of her life as an enslaved person. She reported how abusive her experiences were from both White men and women who were in charge of her. She reported the killings, whippings, slappings, torments, and malnourishments, and the daily negotiations of not having any authority over one's own body, or one's children, suggesting that the owners of enslaved people had gizzards and not hearts, is akin to the earlier reported experiences of interviews featured in this article. She recalled the heightened level of fear that she and other enslaved people endured, and she mentioned the paddy rollers, persons who predate police officers, which provides us with a "multilayered story about intergenerational relations" (Shaw, 2003, 657) with law enforcement. Not residing with your husband because they are "owned" by someone else was another aspect of the enslaved person's experience. Mrs. Spark's use of the word "nigger" is replete in her discussion, showing how employed that word was and is in American lexicon. Studying the narratives of formerly enslaved people gives entry into "exploring, among other topics, family history, labor history, and the general history of southern race relations from the early 19th century well into the 20th [century]" (Shaw, 2003, 655).

Mrs. Sparks' account corroborated the other accounts of abusive labor conditions. Forced to work all day and night long and beaten if one fell to fatigue is an incomprehensible experience that was an experience of enslaved people. The revelation of intolerable labor conditions holds evidence for labor conditions of African American working-class people. Stripped of their own agency over all natural and economic experiences, there was no negotiating such a life except through escape. The power of these narratives is that Mrs. Sparks not only recounts her experiences, but provides an interpretation of the meaning of living as an enslaved person. Not only are we reading about the horror of enslavement, but we are also reading about the horror in re-telling the experience. Spark's articulation has been termed as an African American mother tongue: "back talk, biblical allusion/allegory, concealment, deception, dissembling, guile, hesitations, humor, impertinence, impudence, innuendo, insolence, invective, irony, ironic humor, laughter, lying, masking, misdirection, mumbling, physical antics, rage, sarcasm, sass, satire, secrecy, shifts in point of view, signals, silence, song, understatement, whispering ... tools misled, confused, tricked, or made a fool of the oppressor" (Stover, 2003, 140). Revisiting these narratives provides a continuation of cultural memory, which sustains the connections from one generation to another.

These narratives expands the landscape of literature to examine the human experience of landing in the Colonial Virginia. The significance of the landing of Africans at Point Comfort and the births of Africans into enslavement compounds the human trajectory of generations of families in America. By applying a social justice historiography, we can draw contemporary perspectives by not only reading the narratives to younger generations, we then add the narratives of those successive generations to show the tapestry of the African American experience in a healing and transformative ritual. Attending to generational collateral afflictions connects generations, makes history personal, expands how suffering is defined, and addresses systemic power relationships that African Americans experience. These ancestral narratives are applied as a method to cultural solvency—identifying the assets of cultural survival in order to survive culturally. This is a recovery process so important in human healing and transformation. These narratives reveal a significant era that changed the entire worldview of all people, with African people carrying the ultimate burden of the disruption of culture, memory, psychology, scientific and technological advancement through generations and generations of trauma. Yet, these narratives are personal stories ripe with the voices of ancestors that were able to articular their humanity, and it is left up to those of who are the products of such a vile institution to internalize their stories for our own curative process.

References

Born in Slavery: Slave Narratives from the Federal Writer's Project, 1936–1938. (1936) Richard Slaughter Interview by Claude W. Anderson, Retrieved from Library of Congress, https://www.encyclopediavirginia.org/_Autobiography_of_Richard_Slaughter_1936.

Brown, K.D., & Brown, A.L. (2010). Silenced memories: An examination of the sociocultural knowledge on race and racial violence in official school curriculum. *Equity & Excellence in Education, 43*(2), 139–154.

Coombs, N. (2013). *The Black Experience in America*. NY: Simon & Schuster.

Federal Writers' Project: Slave Narrative Project, Vol. 17, (1936). Virginia, Berry-Wilson. [Manuscript/Mixed Material] Retrieved from the Library of Congress, https://www.loc.gov/item/mesn170/.

Guasco, M. (2014). *Slaves and Englishmen: Human Bondage in the Early Modern Atlantic World*. University of Pennsylvania Press.

Hill, L.M. (1998). Ex-Slave Narratives: The WPA Federal Writer's Project Reappraised. *Oral History, 26*(1), 64–72, Retrieved from http://www.jstor.org/stable/40179473.

Newby-Alexander, C.L. (2017). *Virginia Waterways and the Underground Railroad*. South Carolina: History Press.

Ruef, M., & Fletcher, B. (2003). Legacies of American slavery: Status attainment among southern blacks after emancipation. *Social Forces, 82*(2), 445–480.

Shaw, S.J. (2003). Using the WPA ex-slave narratives to study the impact of the great depression. *The Journal of Southern History*, 69, 3, 623–658.

Stover, J.M. (2003). Nineteenth-century African-American women's autobiography as social discourse: The example of Harriet Ann Jacobs. *College English, 66*(2), 133–154.

Van Sertima, I. (1976). *They Came Before Columbus*. New York: Random House.

Voices from the Days of Slavery: Stories, Songs and Memories—Fountain Hughes (transcript). (1949). Retrieved from the Library of Congress, https://www.loc.gov/podcasts/slavenarratives/transcripts/slavery_hughes.pdf.

West, C.M. (2016). Living in a Web of Trauma. Edt by Carlos Cuevas & Callie Marie Rennison. *The Wiley Handbook on the Psychology of Violence*, Malden, MA.

Posttraumatic Slave Syndrome, the Patriarchal Nuclear Family Structure and African American Male-Female Relationships

NOELLE M. ST. VIL, CHRISTOPHER ST. VIL
and COLITA NICHOLS FAIRFAX

Introduction

One of the less discussed and determined features of family life for Africans who entered into the English North American context in 1619 is marriage. Although data about Anthony and Isabel (Isabella) Tucker as a married couple in present-day Hampton exists, particular details about their lives, details around the birth of their son William in 1624/1625, or their deaths are absent from public records. What an important narrative to highlight because marriage has been an enduring custom throughout the African continent. Throughout the development of what would become America, marriages among enslaved and free Black people were under incredible threats of separation and independence. Therefore, analyzing current conditions of African American marriage, which informs family and community patterns, is an analysis that provides insight into how Black people manage family life. Marriage is on the decline in the United States (Cohn, Passel, Wang, & Livingston, 2011) and disproportionately so among African Americans (Bent-Goodley, 2014; Fairfax, 2014). African Americans have lower rates of marriage and marital stability, higher rates of divorce, and higher rates of single parent–headed households than other racial groups (National Healthy Marriage Resource Center, n.d.). Despite these facts, currently one third of African American adults are married (Cohn et al., 2011) and many African Americans desire marriage (Bent-Goodley,

2014). Marriage acts as a protective factor for African Americans by lifting them out of poverty, providing better educational opportunities for children, reducing the risk of living in high-crime neighborhoods, and positioning them to be pillars of support within their extended families and communities (Bent-Goodley, 2014; Blackman, Clayton, Glenn, Malone-Colon, & Roberts, 2005).

Although African American male–female relationships have a legacy of exhibiting resiliency and strength (Hill, 2003; McAdoo, 2007; Staples, 1999), forced adaptations to structural racism in the United States may have resulted in some attitudes and behaviors that undermine the development of healthy relationships between African American men and women (DeGruy, 2005; Edin & Kefalas, 2005). The discrepancy between the desire to achieve the patriarchal nuclear family structure (PNFS) in the United States and experiences of structural racism is at the crux of understanding adverse relationship outcomes among African American men and women (Franklin, 2000).

The PNFS is a two-tiered system of society that promotes men as the head of their family and treats women as subservient (Edgell & Docka, 2007). In a PNFS, men are decision makers, providers, breadwinners, and protectors (Gerstel, 2011). Women are confined to domestic roles such as cooking, cleaning, and child-rearing (Gerstel, 2011). In the United States, the PNFS is considered to be an ideal (Gerstel, 2011). Historically, any deviations from the PNFS was considered pathological (Moynihan, 1965; Staples, 1999). However, the very essence of the trauma of slavery and continued oppression undermines the ability of many African Americans to obtain the PNFS, resulting in disharmony between African American men and women (Dixon, 2009).

The trauma-informed perspective recognizes the prevalence and impact of trauma in the lives of people (Harris & Fallot, 2001; Levenson, 2017). When people experience trauma, they adapt to survive. The adaption to trauma and the various ways trauma manifests itself is normal. However, the adapted attitudes and behaviors may be unhealthy to successful functioning in daily life (Harris & Fallot, 2001; Levenson, 2017). Aligning with the trauma-informed perspective, this article uses posttraumatic slave syndrome (PTSS) (DeGruy, 2005), a form of historical trauma, as a lens to highlight how striving for the PNFS may be counterproductive to the well-being of many African American male-female relationships.

PTSS is a concept developed by Dr. Joy DeGruy (2005) to illustrate the adverse effects of institutionalized racism in the lives of African Americans. Without understanding how institutionalized racism has created a mismatch between the PNFS and the ability of many African Americans to obtain this American ideal, social work solutions to African American male–female relationships will be well intentioned, but ineffective. Thus, this article uses PTSS to illustrate the adverse attitudes and behaviors that may arise between African American men and women, particularly those experiencing unemployment and incarceration, while trying to obtain the PNFS. In addition, we will discuss the implications for reconciling this mismatch through social work interventions.

Throughout their history in the United States, African Americans have been subjected to traumatic policies and practices that make it challenging to obtain the PNFS (Franklin, 1997; Tucker & Mitchell-Kernan, 1995; W.J. Wilson, 1987, 1996). The difficulty is evident in three periods experienced by African Americans in the United States (Gaskin, Headen, & White-Means, 2005): the slavery generation (1619–1865), legalized segregation and discrimination generation (1865–1965), and the race-neutral generation (1965–present).

The Slavery Generation

For 246 years, 63 percent of African American tenure in the United States, African Americans were treated as the property of whites (Gaskin et al., 2005). Although African Americans married during slavery, their marriages were not legally recognized because slaves were considered property under the law (Franke, 1999). In fact, black male and female relationships were undermined, violated, and traumatized. Male and female slaves needed permission from slave masters to marry (Goring, 2006). Slave masters used marriage as a means to promote sexual reproduction among slaves, leading to an increase in the number of slaves under their control (Goring, 2006; White, 1999). Since the beginning of African American presence in the United States, the African American family was incongruent with the patriarchal nuclear family (Franklin, 2000). A slave master was the head of an African American family. Male slaves were unable to fulfill patriarchal nuclear family roles as husbands, providers, protectors, and fathers (Black, 1997; Staples, 1977). Female slaves worked outside of the home and were forced to be independent, as they could not depend on their husbands for safety and well-being (Franklin, 2000; Kolchin, 1993; White, 1999). Male and female slaves were relegated to the role of physical laborers and their roles were equal, complementary, and necessary for survival (White, 1999). They equally contributed economic resources to the family and had equal influence in the aspects of their day-to-day lives that were within their control (White, 1999). The slave family lived under looming threat that they, their partners, or their children could be beaten, raped, killed, or sold at any time.

Legalized Segregation and Discrimination

For 100 years post slavery, 26 percent of African American tenure in the United States, African Americans experienced legalized segregation and discrimination in the forms of convict leasing and peonage (Gaskin et al., 2005). During this time, there was an increase in African American marriages as it was now recognized by law (Goring, 2006). However, policies were created to ensure that this increase in marriage among African Americans did not result in the attainment of the patriarchal nuclear family (Franke, 1999; Franklin, 1997). To maintain the free labor lost under slavery, the Black Codes were created to restrict the freedom of African Americans and make it easy to arrest them for minor legal infractions. The Black Codes were instituted in many states (Blackmon, 2008). The practice of convict leasing signals the beginning of the prison industrial complex and the disproportionate incarceration of masses of African American men (Fierce, 1994), leaving many African American families without husbands and fathers to be the heads of households.

Peonage or sharecropping, a type of debt slavery where laborers work the land in exchange for a share of the crop, was common among many freed male slaves (Franklin, 2000). During this time many African American men tried to create the patriarchal nuclear family by attempting to domesticate their wives, but they were unsuccessful because the labor of African American women was needed for the economy to prosper (Giddings, 2007). Planters, wanting more production surplus, negotiated a Faustian bargain with the Freedmen's Bureau, which encouraged African American women to go back to work. The bureau designated husbands as heads of households in which they were responsible for labor contracts, and wives were paid less money than their husbands (Franklin, 1997). The bargain increased family disputes and spousal abuse in African American homes (Franklin, 1997). Women had difficulty accepting their husbands' new authority when under slavery they were equal to their husbands and worked together side-by-side (Franklin, 2000). The egalitarianism experienced by African American men and women under slavery is what sustained African American marriages (Giddings, 2007). The Faustian bargain ushered patriarchy into the African American family sphere and resulted in a decrease in African American women's desire to marry and so a decline in marriage among African Americans (Bent-Goodley, 2014).

The Race-Neutral Generation

The last 48 years, 11 percent of African American tenure in the United States, may be called the race-neutral period, which is a reference to the rhetoric about a post-racial America in the context of pervasive structural racism that continues today (Gaskin et al., 2005). Two of the most pressing issues for African American marriages and relationships are the unemployment rate of black men and the rate of mass incarceration. The unemployment rates of African Americans are nearly twice as high as the unemployment rates for white Americans (8.4 versus 4.3; Bureau of Labor Statistics, 2017) with African American men experiencing higher unemployment rates than African American women (7.8 versus 6.4; Bureau of Labor Statistics, 2018). These figures suggest that it is significantly difficult for many African American men to achieve the breadwinner role, which is central to the PNFS. Compounded with the unemployment rate is the incarceration rate of African American men, who account for only 6 percent of the general population but represent nearly 50 percent of the prison population (Perry & Bright, 2012). Mass incarceration of African American men leads to husbandless and fatherless households and makes it difficult for those formerly incarcerated to find employment, which in turn diminishes their chances for upward mobility and reduces the likelihood of fulfilling the breadwinner role (Pew Charitable Trusts, 2010). The inability of many African American men to realize the breadwinner role has resulted in adaptations to an oppressive structure, which has resulted in significant levels of stress between African American men and women (Franklin, 1997, 2000). This adaptation and stress are described using PTSS as a lens.

PTSS

PTSS is a conceptual framework, developed by Dr. Joy DeGruy (2005), that seeks to explain the connection between centuries of oppression experienced by African Americans and the prevalence of contemporary beliefs and behaviors that they hold. According to DeGruy (2005),

> Post Traumatic Slave Syndrome is a condition that exists when a population has experienced multigenerational trauma resulting from centuries of slavery and continues to experience oppression and institutionalized racism today. Added to this condition is a belief (real or imagined) that the benefits of the society in which they live are not accessible to them [p. 121]

As a result of living in an oppressive society, DeGruy (2005) suggested, predictable patterns of behavior tend to occur that are counterproductive to the well-being of African Americans. The key patterns of behaviors reflective of PTSS are vacant esteem, ever-present anger, and racist socialization (DeGruy, 2005). *Vacant esteem* refers to the state of believing that one has little or no worth and is typically derived from society's declaration of inferiority and belief in white supremacy. The ever-present anger is the response of African Americans being marginalized in mainstream society. African Americans express through anger their frustration of experiencing barriers to upward mobility and their fear of being unable to do so. *Racist socialization* refers to the adoption of white norms and values by African Americans.

Behaviors Reflective of PTSS in African American Relationships

PTSS, as it pertains to African American male–female relationships, refers to the adaptations to oppression that prevent many African Americans from attaining the PNFS and leads to coping mechanisms that make it difficult to sustain healthy male–female relationships. The three coping mechanisms and their relevance to African American male–female relationship are presented in the following sections (also see Table 1).

Adaptive Behavior 1: Vacant Esteem

African American men who face socioeconomic disadvantage may find it difficult to achieve the breadwinner role due to blocked economic opportunities and may feel the need to compensate by subscribing to other portions of traditional masculinity such as an overemphasis on physicality (Mosher & Tompkins, 1988; Oliver, 2006; Seaton, 2007). In these relationships, physical domination is expressed through sexual conquest (Oliver, 2006). Under strained economic conditions, and in an effort to increase self-esteem, masculinity may move from the acquisition of socioeconomic goods to the belief that the more women one sleeps with, the more masculine he becomes (Hill Collins, 2004). Because some black men are unable to financially provide for their families, they may feel inadequate and undeserving of marriage (Dixon, 2009) and may endorse an alternative form of masculinity that was created for them under slavery, when their worth was defined by physical ability and sexual prowess (Akbar, 1996; A.N. Wilson, 1992).

As a result, some African American women who have relationships with African American men espousing this masculinity may adapt. Although many African American women desire monogamous relationships with African American men (Banks, 2011; McLellan-Lemal et al., 2013), some feel that this is unattainable (McLellan-Lemal et al., 2013; W.J. Wilson, 1996). Some African American women figure that if they cannot have monogamous relationships, they should use sex for material gain (Hurt, McElroy, Sheats, Landor, & Bryant, 2014; McLellan-Lemal et al., 2013). This adaptation is synonymous to the role of the slave woman as a sexual object (Akbar, 1996) and aligns with the U.S. cultural value of capitalist consumerism (the attainment of material goods) (Dixon, 2009).

Adaptive Behavior 2: Ever-Present Anger

Ever-present anger is misplaced hostility and frustration of some African Americans due to their inability to subscribe to traditional gender roles. Instead of acknowledging the barriers created by systematic racism and oppression, some African American men may hold African American women responsible for their inability to obtain traditional masculinity (Franklin, 2000). They may feel slighted by the advancement of African American women in the workforce and educational realms (African American women outperform African American men in earning college degrees; see Musu-Gillette et al., 2017) and insecure about their masculinity due to their inability to achieve breadwinner status (Aldridge, 2008). As a result, some African American women may feel unappreciated by African American men and belittle them for their inability to provide financially (Franklin, 2000). Within relationships, these feelings may cause continual conflict between some African American men and women (Aldridge, 2008).

Adaptive Behavior 3: Racist Socialization

Racist socialization is the idealization of the nuclear family structure in U.S. society, which includes a mother, a father, and their young children residing in a home, and also the gender roles played by each person. The idea of the nuclear family and accompanying traditional gender roles is pervasive in the United States and is promoted through media, policies, and practices (Franklin, 1997; Gerstel, 2011). The emphasis on the promotion of the nuclear family and traditional gender roles has resulted in many African Americans idealizing this model despite their inability to obtain it (Crosbie-Burnett & Lewis, 1993, Franklin, 2000). Many African Americans, particularly those who are economically vulnerable, live in extended families (that is, families that extend beyond the nuclear family to include grandparents, aunts, uncles, cousins) and may not subscribe to traditional gender roles (Hill, 2003; Stack, 1975; Staples, 1999). Extended family living and nontraditional gender roles have helped many African American couples endure economic challenges, manage demands of parenting, and maintain good mental health (Crosbie-Burnett & Lewis, 1993; Franklin, 1997, 2000; Hill, 2003; St. Vil, McDonald, & Cross-Barnett, 2018). African Americans who desire to live within a nuclear family structure or embrace traditional gender roles within relationships, but are unable to obtain these ideals (Dixon, 2009; Gerstel, 2011), may experience vacant esteem and ever-present anger.

Implications for Social Work

Interventions to address African American relationships must first understand and recognize the connection between present-day behaviors and attitudes of African Americans, and historical and continual oppression, which makes it difficult for some African Americans to achieve the PNFS. PTSS is a macro-level concept with macro- and micro-level outcomes. Thus, interventions should reflect a personal transformation whereby the client is able to confront trauma and systemic abuse that have affected their functioning and abilities to engage in healthy relationships while advocating, in partnership with social workers, for a more equitable and just system. Integrating African-centered social work, which relies on African philosophies, history, and culture (Schiele, 1992), into practice with African Americans and engaging in community-based participatory research (CBPR) may be effective in addressing historical trauma on multiple levels.

Social workers can become knowledgeable of and integrate African-centered social work into practice with African Americans. African-centered social work principles include "recognizing the importance of family and community," "encouraging individual and collective functioning," and "acknowledging the critical ways people are interdependent" (Bent-Goodley, Fairfax, & Carlton-LaNey, 2017, p. 3). Through these principles, social workers can partner with African Americans to create prevention interventions that are culturally congruent, celebrate the strength of extended families and alternative family structures, and challenge the masculine and feminine identities ascribed by the PNFS. This may be similar to work described by Tony Porter (2015) in his book, *Breaking Out of the Man Box: The Next Generation of Manhood*, which challenges male socialization and its connection to violence against women. However, his work can be extended by targeting masculinity and femininity and placing an emphasis on the intersection of race and socioeconomic status. Ultimately, the principles of African-centered social work will allow African Americans to come to know their strengths, understand the world in which they live, and position themselves to thrive (McAdoo, 2007).

While incorporating African-centered social work into social work practice with African Americans, it is imperative that the effects of historical trauma are addressed using evidence-based interventions developed in partnership with African American communities. Therefore, it is critical that social workers engage in CBPR, which emphasizes the importance of collaboration with the community in all phases of the research process to facilitate change (Holkup, Tripp-Reimer, Salois, & Weinert, 2004). For example, Heart (1998) engaged in CBPR to create a historical trauma intervention model of addressing unresolved grief among the Lakota. The psychoeducation intervention model included (a) education about historical trauma to increase awareness of the impact of trauma; (b) sharing the effects of trauma in a traditional context to provide cathartic relief; and (c) initiating grief resolution, including a reduction in grief, increase in positive identity, and a commitment to individual and community healing.

CBPR is not limited to micro- and mezzo-level outcomes but can also be used to challenge systemic racism and promote social justice. Cacari-Stone, Wallerstein, Garcia, and Minkler (2014) developed a conceptual model for bridging evidence with policy. According to their model, the macro-level context (for example, historical and contemporary trauma leading to high unemployment rates and incarceration rates among African Americans) sets the stage for using CBPR to engage in policy change. Community issues can be made a priority among policymakers through evidence (the collection of data to demonstrate that a problem exists) and civic engagement (public testimony in town hall meetings, public hearings, and media advocacy). Social workers in collaboration with community members can develop policy strategizes through "systematic problem identification, setting the agenda by bringing the legitimate attention to community issues, constructing policy alternatives, and adopting politically feasible policy objectives" (p. 1617). Ultimately, community based participatory research empowers the community to develop culturally relevant micro-, mezzo-, and macro-level interventions to address historical trauma.

Conclusion

African American marriages have existed in the English North American context since 1619, with the marriage of Anthony and Isabell(a). Their marriage, and the subsequent marriages of generations of Black people are shaped under an abnormal patriarchal context that impact how marriage survives and thrives. The desire of African Americans to model patriarchal norms may contribute to adverse marriage and relationship statistics. The African American experience in the United States disenfranchises many African American families from obtaining this family structure. In response, many African Americans display attitudes and behaviors characteristic of PTSS, which are ineffective in building healthy marriages and relationships. Social workers must understand the mismatch between African Americans' experiences and the PNFS to partner with these communities to develop culturally appropriate and effective prevention interventions for the best optimal outcomes for African American couples.

Table 1: PTSS and African American Relationships

Behaviors Reflective of PTSS	*Definition*	*Manifestation in African American Relationships*
Vacant esteem	Belief that one has little or no worth	Feeling that they and their partners are unworthy of healthy monogamous relationships
Ever-present anger	Expression of frustration to marginalization	Blaming each other for their inability to obtain traditional gender norms of the PNFS
Racist socialization	Adoption of white norms and values	Idealizing the nuclear family structure and traditional gender roles despite their inability to obtain them

Notes: PTSS = *posttraumatic slave syndrome*; PNFS = *patriarchal nuclear family structure.*

References

Akbar, N.I. (1996). *Breaking the chains of psychological slavery*. Tallahassee: Mind Production & Associates.
Aldridge, D.P. (2008). *Our last hope: Black male-female relationships in change*. Bloomington, IN: Author House.
Banks, R.R. (2011). *Is marriage for white people?: How the African American marriage decline affects everyone*. New York: Dutton.
Bent-Goodley, T. (2014). In circle: A healthy relationship, domestic violence, and HIV intervention for African American couples. *Journal of Human Behavior in the Social Environment, 24*, 105–114.

Bent-Goodley, T., Fairfax, C.N., & Carlton-LaNey, I. (2017). The significance of African-centered social work for social work practice. *Journal of Human Behavior in the Social Environment, 27*(1–2), 1–6.

Black, D.P. (1997). *Dismantling Black manhood: A historical and literary analysis of the legacy of slavery.* New York: Routledge.

Blackman, L., Clayton, O., Glenn, N., Malone-Colon, L., & Roberts, A. (2005). *The consequences of marriage for African Americans: A comprehensive literature review.* New York: Institute for American Values.

Blackmon, D.A. (2008). *Slavery by another name: The re-enslavement of Black Americans from the Civil War to World War II.* New York: Anchor Books.

Bureau of Labor Statistics, U.S. Department of Labor. (2017, January 13). *Unemployment rate and employment-population ratio vary by race and ethnicity* [The Economics Daily]. Retrieved from https://www.bls.gov/opub/ted/2017/unemployment-rate-and-employment-population-ratio-vary-by-race-and-ethnicity.htm.

Bureau of Labor Statistics, U.S. Department of Labor. (2018, December 7). *Table A-2: Employment status of the civilian population by race, sex, and age.* Retrieved from https://www.bls.gov/news.release/empsit.t02.htm.

Cacari-Stone, L., Wallerstein, M., Garcia, A.P., & Minkler, M. (2014). The promise of community-based participatory research for health equity: A conceptual model for bridging evidence with policy. *American Journal of Public Health, 104*, 1615–1623.

Cohn, D., Passel, J.S., Wang, W., & Livingston, G. (2011, December 14). *Barely half of U.S. adults are Married—A record low.* Retrieved from http://www.pewsocialtrends.org/2011/12/14/barely-half-of-u-s-adults-are-married-a-record-low/.

Crosbie-Burnett, M., & Lewis, E.A. (1993). Use of African-American family structures and functioning to address the challenges of European-American postdivorce families. *Family Relations, 42*, 243–248.

DeGruy, J. (2005). *Post traumatic slave syndrome: America's legacy of enduring and healing.* Portland, OR: Joy DeGruy Publications.

Dixon, P. (2009). Marriage among African Americans: What does the research reveal? *Journal of African Americans Studies, 13*, 29–46.

Edgell, P., & Docka, D. (2007). Beyond the nuclear family? Familism and gender ideology in diverse religious communities. *Sociological Forum, 22*(1), 25–50.

Edin, K., & Kefalas, M. (2005). *Promises I can keep: Why poor women put motherhood before marriage.* Berkeley: University of California Press.

Fairfax, C.N. (2014). Social work, marriage, and ethnicity: Policy and practice. *Journal of Human Behavior in the Social Environment, 24*(2), 83–91.

Fierce, M. (1994). *Slavery revisited: Blacks and the southern convict lease system, 1865–1933.* New York: City University of New York, Brooklyn College, Africana Studies Research Center.

Franke, K.M. (1999). Becoming a citizen: Reconstruction era regulations of African American marriages. *Yale Journal of Law and the Humanities, 11*, 251–309.

Franklin, D.L. (1997). *Ensuring inequality: The structural transformation of the African American family.* New York: Oxford University Press.

Franklin, D.L. (2000). *What's love got to do with it?: Understanding and healing the rift between African American men and women.* New York: Touchstone.

Gaskin, D.J., Headen, A.E., & White-Means, S.I. (2005). Racial disparities in health and wealth: The effects of slavery and past discrimination. *Review of Black Political Economy, 32*(3–4), 95–110.

Gerstel, N. (2011). Rethinking families and community: The color, class, and centrality of extended kin ties. *Sociological Forum, 26*(1), 1–20.

Giddings, P. (2007). *When and where I enter: The impact of African American women on race and sex in America.* New York: HarperCollins.

Goring, D. (2006). The history of slave marriage in the United States. *Louisiana State University Law Center LSU Digital Commons,* Article 262. Retrieved from https://digitalcommons.law.lsu.edu/cgi/viewcontent.cgi?article=1262&context=faculty_scholarship.

Harris, M., & Fallot, R. (2001). *Using trauma theory to design service systems.* San Francisco: Jossey-Bass.

Heart, M.Y.H.B. (1998). The return to the sacred path: Healing the historical trauma and historical unresolved grief response among the Lakota through a psychoeducational group intervention. *Smith College Studies in Social Work, 68*, 287–305.

Hill, R.B. (2003). *The strength of African American families: Twenty-five years later* (2nd ed.). Lanham, MD: University Press of America.

Hill Collins, P. (2004). *African American sexual politics: African Americans, gender, and the new racism*. New York: Routledge.

Holkup, P.A., Tripp-Reimer, T., Salois, E.M., & Weinert, C. (2004). Community-based participatory research: An approach to intervention research with a Native American community. *Advances in Nursing Science, 27*, 162–175.

Hurt, T.R., McElroy, S.E., Sheats, K.J., Landor, A.M., & Bryant, C.M. (2014). Married Black men's opinions as to why Black women are disproportionately single: A qualitative study. *Personal Relationship, 21*(1), 88–109.

Kolchin, P. (1993). *American slavery 1619–1877*. New York: Will and Wang.

Levenson, J. (2017). Trauma-informed social work practice. *Social Work, 62*, 105–113.

McAdoo, H.P. (2007). *Black families* (4th ed.). Thousand Oaks, CA: Sage Publications.

McLellan-Lemal, E., Toledo, L., O'Daniels, C., Villar-Loubet, O., Simpson, C., Adimora, A.A., & Marks, G. (2013). "A man's gonna do what a man wants to do": African American and Hispanic women's perceptions about heterosexual relationships: A qualitative study. *BMC Womens Health, 13*, 27.

Mosher, D.L., & Tomkins, S.S. (1988). Scripting the macho man: Hypermasculine socialization and enculturation. *The Journal of Sex Research, 25*(1), 60–84.

Moynihan, D.P. (1965). *The Negro family: The case for national action*. Retrieved from https://web.stanford.edu/~mrosenfe/Moynihan%27s%20The%20Negro%20Family.pdf.

Musu-Gillette, L., de Brey, C., McFarland, J., Hussar, W., Sonnenberg, W., & Wilkinson-Flicker, S. (2017, July). *Status and trends in the education of racial and ethnic groups 2017* (NCES 2017-051). Washington, D.C.: U.S. Department of Education, National Center for Education Statistics.

National Healthy Marriage Resource Center. (n.d.). *Supporting an African American healthy marriage initiative*. Retrieved from http://www.healthymarriageinfo.org/wp-content/uploads/2017/12/Supporting-an-African-American.pdf.

Oliver, W. (2006). "The Streets": An alternative African American male socialization institution. *Journal of African American Studies, 36*, 918–937.

Perry, A.R., & Bright, M. (2012). African American fathers and incarceration: Paternal involvement and child outcomes. *Social Work in Public Health, 27*, 187–203.

Pew Charitable Trusts. (2010). *Collateral costs: Incarceration's effect on economic mobility*. Washington, D.C.: Author.

Porter, T. (2015). *Breaking out of the "man box": The next generation of manhood*. New York: Skyhorse Publishing.

St. Vil, N.M., McDonald, K., & Cross-Barnet, C. (2018). A qualitative study of Black married couples' relationships with their extended family networks. *Families in Society, 99*(1), 56–66.

Schiele, J.H. (1992) The contour and meaning of Afrocentric social work. *Journal of Black Studies, 27*(6), 800–819.

Seaton, G. (2007). Toward a theoretical understanding of hypermasculine coping among urban Black adolescent males. *Gender and Sexuality, 15*, 367–390.

Stack, C.B. (1975). *All our kin: Strategies for survival in a Black community*. New York: Harper & Row.

Staples, R. (1977). The impotent African American male. In D.Y. Wilkinson & R.L. Taylor (Eds.), *The African American male in America: Perspectives on his status in contemporary society* (pp. 133–144). Chicago: Nelson-Hall.

Staples, R. (1999). *The Black family: Essays and studies* (6th ed.). Belmont, CA: Wadsworth Cengage Learning.

Tucker, M.B., & Mitchell-Kernan, C. (1995). *The decline in marriage among African Americans*. New York: Russell Sage Foundation.

White, D.G. (1999). *Ar'nt I a woman?: Female slaves in the plantation south*. New York: W.W. Norton.

Wilson, A.N. (1992). *Understanding African American adolescent male violence: Its remediation and prevention*. Brooklyn: Afrikan World Infosystems.
Wilson, W.J. (1987). *The truly disadvantaged: The inner city, the underclass, and public policy*. Chicago: University of Chicago Press.
Wilson, W.J. (1996). *When work disappears: The world of the new urban poor*. New York: Knopf.

Vestiges of Slavery
The Occupational Segregation of Black Women
Rhonda Vonshay Sharpe

Introduction

"What the evidence of the decade after 1619 tells us is inconclusive but not insignificant. It shows with alarming clarity that blacks from the outset suffered from a prejudice that relegated them to the lowest rank in the colony's society, and there are strong hints that bondage for blacks did not follow the same terms as for whites" (Vaughan, 1972). What Vaughan's statement doesn't reveal is that African women were most likely on the lowest rung of society.

Anderson (2012) argues that economic factors complicated Virginia's long history of racism. He posits that better economic conditions led to longer life expectancy in Virginia and allowed for a new labor system, created along racial lines, that allowed Black servants to be owned or assigned to a lifetime of servitude. This new "labor system" motivated the accelerated growth in the import of Africans to be slaves.

The role of the African female slave in America was multifaceted. While it was not common, she plowed fields, served as a lumberjack and did tasks similar to male slave if she was a full hand (Osofsky, 1969). It was more common that she served as a midwife, a role cemented in the female domain and high in prestige (White, 1983). As Black slave women gained more experience with midwifery, they often became known as "doctor women" and expanded their services to include caring for men, women, and children. For some Black slave women, their knowledge of the healing power of herbs would have earned them the reputation as "doctor women."

The modern image of the Black women as caretakers has origins in slavery but very different social status. In slavery times, occupations such as cooking and sewing were considered skilled jobs (White, 1983). Slave women who did these jobs were considered "half hands" and were often women who were pregnant or nursing. Slave women who were skilled enough to make clothes for Whites could keep a portion of their earnings. As many slave meals were communal, Black slave women who were skilled cooks garnered respect from both Blacks and Whites (White, 1983).

The limited occupations for slave men and women influenced employment after the abolishment of slavery. Perea (2011) points out that even after slavery was abolished, most southern Blacks were employed as agricultural or domestic workers, the remnants of slavery.

Virginia's long history of disparate treatment of African women and their decedents can be traced back to the execution of Virginia Christian. Mrs. Ida Belote convinced that Ms. Christian, a domestic worker, had stolen from her, assaulted Ms. Christian. Ms. Christian argued that she had acted in "self-defense" but was executed by the state of Virginia for killing her White employer (Harris, 2014). Bergman (1981) notes that physical violence was not uncommon for housewives, but unlike with other jobs, no criminal penalties were assigned. Criminal penalties were often not assigned for physical abuse against domestic workers, but for different reasons—race. Ironically, she shares the name of the state that executed her.

In 1896, working-class Blacks in Hampton, Virginia, limited to the following occupations:

> Black males secured employment as bakers, brick masons, blacksmiths, farmers, sailors, shoemakers, drivers, watermen, fishermen and crabmeat and oyster processors. Like most working-class African American women in the nation, the vast majority of uneducated Hampton black female wage earners toiled as laundresses and domestic servants. Between 1890 and 1910, ninety percent of southern black women were confined to household work and represented two-thirds of the nation's laundry workers. [Harris, 2014, 924].

In 1896, Hampton's Black middle class was employed as teachers and school administrators, ministers, undertakers, physicians, and politicians (Harris, 2014). Occupation mobility was not only limited by skills but also by race and gender.

Occupational Segregation

The primary consequence of employment discrimination is a difference in the distribution of workers by occupation, assuming equal qualifications (Bergman & Lyle, 1971). If repeatedly based on gender, race, ethnicity, or some combination thereof, employment discrimination can lead to occupational segregation. The historic stratification of work by gender is visible in today's labor market, but the prestige of "skilled" women's work has disappeared.

In the 40 years since Gross coined the term *sex segregation*, a plethora of research has examined the who, what, why, where, and how of gender-segmented labor markets. What these studies show is that women's work is devalued as is evident by low pay. The continued presence of occupational segregation, post the 1964 Civil Rights Act, underscores the paradoxes in socio-legal policies in the United States.

For most, the word *segregation* symbolizes the separation of people into dissimilar schools, neighborhoods, and services. Reskin (1993) posits that segregation is a fundamental process in social inequality that is more nuanced than just physical separation. Segregation operates on a set of characteristics that symbolize preferential or marginalized status resulting in unequal treatment (Reskin, 1993). Researchers have explored the role of societal customs, racism, and stereotype, but exactly what causes labor market segregation is unknown.

Several studies have examined the Black-White occupational segregation phenomena. Albelda (1986) examined the segregation of non–Whites and Whites. She finds a convergence by race, non–Whites converging to Whites, but not by gender, women converging to men. The convergence of non–White women to White women is attributed to the decrease of Black women doing domestic work. King (1992) attributes the large decrease in occupational segregation for Blacks observed in the 1960s and 1970s to civil rights advances. She credits advances from legal challenges for the decrease in occupational segregation of women.

Alonso-Villar and del Río (2013) evaluate changes to the occupational segregation of Black women from 1940 to 2010. They find less occupational segregation of Black women, but that changes are more pronounced between Black women than between Black women and other women. Educated Black women were more segregated by occupation than other women. Education does not seem to be an equalizer for Black women relative to other women but serves as a sorting mechanism for Black women into occupations (Sharpe, 2004). Alonso-Villar and del Río also find that 42 percent of Black women with less than a high school education were concentrated in the following occupations: health aide, nursing aide, child care worker, housekeeping, and cashier.

The above briefly discusses the research on the occupation of segregation of Black women. These studies ignore the history of Black women in the United States, specifically, that many of these women are descendants of slaves. Following the logic of Burgess (1994), this chapter examines the occupational segregation of Black women by linking it to the tasks performed by their enslaved ancestors.

Methodology

This study examines how the vestiges of slavery can be seen in the occupations of Black women in Virginia. The study is limited to the period of 1960–2015. The analysis is descriptive, using cross tables to identify trends in changes in occupational distribution. This study answers the following questions:

1. How has the occupational distribution of Black women changed from 1960 to 2015?
2. What are the top 10 occupations of Black women? How do the top 10 occupations of Black women compare to those of Black men and White women?
3. How has the educational attainment of Black women changed?
4. What were the wages of the top 10 occupations of Black women?

To address these questions, our study makes use of descriptive analyses of data from the 1960, 1970, 1980, 1990, and 2000 Integrated Public Use Microdata Series (IPUMS) and 2010 and 2015 American Community Survey for the state of Virginia. The sample consists of individuals 16–70 years of age. The IPUMS selection criteria are age, gender, race, Hispanic, educational attainment, marital status, wages, occupation, and industry. The top 10 occupations are ranked by the percent of women in each occupation.

This study has several limitations. First, this study does not control for immigration. Second, rankings generated by controlling for race and education may be an inefficient way to identify occupations that need to increase diversity or are biased against Black women. Finally, our ability to suggest causation for any trends identified is restricted because of the descriptive analyses.

Results

Virginia's Black population has been relatively stable, 18 percent, over the past 50 years. (See Table 1.) Black women were the largest racial or ethnic non–White group. Between 1960 and 2015, one out of every five women in Virginia identified as a Black woman. (See Table 2.) Nearly one out of every three women in Virginia identified as a woman of color over the same period. Virginia has evolved from a Black-White state in 1960 to a state where nearly one in three residents was a person of color in 2015. The increase in the diversity of Virginia's residents provides a new source of labor with varied labor market skills.

To explore further the impact these skills may have had on the employment of Black women, Table 3 provides the 1960 ranking of the top 10 occupations and unemployment of women. The occupations were ranked by the percentage of Black women in an occupation. In 1960 most women were unemployed or never worked. Most Black women were employed as private or domestic workers. Haynes (1923) reports that in a ranking of those employed as domestic workers, Negro women held second place and outnumbered the Negro male 3 to 1 in this occupation.

The top-ranked occupation for White women was stenographer/typist (8.7 percent), which is ranked 14th for Black women (.76 percent). What is striking about the 1960 occupation distribution reported in Table 3 is that nearly 90 percent of Black women were accounted for using these ten occupation codes and unemployed. On average, these occupation codes account for nearly two out of every three women (Total column) compared to nine out of every ten Black women.

Table 1. Population Distribution by Race, Ethnicity and Gender: 1960–2015

Asian	1960	1970	1980	1990	2000	2010	2015
Male	0.1%	0.2%	0.6%	1.2%	2.2%	2.7%	3.1%
Female	0.1%	0.2%	0.7%	1.4%	2.3%	3.1%	3.7%
Subtotal	0.1%	0.4%	1.2%	2.6%	4.5%	5.8%	6.8%
Black	1960	1970	1980	1990	2000	2010	2015
Male	9.3%	8.1%	8.4%	8.5%	8.7%	9.4%	9.4%
Female	9.8%	8.7%	9.3%	9.4%	9.3%	10.3%	10.2%
Subtotal	19.1%	16.8%	17.7%	17.9%	18.0%	19.7%	19.6%
Hispanic	1960	1970	1980	1990	2000	2010	2015
Male	0.2%	0.2%	0.7%	1.3%	1.9%	4.0%	4.6%
Female	0.1%	0.3%	0.7%	1.1%	2.1%	3.6%	4.2%
Subtotal	0.3%	0.5%	1.5%	2.5%	4.1%	7.6%	8.8%

Native American	1960	1970	1980	1990	2000	2010	2015
Male	0.0%	0.1%	0.1%	0.1%	0.2%	0.1%	0.1%
Female	0.0%	0.1%	0.1%	0.1%	0.1%	0.1%	0.1%
Subtotal	0.0%	0.1%	0.2%	0.3%	0.3%	0.2%	0.2%
White	1960	1970	1980	1990	2000	2010	2015
Male	40.1%	40.8%	39.2%	38.3%	36.0%	33.2%	32.3%
Female	40.4%	41.3%	40.2%	38.5%	37.1%	33.4%	32.4%
Subtotal	80.4%	82.1%	79.4%	76.8%	73.1%	66.6%	64.7%
Percent Male	50%	49%	49%	49%	49%	49%	49%
Percent Female	50%	51%	51%	51%	51%	51%	51%
Total	100%	100%	100%	100%	100%	100%	100%

Table 2. Population Distribution of Women
by Race and Ethnicity: 1960–2015

Women	1960	1970	1980	1990	2000	2010	2015
Asian	0%	0%	1%	3%	5%	6%	7%
Black	19%	17%	18%	19%	18%	20%	20%
Hispanic	0%	1%	1%	2%	4%	7%	8%
Native American	0%	0%	0%	0%	0%	0%	0%
White	80%	82%	79%	76%	73%	66%	64%
Total	100%	100%	100%	100%	100%	100%	100%

Table 3. Top 10 Occupations for Women
by Race and Ethnicity: 1960–2015

1960						
1950 Occupation Codes	White	Black	Native American	Asian	Hispanic	Total
Unemployed or Never Worked	42.11	39.85	53.13	56	35.23	41.67
Private Household Worker	1.17	22.06	3.13	0	1.14	5.23
Operative and Kindred	8.22	5.77	6.25	2.67	3.98	7.72

1960						
1950 Occupation Codes	White	Black	Native American	Asian	Hispanic	Total
Service Workers, Except Private Household	0.36	5.58	0	1.33	0	1.38
Teachers	3.48	2.77	0	0	4.55	3.34
Farm Laborers, Wage Workers	0.21	2.72	3.13	0	0	0.7
Cooks, Except Private	0.43	2.55	0	1.33	0.57	0.84
Laundry and Dry Clean	0.55	2.46	0	0	0.57	0.92
Waiters and Waitresses	2.57	1.83	9.38	6.67	2.27	2.43
Charwomen and Cleaners	0.07	1.14	0	0	0	0.28
Attendants, Hospital and Other Institution	0.58	1.06	0	0	0	0.67
Total Percentage Top 10 Occupations	59.17	86.73	75.02	68	48.31	64.51
2015						
2010 Occupation Codes	White	Black	Native American	Asian	Hispanic	Total
Unemployed, or Never Worked	19.85	20.77	20.69	22.36	18.76	20.11
Cashiers	2.37	3.99	3.45	3.8	3.13	2.79
Nursing, Psychiatric, and Home Health Aides	0.99	3.79	0	0.53	0.62	1.41
Customer Service Representatives	1.38	2.87	3.45	1.39	1.64	1.65
Secretaries and Administrative Assistants	3.86	2.69	4.6	1.44	2.1	3.38
Retail Salespersons	1.71	2.2	3.45	2.64	2.36	1.91
Elementary and Middle School Teachers	4.64	2.04	6.9	1.39	1.69	3.79
Registered Nurses	3.12	1.98	3.45	2.45	0.77	2.72
Personal Care Aides	0.68	1.98	0	0.34	0.92	0.89
Maids and Housekeeping	0.71	1.77	2.3	0.87	5.38	1.21
Managers (Including Postmaster)	2.56	1.69	1.15	2.74	2.51	2.42
Total Percentage Top 10 Occupations	41.87	45.77	49.44	39.95	39.88	42.28

To show how the 1964 Civil Rights Act might have impacted more recent changes, 1960 is used as a benchmark. Haynes (1923) suggests that the decrease in domestic workers in the South was in part due to migration to Northern cities and a decrease in employment as farmers or as a laundress. Figure 1 shows the trends in employment in domestic and farming occupations. Note the large drop in private household workers between 1960 and 1970 and the decrease in the percent of Black women employed in domestic-related jobs and farming.

By 2015, none of the 1960 occupations, except unemployed and teacher, are listed in the top 10 for Black women. However, the 2015 occupation codes shifted from *domestic* to *caregiving* occupations, which we can link to midwifery and "doctor woman" during slavery. The percentage of Black women in the caregiving occupations that do not require a bachelor's degree is near twice the average for all women. (See Table 3.) Hence, Black women are still over-represented in low-skilled and low-paying occupations that have links to caregiving during slavery.

Table 4 and Table 5 provide the top 10 occupations for Black men and women and White women using the occupation codes for 1950 and the occupation codes for 2015. The purposes of these tables are to show changes in the occupational distribution given changes in the coding of occupations. For example, in 1950 the occupational code was "private household worker," but the 2010 occupational codes separate personal care from maid and housekeeping duties. Note that for 1960 the top 10 occupations and unemployment account for nearly 90 percent of all Black women independent of the occupational coding used: 87.79 percent for 1950 codes compared to 87.18 percent for 2010 codes.

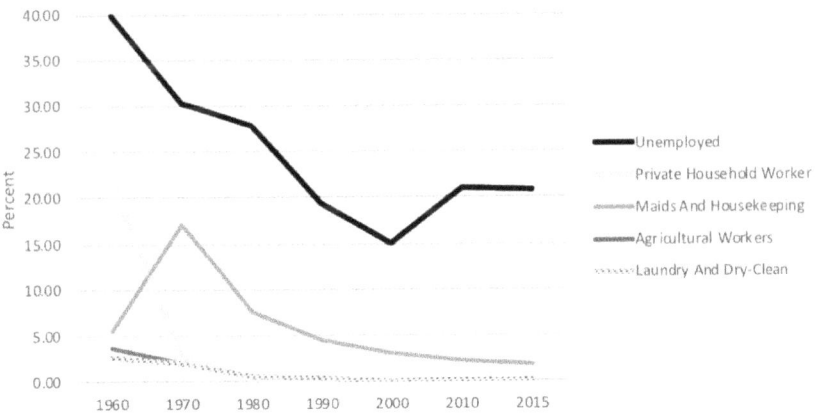

Trends in Domestic Employment for Black Women 1960–2015.

The refining of the occupation codes from 1950 to 2010 and the creation of new and more specialized occupations may give the appearance of more opportunities for Black women, especially when compared to the 1950 occupation codes. Using the 2010 occupation codes, in 2015 only 9.47 percent of Black women were employed in the top 10 occupations compared to 18.88 percent using the 1950 occupation codes. However, the previous discussion about Table 3 illustrates that while this may be true in the absolute sense, it is not true for the broad occupation classifications, i.e., occupations related to domestic work or caregiving.

While the percent of Black women who are elementary and middle school teachers in 2015 is essentially the same as in 1960 (2 percent), more White women are elementary and middle school teachers (4.64 percent vs. 2.49 percent). The percent of White women who are waitresses has declined from 2.57 percent in 1960 to 1.63 percent in 2015. For Black women, the percent working as waitresses declined from 1.83 percent in 1960 to .39 percent in 2000 and then increased to 1.3 percent in 2015. The percent of Blacks in agriculture and personal care is zero by 2015. (See Table 5.)

Table 4. 1950 Occupation Codes, Top 10 Occupations, Black and White Women: 1960–2015

Black Women	1960	1970	1980	1990	2000	2010	2015
Unemployed or Never Worked	39.85	30.13	27.24	19.3	14.96	21	20.77
Private Household Workers	22.06	13.75	5.0	2.04	0	0	0
Operative and Kindred	5.77	11.09	9.58	8.35	5.91	3.08	2.81
Service Workers, No Private Households	5.58	5.3	1.88	1.8	0.59	0.49	0.53
Teachers	2.77	3.43	3.9	3.98	5.12	4.69	3.52
Farm Laborers, Wage Worker	2.72	1.79	0.53	0.45	0	0	0.02
Cooks, Except Private Households	2.55	2.78	2.85	3.38	2.17	2.91	2.85
Laundry and Dry-Cleaning Workers	2.46	2.02	1.07	0.75	0	0.3	0.26
Waiters and Waitresses	1.83	1.79	1.32	0.83	0.39	0.65	1.3
Charwomen and Cleaners	1.14	2.59	2.74	2.66	3.15	2.16	1.77
Attendants, Hospital and Other Institution	1.06	1.98	3.71	4.81	2.56	5.32	5.82
Total Percentage Top 10 Occupations	87.79	76.65	59.82	48.35	34.85	40.6	39.65

Black Men	1960	1970	1980	1990	2000	2010	2015
Laborers	18.22	14.32	11.34	10.22	8.41	6.51	6.25
Unemployed, or Never Worked	16.58	11.37	15.69	12.98	12.28	22	23.37
Operative and Kindred Workers	8.63	11.2	9.77	8.64	9.7	6.12	4.38
Farm Laborers, Wage Workers	6.06	3.65	1.61	0.8	0.86	0.82	0.21
Truck and Tractor Drivers	5.54	4.31	4.42	5.34	4.53	3.79	3.87
Farmers (Owners and Tenants)	4.79	1.56	0.39	0.23	0	0.04	0.02
Janitors and Sextons	3.69	5.46	5.72	4.63	3.02	2.88	3.8
Members of The Armed Services	3.49	6.32	6.58	7.04	5.17	2.55	2.51
Clerical and Kindred Workers	1.68	2.95	3.78	3.53	4.53	5.06	4.23
Service Workers, No Private Households	1.54	2.17	1.35	1.33	0.65	1.02	0.93
Lumbermen, Raftsmen, and Woodchoppers	1.52	1.11	0.6	0.41	0.86	0.11	0.19
Total Percentage Top 10 Occupations	71.74	64.42	61.25	55.15	50.01	50.9	49.76
White Women	**1960**	**1970**	**1980**	**1990**	**2000**	**2010**	**2015**
Unemployed, or Never Worked	42.11	31.33	26.97	19.11	15.86	19.67	19.85
Stenographers, Typists, and Secretaries	8.68	10.9	8.83	7.28	7.4	4.88	4.1
Operative and Kindred Workers	8.22	8.48	5.78	4.79	2.79	1.71	1.48
Clerical and Kindred Workers	6.87	7.16	7.87	8.19	8.13	7.75	7.3
Salesmen and Sales Clerks	6.76	5.79	4.1	3.78	3.62	3.03	2.73
Teachers	3.48	4.87	4.81	5.11	6.41	6.78	6.82
Waiters and Waitresses	2.57	2.64	2.46	1.87	1.73	1.67	1.63
Bookkeepers	2.04	2.73	2.45	2.38	2.34	1.51	1.23
Nurses, Professional	1.69	1.94	2.19	2.53	3.04	3.28	3.6
Managers, Officials, and Proprietors	1.35	1.39	4.04	7.11	10.19	9.63	10.07
Cashiers	1.25	1.61	2.98	3.43	2.88	2.49	2.37
Total Percentage Top 10 Occupations	85.02	78.84	72.48	65.58	64.39	62.4	61.18

Table 5. 2010 Occupation Codes, Top 10 Occupations, Black and White Women: 1960–2015

Black Women	1960	1970	1980	1990	2000	2010	2015
Unemployed or Never Worked	39.86	30.25	27.90	19.30	14.96	21.00	20.77
Personal Care and Service Workers, All Other	21.77	2.70	0.29	0.21	0.00	0.00	0.06
Maids and Housekeeping	5.56	17.10	7.59	4.48	3.15	2.16	1.77
Other Production Workers	4.31	4.46	2.27	1.27	1.18	0.61	0.47
Agricultural Workers	3.71	2.06	0.49	0.29	0.00	0.00	0.02
Laundry and Dry-Cleaning Workers	2.72	2.06	0.61	0.38	0.00	0.22	0.24
Chefs and Cooks	2.55	3.01	2.54	3.20	1.57	1.82	1.43
Elementary and Middle School Teachers	2.05	2.36	2.78	3.02	3.54	2.73	2.04
Waiters and Waitresses	1.83	1.79	1.32	0.83	0.39	0.65	1.30
Food Preparation Workers	1.60	0.00	0.41	0.40	0.20	0.49	0.67
Childcare Workers	1.22	1.45	1.71	1.19	0.98	1.94	1.47
Total Percentage Top 10 Occupations	87.18	67.24	47.91	34.57	25.97	31.62	30.24
Black Men	**1960**	**1970**	**1980**	**1990**	**2000**	**2010**	**2015**
Material Moving Workers	17.26	7.14	0.53	0.32	0.22	0.02	0.17
Unemployed or Never Worked	16.58	17.4	21.93	12.98	12.28	22	23.37
Other Production Worker	8.01	5.5	3.58	2.52	2.16	1.62	1.08
Agricultural Workers	6.76	3.78	1.6	0.75	0.86	0.8	0.21
Driver/Sales Workers	6.67	5.74	5.08	5.54	4.53	3.83	3.91
Farmers, Ranchers, and Agricultural Managers	4.79	1.64	0.67	0.37	0	0.04	0.02
Janitors and Building Cleaners	3.69	5.46	5.62	4.41	3.02	2.73	3.38
Military, Rank Not Specified	3.49	0.29	0.34	0.07	0.65	0.87	0.47
Logging Workers	1.52	1.11	0.6	0.41	0.86	0.11	0.19
Baggage Porters, Bellhops, and Concierges	1.46	0.25	0.03	0.11	0	0.04	0.13
Personal Care and Service Workers, All Other	1.44	1.11	0.13	0.09	0	0.04	0.02
Total Percentage Top 10 Occupations	71.67	49.42	40.11	27.57	24.58	32.1	32.95

White Women	1960	1970	1980	1990	2000	2010	2015
Unemployed or Never Worked	42.11	31.53	27.48	19.11	15.86	19.67	19.85
Sales and Related Workers	6.82	0.48	2.47	1.99	0.29	0.16	0.18
Office Clerks, General	5.52	2.85	2.71	1.54	1.15	1.08	1.17
Secretaries and Administrative Assistants	5.45	7.73	7.41	6.36	6.98	4.56	3.86
Other Production Workers	4.1	1.93	0.93	0.61	0.29	0.3	0.25
Word Processors and Typists	3.23	3.17	1.41	0.95	0.41	0.32	0.26
Waiters and Waitresses	2.57	2.64	2.46	1.87	1.73	1.67	1.63
Elementary and Middle School Teachers	2.49	3.17	3.32	3.69	4.15	4.65	4.64
Sewing Machine Operators	2.1	2.67	1.83	1.55	0.37	0.19	0.13
Bookkeeping, Accounting, and Auditing Clerks	2.04	2.73	2.45	2.38	2.34	1.52	1.23
Registered Nurses	1.69	1.92	2.07	2.35	2.75	2.86	3.12
Total Percentage Top 10 Occupations	78.12	60.82	54.54	42.4	36.32	36.98	36.32

The intra-racial comparison of Black men and women highlights differences in the occupational distribution of Blacks. (See Table 6.) In 1960, less than 1 percent of Black men were employed as private household workers compared to 22 percent of Black women. In 1960, Black men and women were similarly employed as attendants at hospitals. By 2015, Black men and women were similarly employed as retail salespersons, 2 percent, though more Black men than women were employed as managers, 2.39 percent vs. 1.69 percent. In 2015, none of the top 10 occupations for Black men were caregiving occupations, although several are manual labor related. (See Table 5.)

Table 6. Top 10 Occupations for Black Men and Women: 1960–2015

1960			
1950 Occupation Codes	Male	Female	Blacks
Unemployed or Never Worked	16.58	39.85	28.52
Private Household Workers	0.75	22.06	11.69
Operative and Kindred Workers	8.63	5.77	7.16
Service Workers, Except Private Households	1.54	5.58	3.62
Teachers	0.74	2.77	1.78

1960			
1950 Occupation Codes	Male	Female	Blacks
Farm Laborers, Wage Worker	6.06	2.72	4.35
Cooks, Except Private Households	1.23	2.55	1.91
Laundry and Dry Cleaner Operatives	0.6	2.46	1.56
Waiters and Waitresses	0.5	1.83	1.18
Charwomen and Cleaners	0.24	1.14	0.7
Attendants, Hospital and Other Institution	1.09	1.06	1.08
Total Percentage Top 10 Occupations	37.96	87.79	63.55
2015			
2010 Occupation Codes	Male	Female	Blacks
Unemployed or Never Worked	23.37	20.77	22.02
Cashiers	1.76	3.99	2.92
Nursing, Psychiatric, and Home Health Aides	0.53	3.79	2.23
Customer Service Representatives	0.76	2.87	1.86
Secretaries and Administrative Assistants	0.3	2.69	1.54
Retail Salespersons	2.04	2.2	2.12
Elementary and Middle School Teachers	0.57	2.04	1.34
Registered Nurses	0.25	1.98	1.15
Personal Care Aides	0.17	1.98	1.11
Maids and Housekeeping	0.45	1.77	1.13
Managers (Including Postmasters)	2.32	1.69	1.99
Total Percentage Top 10 Occupations	32.52	45.77	39.41

The percentage of Black women with at least a high school diploma increased from 22 percent in 1960 to nearly 88 percent in 2015. (See Table 7.) Despite the increase in the percentage of Black women with at least a high school diploma, three of the top 10 occupations in 2015 for Black women were identified by Alonso-Villar and del Río (2013) as occupations that do not require a high school diploma and were low paying. Although this study does not address occupational segregation by educational attainment, Table 7 suggests that the improvement in the average human capital of Black women did not improve their occupational status as measured by the percentage of Black women in these low-skilled and low-paying occupations. The counter is that as educational attainment increased, the top 10 occupations account for fewer Black women, suggesting an expansion of employment opportunities.

Table 7. Degree Attainment of Black Women (Percent)

	1960	1970	1980	1990	2000	2010	2015
No Diploma	78.45	69.45	51.27	31.35	21.46	15.68	12.5
High School	16.83	23.89	36.62	54.04	55.12	56.18	55.73
Associate	1.53	2.44	5.08	4.25	6.3	7.38	8.55
Bachelor's	3.19	4.23	7.04	7.19	12.01	12.75	13.7
Master's	0	0	0	2.51	4.72	6.53	7.88
Professional	0	0	0	0.42	0.39	1.01	0.83
Doctorate	0	0	0	0.23	0	0.47	0.83
Total HS or Above	21.55	30.56	48.74	68.64	78.54	84.32	87.52

Stymied earnings and wage inequality are a consequence of a stratified (segregated) labor market. Of the 1960 top 10 occupations for Black women, Black women who were teachers had median earnings that were higher than the national median earnings for women. (See Table 8.) Their earnings were 97 percent of the national median earnings of Black men and 1.5 times the national median earnings for Black women. For 2015, the median earnings for Black teachers in Virginia were higher than the median household income for Blacks.

Table 8. Median Wages Earned for Top 10 Occupation of Black Women: 1960–2015

2010 Occupation Codes	1960	2015
Elementary and Middle School Teachers	$30,255	$48,620
Chefs and Cooks	$6,728	$12,261
Laundry and Dry-Cleaning Workers	$6,474	$24,944
Other Production Workers	$4,782	$10,570
Maids and Housekeeping Cleaners	$4,274	$14,586
Food Preparation Workers	$2,243	$15,854
Waiters and Waitresses	$2,581	$9,724
Personal Care and Service Workers	$2,581	$16,489
Childcare Workers	$889	$4,862
Agricultural Workers	$381	$21,139

2010 Occupation Codes	1960	2015
National Medians		
Black Men	$31,169	$36,989*
Black Women	$19,371	
White Women	$28,579	$62,950*
Women	$27,927	$40,742
Family	$47,392	$56,516

Wages have been adjusted to reflect 2018-dollar value.
*Is the value for the racial group.

Conclusion

Reskin (1993) notes that men and women both desire jobs that are characteristically "male" jobs. This logic can be extended to White and Black women; that is, Black women desire jobs that have historically been "reserved" for White women. A comparison of Table 5 and Table 6 shows that Black women have had some movement into occupations historically reserved for White women. However 100 years after the abolishment of slavery, Black women were still concentrated in caregiving occupations that can be linked to slavery. Four of the top 10 occupations in 2015 were akin to the "doctor woman." As we observe the 400th year since the arrival of enslaved persons to Virginia (United States), like so many discriminatory behaviors, the vestiges of slavery are hidden in plain sight—segregation of the labor market.

References

Albelda, R.P. (1986). Occupational Segregation by Race and Gender, 1958–1981. *Industrial and Labor Relations Review*, 404–411.

Alonso-Villar, O., & del Río, C. (2013). *The Occupational Segregation of Black Women*. Retrieved from http://www.ecineq.org/ecineq_baril3/FILESxBaril3/CR2/p234.pdf.

Anderson, P. (2012). Supporting Caste: The Origins of Racism in Colonial Virginia. *Grand Valley Journal of History*, 1–17.

Bergman, B.R., & Lyle, J.R. (1971). The Occupational Standing of Negroes by Areas and Industries. *The Journal of Human Resources*, 411–433.

Burgess, N.J. (1994). Gender Roles Revisited: The Development of the "Woman's Place" Among African American Women in the United States. *Journal of Black Studies*, 291–401.

Current Population Report: Consumer Income. (1961, June 9). Retrieved from Bureau of the Census: https://www2.census.gov/prod2/popscan/p60-036.pdf.

Harris, L. (2014). The "Commonwealth of Virginia vs. Virginia Christian": Southern Black Women, Crime & Punishment in Progressive Era Virginia. *Journal of Social History*, 922–942.

Haynes, E.R. (1923). Negroes in Domestic Service in the United States: Introduction. *The Journal of Negro History*, 384–442.
King, M.C. (1992). Occupational Segregation by Race and Sex, 1940.
_____. *Monthly Labor Review*, 30–37.
Osofsky, G.E. (1969). *Puttin On Ole Massa*. New York: Harper and Row.
Perea, J.F. (2011). The Echoes of Slavery: Recognizing the Racist Origins of the Agricultural and Domestic Worker Exclusion from the National Labor Relations Act. *Loyola University Chicago, School of Law LAW eCommons*, 95–138.
Poverty and Income in the United States 2015. (2016, September). Retrieved from Current Population Reports: https://www.census.gov/content/dam/Census/library/publications/2016/demo/p60-256.pdf.
Reskin, B. (1993). Sex Segregation in the Workplace. *Annual Review of Sociology*, 241–70.
Sharpe, R.V. (2004). Does Educational Attainment Reduce Labor Market Discrimination? *International Association for Feminist Economics*. Oxford, England.
Vaughan, A.T. (1972). Blacks in Virginia: A Note on the First Decade. *The William and Mary Quarterly*, 469–478.
White, D.G. (1983). Female Slaves: Sex Roles and Status in the Antebellum Plantation South. *Journal of Family History*, 248–261.

Building a Nation

United States Black Founders, Racial Ideology and the Crisis of Black Citizenship

LaGarrett J. King

> "History is a people's memory, and without a memory, man is demoted to lower animals."
>
> —Malcolm X

On January 8, 2018, the 400 years of African American History Commission Act became law (400 Years of African American History Commission Act, 2018). The legislation, led by Representative Bobby Scott and Senators Tim Kaine and Mark Warner of Virginia, was created to commensurate the 400-year anniversary of the *first twenty and odd Negroes* stolen from West and Central Africa to Tsenacommacah, its native name, or Point Comfort, Virginia. The *twenty and odd Negroes* were exchanged for food and we believe sold into slavery. A few days later, an additional seven to nine Africans were also bought and sold in the area for exchange for food. This historical moment marked the beginning of over 200 years of African oppression through the horrid practice of chattel slavery.

The Commission's duties are to plan, develop, and implement programs and activities, as well as provide grants to communities and nonprofit organizations to develop programs and events that will shed light onto Black American history since 1619. The bill calls for Black history that will highlight enslavement but also include histories salient to the Black American experience. The commission wants to support programs that "fully tell the story of Black Americans, their contributions, and their resilience over the last 400 years" (Scott, 2016). The 15-member commission, made up of government and nongovernment citizens, will serve until 2020 and private donations will be used to support these endeavors.

As a Black History Educator, I am excited about the possibilities connected with the commission's duties. The 400 year African American History Commission Act is part of a legacy at legislating Black history both at the federal and state levels since the 1960s (King, 2018). The law is an extension of various Black history policies meant to bring awareness to Black history that has been for so long misinterpreted. These Black history policies include state mandated Black history curriculum and teaching for K-12 students as well as the National Museum of African American History and Culture (King, 2018). I am hopeful that the commission will promote Black history that will be carefully crafted with nuance, rigor, and critically. Yet, I am cautious given how Black history, historically, has been co-opted by the mainstream to promote miseducation and to resolve White America of guilt and shame (King, 2018; Woodson, 2006).

I have two major concerns. First, language use within the law such as "encouraging patriotic activities" brings pause given how the United States has traditionally conceptualized patriotism as an act that requires non-questioned loyalty and void of any dissent (Busey & Walker, 2017; Westheimer, 2009). My hope is that the commission's definition is closely aligned with patriotism that understands its democratic values where being critical and dissension are salient patriotic virtues.

Second, I am worried that sponsored activities will add to what Michael Guasco (2018) termed, the fallacy of 1619. The fallacy of 1619 are narratives that:

1. Center White Christian European perspectives as the official narrative,
2. Ignore African exploration to the new lands, even predating Christopher Columbus,
3. Overlook the transnational nature of the slave trade, which includes the Portuguese, Spanish, English, French, Dutch and others happening as early as the late fifteenth century, and
4. Disregard African experiences and perspectives

The year 1619 has taken a prominent view in how society interprets United States history. Most times, the narratives focus too much on a nostalgic American founding that identifies Europeans in palatable terms such as colonists or explorers. The term invaders or colonizers maybe more applicable given that Indigenous groups occupied the lands first. Guasco (2018) notes that 1619 sometimes ignores that the English were outsiders but ensures that Africans were foreign to the lands. This approach is ahistorical, non-contextual, ignores Black agency, and promotes a deficit historical lens about Black people.

The fallacy of 1619 engraves an epistemological rendering of Black people as slaves. In other words, Black people are forever remembered as slaves, which is such as small (albeit influential) portion of Black history. The fallacy of 1619 also reduces Black people's contributions to United States. At best, persons may admit that enslaved people helped build the infrastructure of the country or helped establish the United States as an economic power through cotton and other resources (Baptist, 2016).

In this chapter, however, I would like to alter those narratives that situate Black people as simple slaves who were commodified for the wealth of the United States. I contend that Black people not only contributed to "America" as enslaved individuals but Black people helped shape American democracy as well. I am attempting to reshape our understanding that Black people's contributions were not solely physical but also intellectual.

This chapter, therefore, will focus on the concepts of Black American Founders of the United States of America. I define Black American Founders as men and women of African ancestry who lived during the colonial period and pre-emancipation era, whose ideas and actions helped build several social institutions in the United States, challenged the White Founders ideas regarding democracy, and redefined race. The Black Founders' discussion challenges what I believe is a prevailing discourse (maybe innocuous or not) that struggles to dismiss our slavery's past. I contend that how we imagine slavery (in its historic sense) and its connection with Black people is still prevalent. I argue that Blackness is still synonymous with slave and has had implications to how we understand Black people and their continued quest for full citizenship.

My point connects to how whenever Black American citizens, exert themselves as agents of their freedom, opposing and sever actions are taken, usually by White people, against Black people, many times resulting in violence (Anderson, 2016). I believe those horrid actions are a result of how we understand history and our understanding of who Black people were and still are. I surmised that history plays a powerful role in how we perceive identity. History tells us who we are and gives us impressions about the other. History is more than stories of the past; something we are afraid to repeat, it is our memory of who we are as a people against other people and cultures. History also lives within our consciousness and what we learn is difficult to break from our unconscious mind. History is generational and is passed down through stories, cultural artifacts, and the school curriculum or as Christine Sleeter (2018) puts it, the past doesn't simple disappear.

My chapter situates Black Founders as part of the early Black Freedom Movement and extends our understanding how Black people understood and enacted ideas of democracy.

There are three sections of this paper. First, I engage with the concept of the afterlife of slavery theorized by Saidiya Hartman (1997). As we enter the 400-year anniversary of enslavement on U.S. soil, it is important to recognize the impact of the institution in contemporary society. Additionally, slavery's afterlife continues to influence how Blackness is seen and imagined, which interferes with how Black people are treated as citizens and humans. My discussion then pivots to Black American Founders of the United States of America. I argue that much of what we know about and treat Black people is connected to how we understand Black people in 1619 and during slavery. Slavery, in this case, is more than a state of bondage; it is an ideology that is influenced by how our history is taught and understood. I define Black American Founders and stress that Black Founders are different from what we know as White Founding Fathers. Last, my concluding thoughts will center on something very radical, I give a few suggestions as to how we should rethink Black people and Black history.

The Afterlife of Slavery

The 13th amendment, passed by Congress on January 31, 1865, and ratified by the states on December 6, 1865, legally ended the institution of slavery except for those who were convicted of crimes (Alexander, 2012). While Black persons were no longer legally in bondage, lingering implications of chattel slavery continued to negatively influence Black life. Saidiya Hartman has called this phenomenon the afterlife of slavery. According to Hartman (1997), the afterlife of slavery is the recognition that the transatlantic slave trade to the Americas and the institution of slavery lasted well after the passing of the 13th amendment and continues to be impactful on the lives of Black people 200 years later. Central to the afterlife of slavery is the notion that Black life is expendable within an anti-black capitalist society.

The afterlife of slavery is twofold. First, the afterlife of slavery has created an ongoing *crisis of citizenship* (Hartman, p. 117) for Black Americans who are liminally American and African. Akin to what Dubois (1999) remarked as double consciousness where " one feels his twoness—an American, a Negros, two souls, two thoughts, two reconciled striving; two warring ideas in one dark body" (p. 1), Black Americans experience what I call conflicting ontologies. Conflicting ontologies are when many Black Americans, our sense of self, our being, has been Americanized yet our Blackness is contentious within Americanized spaces. Our status as Black Americans and our history is constantly (and I would argue maybe purposely) being erased, challenged and othered. Many Black Americans have a yearning to connect to our homelands in Africa. Yet, we are not African; we are ultimately strangers and outsiders on the continent. The transatlantic slave trade and slavery brought about what Kenya scholar Ngugi wa Thiong'o (2009) has called dismemberment. The process of stripping enslaved Africans of their Africanness and from Africa, the loss of their names, language, customs, and legacy, had long-term effects on Black American's identity. The afterlife of slavery presents itself through Black American's constant fight with humanity and a sense of belonging between two worlds, Africa and the Americas.

Second, the afterlife of slavery heavily relies on a consistent racialized ideology that has classified humanity. The creation of race and the institution of slavery in the Americas occurred almost simultaneously and situated those who were considered White at the top of the racial hierarchy while those who were considered Black were situated at the bottom of this raced system. Through this classification, Black or African became synonymous with slave. Europeans started falsifying Africa as the Dark Continent with uncivilized inhabitants who had no history or culture (Jordan, 2013; Munimbe, 1988). Being Black or African, therefore, was classified as a lower form of humanity or what Charles Mills (1998) referred to as *subpersons* or even what Frantz Fanon (1968) has called the *zone of nonbeing*. Therefore, using African persons as slaves was used to justify slavery because the institution became a means to civilize and humanize.

The racialized idea of Blacks as slave has been instrumental as we think of the afterlife of slavery. The passing of the 13th amendment did not interfere with the racist idea that Black persons were subpersons. In many ways, black continues to be synonymous with slave. Michael Dumas (2016) explains that currently Black people in society are:

> socially and culturally positioned as slave, dispossessed of human agency, desire, and freedom. This is not meant to suggest that Black people are currently enslaved (by whites or by law), but that slavery marks the ontological position of Black people. Slavery is how Black existence is imagined and enacted upon, and how non–Black people—and particularly whites—assert their own right to freedom, and right to the consumption, destruction, and/or simple dismissal of the Black [p. 13].

Dumas's notion of Black people as socially and culturally positioned as a slave is an intriguing concept and one that Hartman has stressed has not been undone in the minds of White America. Blackness is in a constant state of surveillance and Black voices continually marginalized. There is considerable evidence that insist that Black people continued to suffer from second-class citizenship where non-progressive racist policies hindered and ignored Black people needs (Glaude, 2017). For example, U.S. policies connected to housing and redlining, transportation via interstate development, health care, criminal justice decisions, and educational policy have slowed Black people's progress both economically and socially. Therefore, many Black people suffer from "skewed life chances, limited access to health and education, premature death, incarceration, and impoverishment," (p. 6) all indicators of the afterlife of slavery.

Despite Black oppression in the United States, Black Americans, in all historical eras in the United States exhibited agency to fight against oppression and second-class citizenship. Currently, the Black Lives Matter Movement and Colin Kaepernick are the current responses to the afterlife of slavery and have been front and center in American society and politics. Yet, these two movements have become polarizing issues. Black Lives Matter, an international network of decentralized activists groups, began as a twitter hashtag in response to the acquittal of George Zimmerman's killing of Black teenager, Trayvon Martin. The organization's mission centers on creating an equitable society with police and criminal justice reform as one of its many missions (Garza, 2014; Taylor, 2016). Kaepernick, a former professional football player, began a protest movement, kneeling during the national anthem before professional football games, to bring attention to Black Lives and other injustices that happen towards Black citizens (Parlow, 2017).

What I am interested in with these two movements are the visceral responses, made mostly by older and conservative White American citizens and conservative news outlets such as FOX News, who claim that BLM and Kaepernick are divisive, racist, and antipolice (Lim, 2016). Opponents of the these movements, claim that the way the protests were enacted were wrong and destructive; instead protests should be more subtle, quiet, and non-violent, similar to what many feel was the approach by a Martin Luther King's led Civil Rights Movement (Dyson and Jagerman, 2000; Alridge, 2006). I argue that BLM and Kaepernick are polarizing based on a historical memory of situating Black people as slaves. This Black-people-as-slave paradigm is engrained in our society starting with the official k-12 history curriculum most people learn as early as elementary school (Busey & Walker, 2017; King, 2018).

The first time people learn about Black people is typically through the enslavement narrative. Traditionally, K-12 history curriculum begins with the disjointed narrative about the twenty and odd Negroes arriving to Virginia in 1619 and then morphs into stories of Black people starting as indentured servants and then moving to enslavement, a lifetime condition. The narrative continues to talk about the institution of slavery as primarily a southern phenomenon. The curriculum may mention a few slave insurrections, typically ones that were unsuccessful with some talks about Black people's contributions towards the American Revolution for both the colonists and British. Lastly, the traditional history curriculum talks about the Civil War and largely presents slavery as one of the causes of the war. Black solider contributions to the Civil War is spoken about and then the narrative moves forward to Reconstruction.

These narratives have largely been how young children learn about Black people's early contributions to United States. The narrative heavily focuses on a passive and paternalistic Black history narrative where enslaved individuals are powerless bystanders as the United States grows as a democratic power (Busey & Walker, 2017; Loewen, 2010). In many respects, one can look at the official narrative as Black people hindering and being a problem for democracy (Ladson-Billings, 2003). For example, Black people and slavery were major issues during the Constitutional Convention, Missouri Compromise, the Fugitive Slave Acts, and of course, the Civil War and Reconstruction. The official narrative teachers that any progress made by Black people as emerging citizens, White people (mostly White men) fought and sometimes won on their behalf.

This sort of historical memory gives the impression that Black people did not fight for or earn their freedom. Instead, because of brave, nice, and progressive Whites, Black people were simply given their freedom. To be clear, my statements are not to discredit or lessen history's White allies; instead, I want to bring attention to how Black people were agents in their own freedom movements and helped push for and challenged democracy. If we are to believe that History is about identity, it makes sense that the historical memory of Black people is one the centers them as a disadvantaged and powerless group of people who needed help not only to relieve them as their status of slave but also certify their humanity.

I argue that this sort of ideology explains the visceral reactions towards how Black freedom fighters decide to fight for citizenship rights. In essence, opponents may believe that Black people have little to no rights to complain, protest, and/or challenge the established democracy and, by proxy what happens to them, because they were not contributors to any of its ideas and governance. Hence, they were slaves and would still be slaves if White people wanted them to be.

I contend this sort of belief stems from our lack of knowledge and the stories we continue to tell about Black people's colonial past. In an effort to move us beyond these troubling narratives, a new paradigm of how we see and understand Black people has to be developed. It is important, therefore, as we commensurate 1619 and Black American contributions, we re-envision their role as not simply as oppressive and enslaved but as people with agency who developed this nation. My approach is to make the case for Black Americans Founders of the United States of America.

Founding Fathers Defined

Before defining Black Founders, it is important to describe how traditionally we have defined United States Founders. R.B. Bernstein (2009) noted that Founding Fathers were first coined by Senator and former President William Harding. Harding defined founders as men who framed and adopted "a series of documents of political foundations, constitutions, declarations, Bill of Rights, treaties, and laws" (p. 8). Founders also became those who participated in the American Revolution. The most salient Founders were the ones who participated in the Second Continental Congress of 1776 and the Constitutional Convention of 1787 (Bernstein, 2009). They were the intellectual founders who adopted and established what is considered the philosophies of American democracy. The pantheon of Founders include George Washington, Thomas Jefferson, James Madison, Benjamin Franklin, John Adams, Alexander Hamilton, and John Jay.

While White Founders were responsible for establishing a representative democracy framework in the New World, it is hard to ignore that many of them were slaveholders and believed that Black people were less than human. Chief Justice Robert Brook Taney even stated in his proslavery opinion in *Dred Scott v. John F.A. Sanford* (1857) that the White Founders never intended to extend citizenship rights to Black Americans leading Thurgood Marshall's (1987) to surmise that the "Constitution was defective from the start" (p. 1338). Marshall, the first Black American Supreme Court justice, noted that the contemporary Constitution is a living document espoused through the efforts of "those who refused to acquiesce in outdated notions of liberty, justice, and equality and who strived to better them" (p. 1341). Fast forward 21 years from Marshall's comments, then Senator and Presidential candidate, Barack Obama noted that the Constitution was ultimately unfinished and was stained by the nation's original sin of slavery (Obama, 2008).

The founding document, the Constitution, continued to establish a racial and ethnic hierarchical structure that limited Black American's governmental voice and citizenship rights, therefore, creating different Americas. One America was for the White elite and others consisted of Black, Native American, Asian, and poor Whites. The Founders, who spoke for White America, were not the Founders of Black America or for other marginalized communities.

Black American Founders

Lerone Bennett (1993) is instrumental in helping understand and define Black American Founders. His book, *The Shaping of Black America*, as well as his articles in the popular Black magazine, *Ebony*, noted that the birth of White America was not the birth of Black America and challenged readers to think of Black America as separate of White America. Black people, in a sense, established a separate country within a country and had separate founders. Bennett surmised that Black Founders were men and women of African ancestry who were early pioneers of America that extended from the middle of the eighteenth century to the middle of the nineteenth century. He noted that the fifty-year period from 1787 to 1837 were the most prominent years for Black American Founders of the United States of America.

It is important to note that we should not think of Black American Founders as a darker pigmented replacement of White Founders, meaning that Black Founders did not mimic or carry the same philosophical principles as their White counterparts. Black Founders should be viewed as oppositional historical characters whose ideas and practices were contentious to most White Founders ideas about democracy. Black Founders can be classified into three categories.

Enslaved Black people
Creators of social institutions
Race leaders

Enslaved Black American Founders are understood in two ways. First, enslaved Black people are responsible for establishing the United States as a global economic power. According to Edward Baptist:

> [African Americans] practices [in cotton production] rapidly transformed the southern states into the dominant force in the global cotton market, and cotton was the world's most widely traded commodity at the time.... The returns from cotton monopoly powered the modernization of the rest of the American economy, and by the time of the Civil War, the United States had become the second nation to undergo large-scale industrialization [xxi].

The cotton plantation economy was the lifeblood of the Southern economy as well as influenced the nation's financial markets and was one of world largest exports. In addition to cotton, the U.S. enslavement yielded considerable profits from its other cash crops like sugar, tobacco, and rice. Enslaved Black people, through all their positions, help sustained the nation's economy. They also helped build the infrastructure of this country including constructing Washington, D.C., the nation's capital. Enslaved

Black people developed their own culture, one that involved a mix of different African cultural groups. These cultures would influence United States culture for decades. Enslaved Black people sacrifice much for the development of White America and one would argue that without their expertise and work, the United States would not have been created.

Second, enslaved Black people who resisted and fought their conditions were Black Founders. Slave insurrections/revolts are the most known form of resistance. With more than 200 enslaved resurrections, enslaved Black people not only fought to secure freedom from enslavement but they were fighting against the system of enslavement. Overthrowing slavery's social structure was to also diminish and fight against the capitalistic structure that upheld the system. Additionally, those enslaved persons who escaped plantations as well as who would be considered maroons are classified as founders for distinct ways. For the enslaved who escape to non-slave territories and for maroon communities, similar to enslaved revolts, they were resisters who challenged and damaged the social system of slavery. Enslaved Black Americans were the first part of the Black freedom movements meant to challenge White Founders racist ideas about Black people and the institution of slavery as a humanizing mechanism.

While Black enslaved people can be considered as Black Founders, it was the Black freedmen/women who had a little more latitude and space to develop systems of freedom. The second category of Black Founders were those who established social institutions that not only served Black freemen and women but would eventually serve those enslaved people into freedom. Black Founders established throughout the late 1700s and early 1800s spaces for Black life including religious, social, political, and economic institutions as well as arts and cultural centers, churches, insurance groups, newspapers and other literary organizations, and Masonic lodges. These places served as safe racial spaces that allowed Black people to be with Black people without the fear of racism. The African Methodist Episcopal Church (founded by Richard Allen and Absalom Jones); *The Freedom's Journal* (edited by Samuel Cornish and John B. Russwurm); and the African Masonic Lodge (established by Prince Hall) serve as examples of these institutions. Additionally, Black women founders were instrumental in creating family and women centric organizations such as the African Female Benevolent Societies (Newman, 2008).

The third category of Black Founders were race leaders who promoted what I have termed critical intellectual agency or CIA (King, 2014). CIA refers to how "Black Founders intellectually challenged the philosophical, social, and moral underpinnings of United States egalitarianism" (King 2014 92). Newman (2013) noted that Black Founders promoted a moral revolution that centered on societal transformation through challenging inequalities by breaking social and political structures that oppressed racially and ethnically diverse groups. *Critical intellectual agency* is about racial justice and how Black Founders repudiated White Founders views about Black Americans and race.

Black Founders understood that while some White Founders were not promoters of enslavement, many were complicit in believing the popular racial theories of the era. That is, most Black people's humanity was seriously flawed and they were naturally inferior. Those beliefs were salient to White Founders who set up governments (Federal, state, and local) with policies steeped in anti-blackness and indifference. Black Founders' critical intellectual agency held a basic premise to challenge those ideas of inferiority.

Black founders who were race leaders and promoted critical intellectual agency are twofold. First, Black Founders challenged White Founders on the ideology of universal emancipation. Black founders were cognizant of the ideas of the Constitution and understood that equality did not to extend to Black people; therefore, they wanted a moral revolution with racial justice as the centerpiece (Newman, 2008). In efforts to appeal to Black freedom and emancipation, we can turn to Black American Revolutionary soldiers.

Black American revolutionary soldiers fought not out of love of a country that oppressed them but out of love of the race and desires to be free of enslavement and second-class citizenry. Second, their presence repudiated the racist ideas that Black people were not brave and capable of military service. Their existence not only demonstrated physical strength but also required a certain mental capability. In other words, Black revolutionary soldiers were fighting for freedom, not for America but for them, their families, and the Black race as a whole. Some examples of these Black revolutionary race leaders include James Armistead Lafayette, Peter Salem, and Prince Estabrook to name a few.

Understanding that Black Revolutionary soldiers fought for Black freedom and not loyalty troubles the popular phrasing that they were Black patriots. More Black persons sided with the British forces than the colonist at first because the British promised Black freedom first. Once the American colonists promised Black persons freedom for exchange for service, then many Black persons joined the Continental army. Black revolutionary soldier "can best be understood by realizing that his major loyalty was not to a place, not to a people, but to a principle" (Nash, 2013, p. xx) Black American revolutionary soldiers were fighting the "African Americans' Revolution," (Nash, 2013) a separate cause from the majority of Whites Americans who were fighting in the American Revolution.

Second, Black Founders exhibited critical intellectual agency by attempting to change the meaning of Blackness and race promoted by many White Founders. As stated earlier, many White Founders considered Black people subhumans and that belief prompted the arguments for the institution of enslavement as some type of humanizing mechanism. Those considered to be Black founders fought against these racist caricatures through various approaches including literary prose. Throughout the eighteenth and nineteenth century, Black founders wrote speeches, pamphlets, and newspaper articles about their rights to be full citizens, typically using ideas promoted by White Founders. According to the *Black Antislavery Writings Project*, more than 1500 documents were written by Black people about their rights to freedom and ideas about race (Newman, 2008). Persons such as Daniel Walker, Daniel Coker, and Phillis Wheatley spoke out against racial injustice and racist ideas against Black people. Their words were meant to promote racial justice and contradict the racial theories of the time.

Benjamin Banneker's letters to Thomas Jefferson serves as an appropriate example of contradicting racial theories of the time. Banneker, the scientist, inventor, and astronomer, was most well known based on his contribution to surveying Washington, D.C., and his almanacs. His 1792 almanac contained a letter to then Secretary of State, Thomas Jefferson about his thoughts about race in Jefferson's book, *The Notes on the State of Virginia*. *Notes*, a book about various issues concerning Virginia, contained some of Jefferson's thoughts about race. Jefferson wrote about his confliction with race, stating that the institution was evil but Black people were subhumans and naturally inferior to White people. Banneker challenged Jefferson to resend his pro-slavery stance, support abolition, reevaluate his thoughts about the Black people's intellectual prowess, and chastised the White Founder's moral authority. Banneker's letter was not simply a letter to Jefferson but it became a commentary on the egregious racialization in American and it established the antecedent for anti-slavery advocacy.

Conclusion

In this chapter, I surmised that the way we understand the institution of slavery and 1619 continues to haunt the United States as a country. Through our historical memory, we come to understand Black people as slaves. To be clear, slave is not meant to understand Black people in bondage but to treat, police, and surveilled Black bodies because our historical memory support thinking that Black people should lack "human agency, desire, and freedom" (Dumas, 2016, p. 13). I noted that because we do not learn as a society that Black people were agents for their freedom, contemporary understandings about Back history may infer that Black people were simply given their freedom and did not earn it. This understanding can have detrimental influence in how people understand a group of people in the contemporary.

I argued for a reconceptualization of Black history, one that does not simple see Black people as slaves, without agency, but one as Founders to America, who helped established or at least hold the White Founders accountable for democracy. Understanding Black Americans as founders of American democracy may alter how we see Black people, not as problems but as solutions to the egalitarian state.

Black Founders were uniquely Black and set the precedent in social justice. They understood that the country was not set up for them and they attempted to fix it. Some of their legacies are still prominent today such as the AME church. They challenged the White Founders misguided racial prejudices and made their voices known. While Black Founders can be classified as establishing a separate nation within a nation, they are uniquely American, and our country is better because of their sacrifice.

As a Black history educator, I am optimistically cautious for the 2019 events commemorating 400 years of Black people on the soil of the United States. As a society, we need spaces to engage with rigorous Black history, narratives and pedagogies that inspire, yet are critical to the systemic challenges we face as a country to fully uphold our ethos. We need Black history that is revisionist, but not to the determent of truth. We need a Black history that is diverse, multidimensional, and intersectional, a history that moves us from the watchful eye of Eurocentrism. We need a Black history that is uniquely Black, which comes from Black people perspectives and epistemologies. We need to understand that Black American history is not what we know to be American history. Black history has its own starting points, its own meanings, and its own purpose. Without those principles, we are just learning White history in Black face.

References

400 year African American Commission Act, Pub. L. No. 115–102. STAT. 2248. (2018)

Alridge, D.P. (2006). The limits of master narratives in history textbooks: An analysis of representations of Martin Luther King, Jr. *Teachers College Record, 108*(4), 662.

Alexander, M. (2012). *The new Jim Crow: Mass incarceration in the age of colorblindness.* The New Press.

Anderson, C. (2016). *White rage: The unspoken truth of our racial divide.* Bloomsbury Publishing USA.

Banneker, B., Jefferson, T., & Sauer, G. (1999). *Copy of a Letter from Benjamin Banneker to the Secretary of State, with his Answer*. Carnegie Mellon University's English Department.
Baptist, E.E. (2016). *The half has never been told: Slavery and the making of American capitalism*. Hachette UK.
Bennett, L. (1993). *The shaping of black America*. Penguin Group USA.
Bernstein, R.B. (2009). *The founding fathers reconsidered*. Oxford University Press.
Busey, C.L., & Walker, I. (2017). A dream and a bus: Black critical patriotism in elementary social studies standards. *Theory & Research in Social Education, 45*(4), 456–488.
Dred Scott v. Sanford, 60 U.S. 393 (1857).
Du Bois, W.E.B., & Marable, M. (2015). *Souls of black folk*. Routledge.
Dumas, M.J. (2016). Against the dark: Antiblackness in education policy and discourse. *Theory into Practice, 55*(1), 11–19.
Dyson, M.E., & Jagerman, D.L. (2000). *I may not get there with you: The true Martin Luther King, Jr* (Vol. 233). Simon & Schuster.
Fanon, F. (1968). *The wretched of the earth: The handbook for the black revolution that is changing the shape of the world*. Grove Press.
Garza, A. (2014) A herstory of the #BlackLivesMatter Movement. Retrieved from http://www.thefeministwire.com/2014/10/blacklivesmatter-2/.
Glaude Jr, E.S. (2017). *Democracy in black: How race still enslaves the American soul*. Broadway Books.
Guasco, M. (2018). The Fallacy of 1619: Rethinking the History of Africans in Early America. Retrieved from https://www.aaihs.org/the-fallacy-of-1619-rethinking-the-history-of-africans-in-early-america/.
Hartman, S. (2008). *Lose your mother: A journey along the Atlantic slave route*. Macmillan.
Jefferson, T. (1999). *Notes on the State of Virginia*. Penguin.
Jordan, W.D. (2013). *White over black: American attitudes toward the Negro, 1550–1812*. UNC Press Books.
King, L.J. (2014). More than slaves: Black founders, Benjamin Banneker, and critical intellectual agency. *Social Studies Research and Practice, 9*(3), 88- 105.
King, L.J. (2017). The status of Black history in U.S. Schools and Society. *Social Education, 81*(1), 14–18.
Ladson-Billings, G. (Ed.). (2003). *Critical race theory perspectives on the social studies: The profession, policies, and curriculum*. IAP.
Lim, N. (2016). Rudy Giuliani: Black Lives Matter "inherently racist." *CNN*. See: https://edition.com/07/11/politics/rudy-giuliani-black-libes-matter-inherently-racist.
Loewen, J.W. (2018). *Teaching what really happened: How to avoid the tyranny of textbooks and get students excited about doing history*. Teachers College Press.
Marshall, T. (1987). Reflections on the bicentennial of the United States Constitution. *Harv. L. Rev., 101*, 1.
Mills, C.W. (2014). *The racial contract*. Cornell University Press.
Mudimbe, V.Y. (1988). *The invention of Africa*. Bloomington, IN: Indiana University Press.
Nash, G.B. (2013). The African Americans' Revolution. In *The Oxford Handbook of the American Revolution* (p. 250). Oxford University Press.
Newman, R.S. (2008). *Freedom's prophet: Bishop Richard Allen, the AME Church, and the black founding fathers*. NYU Press.
Obama, S.B. (2008). A more perfect union. *The Black Scholar, 38*(1), 17–23.
Parlow, M.J. (2017). Race, Speech, and Sports. *U. Rich. L. Rev., 52*, 923.
Scott, B. (2017). 400 Years of African-American History Commission Act. Retrieved https://bobbyscott.house.gov/media-center/floor-statements/400-years-of-african-american-history-commission-act-0.
Sleeter, C. (2018). *The inheritance: A Novel*. Monterey Publishing: Sleeter Publishing.
Taylor, K.Y. (2016). *From# BlackLivesMatter to black liberation*. Haymarket Books.
wa Thiong'o, N. (2009). *Something torn and new: An African renaissance*. Civitas Books.
Westheimer, J. (2009). Should social studies be patriotic?. *Social Education, 73*(7), 316–320.
Woodson, C.G. (2006). *The mis-education of the Negro*. Book Tree. San Diego, CA.

Epilogue
E Pluribus Unum, *Out of Many, One*

Sophia A. Nelson

America is the story of us. The collective us. The us. The we, the ones who came to this great frontier more than 400 years ago and braved the seas, the storms, and the difficult seasons of life so that "we the people" could build a nation of great prosperity.

Many believe that they know our story, but they do not. Our story is complicated. It is one of great promise, and idealism. Yet, it is also one of cruelty and racial degradation.

Yes, ours is a story of explorers, pioneers, and trailblazers. Ours is a story of people who transformed their dreams into reality and turned the struggles of our founding into our present-day favor. Our Founders were indeed great visionaries, truth seekers, and people of great faith. Puritans of virtue. They were brave and adventurous people who dared to dream "the ideal" new world that had never been dreamed of or charted before.

Virginia, the first colony, was rugged and dangerous terrain. Settled by a cadre of Dutch merchants, British prisoners, Irish indentured servants, planters, and men seeking a new land of opportunity and prosperity. And, in seeking that freedom and liberty for themselves, in 1619 they violated the very freedoms they themselves had obtained.

They brought in "20 and odd Negroes," as the record reads, originating from Angola. These slaves were stolen from a Portuguese slave ship, then transported to an English warship flying a Dutch flag, and were eventually sold to colonial settlers. At this time, the slave trade between Africa and the English colonies had not yet been established, and it is unlikely that the 20 or so newcomers became slaves upon their arrival. They were perhaps considered indentured servants, who worked under contract for a certain period (usually seven years) before they were granted freedom and the rights accorded to other settlers.

This, of course, is a topic of debate. And one worth debating, for sure. Their historic arrival, however, marked the beginning of an immoral and brutal trend in colonial America, in which the people of Africa were taken unwillingly from their motherland and subject to lifelong enslavement. The robust economic growth of the English colonies was caused almost entirely by the exploitative institution of slavery, which hit its height by the 1660s through the 1760s.

Among laws affecting slaves most insidiously, helping to perpetuate slavery and racial classifications for generations, was one passed in 1662, which said that children born in the colony would take the social status of their mothers, regardless of who their fathers were. This law was in direct contrast to English common law of the time, and resulted in generation after generation of enslaved persons, including *mixed-race* children and adults, some of whom were nearly wholly white being classified as Negro and not subject to inheritance or social status. Among the most notable were *Sally Hemings* and her siblings, fathered by planter *John Wayles*, and her four surviving children by *Thomas Jefferson*.

Increasingly toward the end of the seventeenth century, large numbers of *slaves* from Africa were brought by *Dutch* and English slave ships to the Virginia Colony, as well as to *Maryland* and other southern colonies. On the large tobacco plantations, planters used them as *chattel* (owned property) to replace indentured servants (who were obligated to work only for a set period of time) as field labor, as well as to serve as household and skilled workers. As slaves, the Africans were not working either by agreement, or for a limited period. The labor-intensive tobacco and later *cotton* plantations of the South were dependent on slavery for profitability.

Yet, despite all of this, the American ideal of liberty, freedom, and equality for all, persisted. Prosperity. Family. Farms and fortunes were built on the backs of enslaved people. The ideal that made the world take notice of the small new nation in 1776 persists to this day, despite all the evidence in 2019 that we are still a nation deeply divided by race.

2019 is an important year in the history of Virginia, as we will commemorate the 400th year the first slaves were brought to America's first colony. The book that you have just read is a compilation of thought and academic analysis of the genesis of slavery in the English Colonies, and its continuance in the American colonies up until 1863. It is an appropriate acknowledgment of the history of enslavement and its vestiges, which can still be found in every social institution today. Those of us who are involved in the anniversary's remembrance believe it is time for a call to action.

The goal of this book is to help us reframe the discussion around the impact of slavery here in America, not to offer a retelling of the story as folklore and legend. Instead of the enslaved people being an afterthought, they will be placed squarely at the center of the unfolding of the American story. 1619 is the year that changed the economic trajectory of America and ensured that it would be the engine of wealth and capitalism around the world.

The time has come for a more detailed look at the impact of how Jefferson and the "Founders' vision" for a "united" America in 1780 (when they asked Charles Thompson to come up with a seal and motto, which read *E Pluribus Unum,* Out of Many, One) still impacts us to this day in 2019. The reality is, we are not a nation united. Our politics are divided. Just as our nation is divided. Our politics have dissolved into screaming, shouting, and silencing the voices of *we the people*. The time has come for us as Americans to wake up. And heed the call of the Founders to be aware of the rise of tyrants due to our lack of civic oversight and engagement. We the people must raise our voices and be heard once again. But what we need now is something far greater: an epiphany of the American soul. We need to focus on our oneness and sameness in a way that we have not since our great democratic republic was formed in 1776. I am not talking about sameness of thought. Because it is our ability to be different—to think differently and to believe differently—that makes America great. I am talking about *we the people* having the courage to stand up and embrace the very inclusion, equality, and diversity that Thomas Jefferson wrote so eloquently about in the Declaration of Independence.

About the Contributors

Maureen **Elgersman Lee** holds a doctorate in humanities with an emphasis on African American studies from Clark Atlanta University, and has held teaching appointments at universities in Georgia, Maine, and Virginia. She is a former executive director of the Black History Museum and Cultural Center of Virginia and serves on the Fort Monroe Authority Board of Trustees. She publishes on the history of Black women, slavery, and Black communities.

Colita Nichols **Fairfax** is a professor of social work, Honors College Senior Faculty Fellow, and Inaugural Faculty Fellow in the Center for African American Public Policy at Norfolk State University. Her research interests include social history and policy analysis. In addition to several articles, she is the author of *Hampton, Virginia* (2005), and *Timeless History and Service of the Iota Omega Chapter, Alpha Kappa Alpha Sorority, Incorporated, 1922 to Our Time* (2017). She edited *Social Work, Marriage Ethnicity* (2016). She is chairman of the Commonwealth of Virginia's State Board of Historic Resources. She holds a Ph.D. in African American studies from Temple University.

James A. **Forbes, Jr.**, is the Harry Emerson Fosdick Distinguished Professor at Union Theological Seminary, New York City. He is the author of *The Holy Spirit and Preaching* and *Whose Gospel*. He is a member of the Board of Overseers of the Mailman School of Public Health, of Columbia University, and the Board of Directors of the Samuel Dewitt Proctor Conference.

Anthony Q. **Hazard, Jr.**, is an associate professor in the Ethnic Studies Department with a courtesy appointment in the Department of History at Santa Clara University, USA. He is the author of *Postwar Anti-Racism* (Palgrave Macmillan 2012). He has held the Postdoctoral Fellowship in Science in Human Culture at Northwestern University, and the Inclusive Excellence Postdoctoral Fellowship at Santa Clara University.

Valerie M. **Joyce** is the chair of the Theatre and Studio Art Department at Villanova University, where she teaches musical theatre, theatre pedagogy, and script analysis. She received her Ph.D. in theatre history and performance studies from the University of Maryland. Her research interests include musical theatre, early American theatre, and African American female playwrights. Her published work appears in *The Palgrave Handbook of Musical Theatre*

Producers, *Pennsylvania History Journal, JADT,* and *Complutense Journal of English Studies.*

LaGarrett J. **King** is an associate professor of social studies education and the founding director of the CARTER Center for K–12 Black History Education at the University of Missouri. His research centers on the teaching and learning of Black history in schools and society. Additionally, he researches critical theories of race, critical multicultural teacher education, and the history of curriculum. He is the editor of an upcoming book, *Perspectives in Black History in Schools,* and co-author of an upcoming book, *Teaching American Slavery.*

Sophia A. **Nelson** is a journalist and author of three nonfiction books. Her latest book, *E Pluribus One: Reclaiming Our Founders' Vision for a United America,* was released in 2017. She has written for major national publications such as *The Washington Post,* the *New York Times, USA TODAY, Politico* magazine, *Essence* magazine and *Ebony* magazine. She was nominated for the Pulitzer prize in letters in for her first book, *Black Woman Redefined* (2011).

Christopher **St. Vil** is an assistant professor at the University at Buffalo School of Social Work. He previously held a post-doctoral fellow position in the Department of African American Studies at the University of Maryland, College Park. His research focuses on trauma and the experiences of victims of violent injury. He received his Ph.D. from the Howard University School of Social Work, his MSW from the State University of New York at Stony Brook and is a former Graduate Education Diversity Fellow of the American Evaluation Association.

Noelle M. **St. Vil** has been an assistant professor at the University of Buffalo School of Social Work faculty since 2015. Her research focuses on black male-female relationships, including the impact of structural racism on these relationships, intimate partner violence and relationship typologies. She is conducting a study on the prevalence and willingness to engage in consensual nonmonogamy among African Americans. She has published an article in *Ethnicity and Health* which contextualizes the unique relationship experiences of blacks.

Rhonda Vonshay **Sharpe** is the founder and president of the Women's Institute for Science, Equity and Race. Her research focuses on the academic labor market as it relates to Black women, the educational attainment of Black women and the experiences of Black undergraduate women. She holds master's degrees in mathematics, operations research and economics. She completed her doctorate in economics/mathematics at Claremont Graduate University.

Christel N. **Temple** is professor of Africana Studies and an affiliate of The Graduate Program for Cultural Studies (CLST), the Critical European Culture Studies doctoral program (CED), and the African Studies Program (ASP). She specializes in cultural theory, global Africana literatures, and the intersections of history and literature. She is the author of *Literary Spaces* (2007), *Transcendence and the Africana Literary Enterprise* (2017), and *The Theory of Black Cultural Mythology* (forthcoming). Her work has appeared in *Journal of Black*

Studies, Journal of Multicultural Discourses, and the *Western Journal of Black Studies.*

Peter **Wallenstein** is a historian at Virginia Tech. He previously taught in New York, Canada, Korea, and Japan. Among his many books and other publications are *Tell the Court I Love My Wife: Race, Marriage, and Law—An American History*; "Slavery under the Thirteenth Amendment: Race and the Law of Crime and Punishment in the Post–Civil War South"; and *Cradle of America: A History of Virginia.*

Index

abolition, of slavery and slave trade 27–29, 48, 63, 167
aboriginal peoples and cultures, of Virginia 4–6, 9–10
Adam (biblical) 57–58
Africa: Atlantic 18, 25, 28, 36–38; Atlantic coast 18, 26, 34; Bantu 19–20, 29; Black Africans and 186; North 26, 28; ports, in slave trade 29–30; regional origins of enslaved Africans 18–21; southeastern 18–21, 23; West 8, 28–29, 31, 34, 42, 50, 122, 138–139; west-central 19–21, 40–41, 45; western 27–29, 36–37
African American History (Asante) 96
African Americans 7–9; on American Revolutionary era 63; Black Codes and 5, 10–11, 156; cartooning tradition 85–87; in diaspora in North America 43; ever-present anger, PTSS and 158–160; historical narratives 145; legal status of, race and 55; literary anthologies, 1619 in 98–99; male-female relationships 154–157; marriages 153–154, 156, 162; men 116, 154, 156–159; Njia and 95–96; PNFS and 154–157, 159–160; point of view on 1619 86–87; PTSS 12, 154, 157–162; race-neutral period 157; racist socialization, PTSS and 159–160; relationships, behaviors reflective of PTSS in 158–160, 162; segregation and discrimination 156; the slavery generation 155–156; social work implications of PTSS 160–162; traditional gender roles and 159–160; unemployment, of men and women 157; vacant esteem, PTSS and 158–160; in Virginia, 1790 63–64; women 12–13, 154, 157–159; worldview 80
African Americans (Hine, D.C., Hine, W.C., and Harrold) 85
African Diaspora 15, 43, 45
African Identities (Kanneh) 89
African merchants and political officials, Atlantic world and 25
Africana cultural memory studies, 1619 in 80, 82, 88–91, 98–99

Africana Studies 11, 81; cultural memory 80, 82, 88–91, 98–99; disciplinary views, on 1619 95–98
African-centered worldview 81, 160–161
Africans 1–6, 10, 13, 15–18; chattel property status 7, 198; female storytelling in culture 138–139; in North America 37–43, 40; in North America, as settlers 84–85; people of African descent 55–58, 62–65, 67; *see also* enslaved Africans; 1619, Africans landing in Virginia
Afrocentric worldview 95–96
Afrocentricity (Asante) 80
afterlife of slavery 185–189
Akan 19–20, 33, 41, 48
Albelda, R.P. 168
alcohol, in slave trade 33
Allada 33–34
Alonso-Villar, O. 168, 178
"Amazing Grace" 69, 79
American Revolution 63, 68, 102, 187–188, 192
the Americas 27–28, 39, 186; European colonization of, race theories and 57–58; regional origins of enslaved Africans destined for 18–19; slave trade and 24–25, 29–36, 43–44; transatlantic migration of enslaved Africans to 15–17, 23–24; *see also* North America
Amerindian 15, 45
Ana Njinga (Nzinga) Mbande (queen) 4
Anansi tales 4
Anderson, Claude W. 145, 147
Anderson, P. 166
Anderson, Talmadge 96
Angelou, Maya 72, 76
Anglo-Powhatan War 4
Angola 4, 8, 18–19, 30, 32–34, 90–91
Angolans, in 1619 landing 85, 88, 90–96, 197–198
anti-Semitism 56–57
Antoney (Anthony) and Isabel (Isabella) 5, 89, 109, 153, 162
apartheid 7

205

206   Index

Appomattox 4, 144
Aristotle 56
Asante, Molefi Kete 80, 96
Asian people 15, 61, 170–172
asiento 30, 90
assassination, of King, M.L. 70
Atlantic Africa 18, 25, 28, 36–38
Atlantic coast, of Africa 18, 26, 34
Atlantic migration *see* enslaved Africans, transatlantic migration of
Atlantic slave trade 25–26, 108; *see also* transatlantic slave trade
Atlantic world 25, 115
Azevedo, Mario 97

Bahamas 91
Bahia 41
Bambaras 37–38, 41–42
Banneker, Benjamin 193
Bantu Africa 19–20, 29
Bantu languages and peoples 19, 40–41, 45
baptism 59–60, 113–116, 127
Baptist, Edward 190
Baquaqua, Mahommah Gardo 21–22, 35, 48
Battle, Kathleen 72
Beatrice of Kongo 34
Before the Mayflower (Bennett) 82–83, 87
Belote, Ida 167
Bennett, Lerone, Jr. 82–83, 87, 190
Berlin, Ira 114
Bermuda 88–90
Bernier, François 60–61
Berry, Fannie 142–144
Bey, Elihu 85–87
Bight of Benin 18–23, 32, 35, 37, 42, 45, 48, 50
Bight of Biafra 18, 20, 30–31, 37–38, 40–42, 49
Billings, Walter 125–126, 132
biracial 111
Black American Founders, of United States 13, 184–185, 188–194
Black American revolutionary soldiers 192
Black Americans 185–187; *see also* African Americans
Black Antislavery Writings Project 193
Black Atlantic 25
Black citizenship 7, 187–189
Black Codes 5, 10–11, 156
Black Colleges and Universities 77
Black cultural mythology 11, 80–81
Black Freedom Movement 184, 191
Black history 182–185, 188, 194
Black Lives Matter 187
Black men, top occupations, 1960–2015 174–178
Black North American History 97–98
Black people 7–9, 15, 167; agency of 193–194; America built by 77; as Black American Founders 13, 184–185, 188–194; citizenship rights 7, 188–189; emancipation versus freedom 141–142; enslavement narrative, in K–12 history curriculum 187–188; Jefferson on inferiority of 64–66; population during Virginia's first century 108–110; racialization as slaves 186–187; racist policies against 186–187; second-class citizenship of 186–187, 192; as slaves, fallacy of 1619 and 183–184; song of 10–11, 71–72; U.S. Census and 67; in Virginia colony, status of 115–117; in Virginia population, 1640s 58–59; White people and 72–73; *see also* African Americans; Africans
Black Saga (Christian, C.) 84–85
Black slave women *see* enslaved African women
Black Studies (Michel and Bobo) 97
Black Virginians 102, 114
Black Wall Street, in Tulsa, Oklahoma 8, 73
Black women 12–13, 111–117, 154, 157–159; as Black American Founders 191; as caregivers 166–167, 173, 180; domestic employment for, 1960–2015 173; domestic workers 167–168; with high school diploma 178, 179; occupational segregation of 168–169; occupations, median wages earned for top ten, 1960–2015 179–180; occupations, top ten, 1960–2015 174–178; occupations in Virginia, slavery and 169–173, 180; as teachers 174, 179; in Virginia colony 105, 108
Blackness 58, 60, 66–67, 184–186, 192–193
Blue Book, Virginia 1907 Tercentennial 81–82
Blumenbach, Johann Friedrich 62–63
Bobo, Jacqueline 97
Bontemps, Arna 76
The Book of Common Prayer 127
Brazil 17, 24, 27, 29, 41–43
Breaking Out of the Man Box (Porter) 160–161
Britain, American Revolution and 63
Bruno, Giordano 57–58
Buffon, George-Louis Leclerc de 62
Byrd, Susie 142

Caribbean islands 17, 27, 41
Carolinas, enslaved Africans in 39–42
Caucasian race 62–63
CBPR *see* community-based participatory research
Census, U.S. 66–67
chattel property status, of Africans 7, 198
chattel slavery 59–63, 67–68, 182
Cheroenhaka 4
Chesapeake 4, 66–67, 123, 129
Chickahominy 4
children 11, 132; mixed-race 105, 198; transatlantic migration of enslaved African 20–21; in Virginia colony, status of, mothers and 107–108, 111–115
Christian, Charles M. 84–85
Christian, Virginia 167
Christianity 4, 12, 98, 183; baptism and 59–60, 113–116, 127; Jews persecuted during

Index   207

early church 56–57; in Virginia colony 59–60, 125–129, 133–134
Church of England 125–126, 128–129
CIA *see* critical intellectual agency
citizenship 60, 185; Africans landing in Virginia in 1619 and 6–7; Black 7, 187–189; Naturalization Act of 1790 and 6–7; second-class 186–187, 192
Civil Rights Act of 1964 168
Civil Rights Laws, of 1960s 7
Civil Rights Movement 187
Civil War, U.S. 1, 66–68, 102–104, 147, 188
colonial law 110; House of Burgesses 103–105; on interracial marriage 117; race and 55, 59–60, 67, 111; racialized labor and 59–60; on status of children and condition of the mother 115
Colonial Virginia *see* Virginia colony
colonialism: in the Americas, slave trade and 24–25; English 82, 85–86, 89–90, 98, 132, 197–198; exploration, race theory and 56–59
colonization 17, 55–58
Commonwealth of Virginia 1–2
communitarianism 11
community-based participatory research (CBPR) 160–161
condition of the mother 111–115
Congo 18, 37–38, 76
Constitution, U.S. 7, 64, 185, 189
Constitutional Convention, 1789 64
Coombs, N. 142
corporal punishment 44
cotton plantations 190, 198
cowries 32–33, 49
Creole 23–24, 49, 58
crisis of citizenship 185
critical intellectual agency (CIA) 191–192
Cuba 27, 29
Cugoano, Ottobah 98
cultural continuity patterns, of slave trade in the Americas 30–36
cultural memory 2, 11, 80; *see also* Africana cultural memory studies
cultural mythology, Black 11
Curse of Ham, race theory 57
Curtin, Philip D. 16, 49

Dahomey 33–34
dan Fodio, Usman (sheikh) 34, 49
Davis, Hugh 111
DeGruy, Joy 12, 154–155, 157–158
del Río, C. 168, 178
democracy and democratic values 13, 71, 102, 183, 188–190
democratic republic, America as 56, 199
de Ovando, Nicolás 46, 49
Department of Justice, U.S. 105
discrimination 156, 168
domestic workers 167–168, 173
double consciousness 185

Douglass, Frederick 70
Drake, St. Claire 85
Dred Scott v. John F.A. Sanford (1857) 189
Du Bois, W.E.B. 16, 185
Due Process (Civil War) amendments 7
Dumas, Michael 186
Dutch slave ships 83–85, 89–90, 97, 122, 131, 198

e pluribus unum 13, 199
economic development, through slave labor 39
Edelman, Marian Wright 77
Elizabeth City 123
Elizabeth City County 3–5, 145
Elizabeth River Parish 126–129, 133
Ellison, Ralph 75
emancipation 10, 66, 144
Emancipation Proclamation 7, 106, 141–142
employment discrimination 168
Encyclopedia Virginia website 89–91
engendering slavery, in Virginia 108
English 5, 30, 58–59, 103, 123; colonies and colonialism 82, 85–86, 89–90, 98, 132, 197–198; ecclesiastical courts 126–127; language, Mary and 128–131; Native Americans and 101–102; "Virginia Houses" of 129–130
enslaved African women: in Creole societies 23–24; labor of 12–13; motherhood and 11–12, 44–45; narratives of 138–139; roles of 166–167; transatlantic migration of 17–18, 20
enslaved Africans: baptism of 59–60, 115–116; Black American Founders 13, 184–185, 188–193; in Brazil 27, 29, 41–43; "ethnic groups" of 29–30; in European conquest of the Americas 24, 39; homelands of immigrants 40–43; in Islamic world 25–26, 29; lived experiences of 10, 12, 138–151; marriage, male-female relationships and 156; migration 15, 36–39, 44–45; names, identity and 96; in North America 37–46; in North America, homelands of 40–43, 40; persistence of African traditions among 36; personal histories 42–43; personhood, African American literary voices and 98; spirituality and song 10–11; transatlantic migration 15–24; in transatlantic slave trade 17, 27, 29, 34–37, 42–48, 64, 185–186; women, labor of 12–13; women, motherhood and 11–12, 44–45; WPA Slave Narrative Collection interviews 137–151; *see also* 1619, Africans landing in Virginia
enslaved Africans, transatlantic migration of 15–18, 28; children 20–21, females and males 17–18, 20; Middle Passage 6, 10, 15, 21–24, 50, 89; to North America 17, 24–25, 41; regional origins of 18–21
enslavement 10, 12–13, 45, 67, 97; of aboriginal people 5–6; of African

208 Index

Americans, Constitutional Convention of 1789 and 64; in Black history 182; exploitation and 33, 36, 44; judicial and religious sanctions in 35; kidnapping and 8, 88; lived experience of, interviews about 138–151; methods, categories of 33–35; narrative, in K–12 history curriculum 187–188; war and 33–34
Equiano, Olaudah 21–22, 98
Europeans 39, 55, 60, 18; colonialism and exploration, race theory and 56–5; as indentured servants 67, 87–8; race theories 61–6; in slave trade 25, 31–3; women, transatlantic migration of 15, 17, 23–24
ever-present anger, PTSS and 158–160
exploitation, enslavement and 33, 36, 44
exploration and colonialism, race theory and 56–59

Fairbanks, Kimberly 135
Fairfax, Anthony x
Fairfax, Simon 1–2
Fairfax, Thomas 1
fallacy of 1619 183–184
Fanon, Frantz 186
Federal Writers' Project (FWP) 137
female storytelling, in African culture 138–139
Ferguson, Missouri 105
firearms 32, 34
Fisher, Sethard 97–98
Flowerdew Hundred Plantation 3–5, 82, 85
Founders, of America: Black American 13, 184–185, 188–194; White 64, 184, 189–194
400 Years of African American History Commission Act of 2018 182–183
14th Amendment 7
Franklin, John Hope 82, 88, 91
Freedmen's Bureau 156
From Slavery to Freedom (Franklin and Moss) 82, 88, 91
Fugitive Slave Act of 1793 66
Futa Jallon 34
Futa Toro 34
FWP *see* Federal Writers' Project

Ganvie 45
Gbe 33–34, 49
Genesis, Book of 78–79
Geneva Bible 128
Georgia 39–42
Gettysburg Address 102–103, 106
Goetz, Rebecca Anne 60
gold 28, 30–31, 49
Gold Coast 19–20, 26, 30, 37, 40–41, 49; firearms in slave trade 32
Graves, Joseph 57
Greensted, William 112, 114–115, 117
Gregory, James 55
Gronniosaw, James Albert Ukawsaw 98

Guasco, Michael 183
Guinea coast 30–32, 37

Hammon, Jupiter 98
Hampton, Virginia 1, 3–6, 69–70, 145, 147, 153, 167; *see also* Point Comfort
Harding, Vincent 76
Harrison, Thomas 126
Harrold, Stanley 85
Hartman, Saidiya 98–99, 185–186
Harvey, John 125
Hausa states 34
Henige, David 16
Henning, W. 132
Higginbotham, A. Leon 55, 83–84, 88, 97
Higginson, Humphrey 111–114
Hine, Darlene Clark 85
Hine, William C. 85
Hippocrates 56
Hispañola 27
historiography: living, of Mary 12, 121–125, 127–128, 135; of 1619 8; social justice 9, 13, 137–138, 151
Historoire Naturelle (Buffon) 62
Hooker, Olivia 73–78
House of Burgesses 103–105, 107–108, 125
House of Commons Sessional Papers of the Eighteenth Century (Lambert) 21
Hughes, Fountain 139–142, 144
Hughes, Langston 3, 76
Hume, David 64
Hunt, Robert 125

I Will Speak for Myself (Joyce) 121–123, 127–134
Ibibio 41–42, 45
"If I Can Help Somebody" 76–77
Igbo 37–38, 41–42, 104
immigrants and immigration, African 17, 25, 40–43, 40, 45
In the Matter of Color (Higginbotham) 83, 97
indentured servants 124, 197–19; Virginia colony, attempted escape, 1640 55, 58; white 60, 67, 87–88, 132
Indigenous peoples 59–60, 65
institutionalized racism 154–155
interracial fornication 132–133
interracial marriages, banned in Virginia colony 117
Introduction to Black Studies (Karenga) 97
Isabel (Isabella) and Antoney (Anthony) 5, 89, 109, 153, 162
Islam 36, 41
Islamic world, enslaved Africans in 25–26, 29

Jackson, Giles B. 81
Jamaican Muslims 43
James (king) 125
Jamestown Rediscovery website 89

Jamestown settlement 5, 46, 55, 58, 67, 81, 84–85, 102
Jefferson, Thomas 64–66, 68, 139, 193, 199
Jews, medieval period persecution of 56–57
jihad 29, 34, 49–50
Jim Crow 6, 13
John's Island, South Carolina 76
Johnson, Anthony 6
Johnson, Charles 85–87
Johnson, James Weldon 73
Johnson, Mary 109
Juneteenth (Ellison) 75

Kaepernick, Colin 187
Kaine, Tim 182
Kanneh, Kadiatu 89
Kant, Immanuel 64
Karenga, Maulana 97
Kecoughtan 3–4
Key, Elizabeth 111–118
Key, Thomas 111–115
kidnapping, in enslavement 8, 88
Kikongo 4
Kimbundu 4
King, Martin Luther, Jr. 70, 76, 187
King, M.C. 168
Kingdom of Benin 26
Kingdom of Kongo 19, 26
Knight, Thomas Dale 125–126
Knoxville, Tennessee 8
Kongo 37–38, 88
Kongo civil wars 34

labor 103–10; abusive conditions 150–151; racialized 55–56, 59–63; slave 12–13, 25, 27–28, 36, 39
Laird, Roland Owen, Jr. 85–87, 96
Laird, Taneshia Nash 85–87, 96
Lakota 161
Lambert, Sheila 21
Lincoln, Abraham 102–103, 106
Linnaeus, Carolus 61–62
living historiography, of Mary 12, 121–125, 127–128, 135
Lloyds, Cornelius 120–121, 123–124, 126, 128–131, 133
Lloyd's of London 31
"Lord, How Come Me Here" 72–75, 77–79
Louisiana, enslaved Africans in 37, 39, 41–42
Louisiana Purchase 66
Lower Norfolk Court 120, 123, 125, 131–135
Luanda, Angola 34

Malcolm X 182
Mandingos 37–38, 41–42
manilas 32, 50
Margaret and John (ship) 109
Markham, Edwin 74–75
marriage, African American 153–154, 156, 162
Marshall, Thurgood 189

Martin, Trayvon 187
Mary 12, 120–135
Maryland: enslaved Africans in, homelands of 40–41; slave labor in 39; Tidewater region of Virginia and 39–42
masculinity, African American 116, 158–159
Matamba 4
matrilineal society and organization 45, 60
Mattaponi 4
McCartney, Martha 91
memory, identity and 11
Mexico 88–91
Michel, Claudine 97
Middle Passage: length of 23, 23; loss of life during 15, 21–23; mortality rates 22–23; in transatlantic slave trade 6, 10, 15, 21–24, 50, 89
migration, of enslaved Africans 15, 36–39, 44–45; *see also* enslaved Africans, transatlantic migration of
militant Islam, in West Africa 34
military wares, in slave trade 32
Millet, Jean-Francois 74
Mills, Charles 186
"Mina" Coast 19, 48, 50
mixed-race children 105, 198
money, in slave trade 32–33
Morgan, Edmund S. 102
Moss, Alfred 82, 88, 91
Mottrom, John 112–113
multicultural society, Virginia as 1
Muslims 35, 37, 42–43

Nansemond 4
National Museum of African American History and Culture 183
Native Americans 23–24, 101–102
Naturalization Act of 1790 6–7
Ndongo 4
"the Negro," legal status and 56
Negro or Negress, Africans as 10
"The New Division of the Earth" (Bernier) 61
New England, abolition of slavery in 63
new Republic, race and 63–67
New World 8, 15, 56, 102, 125, 189
New York City Draft Riot of 1863 8
Newman, R.S. 191–192
Newton, John 69
Njia: The Way 95–96
Noah (biblical) 57
Norfolk 12
North Africa 26, 28
North America 55, 5; Africans as settlers 84–85; Africans in 37–43; enslaved Africans in 37–46; homelands of African immigrants in 40–43; slave trade to 26, 43–44; transatlantic migration of enslaved Africans to 17, 24–25, 41
The Norton Anthology of African American Literature 99

210 Index

Norwood, Hermond 139–141
Notes on the State Virginia (Jefferson) 64–66, 193

Obama, Barack 77, 189
occupational segregation 167–169
Old World 15, 25
Ouidah, port of 34
Oyo 32–34

Pamunkey 4
Paracelsus 57
patriarchal nuclear family structure (PNFS) 154–157, 159–160
Pedro, John 5
penitential punishment, of Mary 120–121, 126–130, 133–135
people of African descent 55–58, 62–65, 67
Percy's Hundred 5
Perea, J.F. 167
personal histories, of enslaved Africans 42–43
Phillip, John 6
plantation slavery, development in Americas 27
PNFS *see* patriarchal nuclear family structure
Pocahontas 101–102
Point Comfort 67; Africans landing at, 1619 1–4, 58, 69–71, 74, 81, 90–91, 101–102, 122–123, 151, 182; Hampton commemoration of Africans landing at 69–70; *Treasurer* landing at, 1620 4–5
polygenism 57–58
Porter, Tony 160–161
Portugal and Portuguese 26–28, 34, 90–91
post-racial rhetoric, structural racism and 157
posttraumatic slave syndrome (PTSS) 12, 154, 157–162
Potomac 4
Powhatan 4
psychoeducation intervention model 161
PTSS *see* posttraumatic slave syndrome
Puerto Rico 27, 29
Punch, John 55, 58

Quadricentennial commemorations, of 1619 69–72

race 1, 142, 186; Black American Founders on 192–193; Blumenbach on racial groups 62–63; categories, in U.S. Census of 1790 66–67; colonial law and 55, 59–60, 67, 111; ethnicity and, occupations for women in Virginia by 171–172; gender and class, of Black women 116; legal status of people of African descent and 55–56, 67; new Republic and 63–67; physical abuse of domestic workers and 167; religious and scientific constructions of 60–63; segregation by 168; social norm of, chattel slavery and 63
race theory 56–59, 61–62, 64–66, 68
race-neutral period 157
racial identification 67, 96
racial justice 192–193
racial targeting 105
racialization 55, 111, 186–187
racialized labor 55–56, 59–63
racism 7; chattel slavery and 63, 67–68; enslaved Africans in North Americas and 44; institutionalized 154–155; occupational segregation and 168; structural 154, 157; systematic 159, 161; of U.S. policies 186–187; in Virginia, economic factors complicating 166; of White Founders 191–193
racist socialization 158–160
rape, of Mary 12, 120, 130–131, 134
Rappahannock 4
Reconstruction 67–68, 188
resistance, to slavery 36, 38, 43–46, 97
Reskin, B. 168, 180
Richter, Julie 111
Rolfe, John 3, 83, 101–102
Rosewood, Florida, massacre of 1923 8
Royal African Company 30

Sacred Hunger (Unsworth) 21–22, 50
Saghanughu, Muhammad Kaba 43
Sancho, Ignatius 98
São João Bautista (ship) 107
Scott, Bobby 182
second-class citizenship, of Black people 186–187, 192
segregation 8, 13, 156, 167–169
Senegambia 18–20, 26, 28, 30, 40–42, 50; European merchants in 32; wars in 34
settler colony 5–6, 9
sex segregation 168
sexual violence 38, 44, 132
Shakespeare, William 58
The Shaping of Black America (Bennett) 190
Sierra Leone 20, 32, 37, 40–42, 45
1619, Africans landing in Virginia 103, 106, 117, 137, 199; in African American literary anthologies 98–99; in Africana cultural memory studies 80, 82, 88–91, 98–99; Africana studies, disciplinary views on 95–98; Angolans in 85, 88, 90–96, 197–198; Black American Founders and 188–189; citizenship and 6–7; fallacy of 183–184; fifty and one hundred years after 104–105; 400 Years of African American History Commission Act and 182; historical views 82–91; historiography of 81; at Jamestown settlement 5, 46, 81, 84–85; knowledge about 9–13; mass kidnapping 8, 88; origins and experiences in colonies 92–95; Pan-African construction of 88–89; at Point

Comfort 1–4, 58, 69–71, 74, 81, 90–91, 101–102, 107, 122–123, 151, 182; Quadricentennial commemorations of 69–72; summer 101–102; as "20 and odd Negroes" 3, 11, 69, 71–72, 75, 89, 197
1620 90–91; Johnson, M., arrival in 109; *Treasurer* at Point Comfort 4–5; Virginia census 108; White women, in Virginia colony 12, 103–105
skin color 58, 65, 87–88
Slaughter, Richard 145–147
Slave Coast, Bight of Benin as 19, 37, 42, 48, 50
Slave Codes 10, 98
slave exports from Africa, Atlantic migration of 16
slave labor 12–13, 25, 27–28, 36, 39
Slave Narrative Collection, WPA 137–151
slave owners, in North America 44
slave resistance 43–46
slave trade 38–39; abolition of 27–29, 48; African collaborators in 28–29; African ports in 29–30; Africans in North America and 37–40; the Americas and 24–25, 29–36, 43–44; Atlantic 25–26, 108; chronology 46–48; contracts and credit in 31–32; European merchants in 25, 31–32; goods of trade in exchange for slaves in 32–33; methods of enslavement 33–35; money in 32–33; movement of people during 16; to North America 26, 43–44; organization of 27–30; political and social conditions of Atlantic Africa in 36–37; Portugal in 26–28; Royal African Company in 30; transatlantic 17, 27, 29, 34–37, 42–43, 45–48, 64, 185–186; *see also* transatlantic slave trade
slave wars 39
slaveholders, U.S. Constitution and 64
slavery 1; abolition of 27–29, 48, 63, 167; afterlife of 185–189; chattel 59–63, 67–68, 182; engendering 108; Jefferson defending 64, 66; occupations of Black women in Virginia since 169–173, 180; racial hierarchy and 186; racial status and 142; resistance to 36, 38, 43–46, 97; in southern U.S. 63–64; 13th amendment 185; trauma of, PTSS and 6, 12, 154, 157–162, 162; U.S. Constitution and 189; White Founders on 191; *see also* enslaved Africans; enslavement
slaves 32–33; fallacy of 1619 and 183–184; families 155–156; Fugitive Slave Act on 66; racialized idea of Black people as 186–187; Three-Fifths Clause on 64; white European indentured servants versus 67, 87–88; *see also* enslaved Africans
Sleeter, Christine 184
social control 29, 44
social justice historiography 9, 13, 137–138, 151
social work implications, of PTSS 160–162

song, of Black people in America 10–11, 71–72
Songhay 28
South Carolina 39–40, 76
southeastern Africa 18–21, 23
southern U.S., slavery in 63–64
Spanish colonies 27, 30
Sparks, Elizabeth 147–150
Stewart, James 96
Still I Rise (Laird, R.O., Laird, T.N., and Bey) 85–87
structural racism 154, 157
sugarcane 27–28, 56
survival, in Black cultural mythology 80–81
Systema Naturae (Linnaeus) 61
systematic racism 159, 161

Takaki, Ronald 59–60
Taney, Robert Brook 189
terror, in slave trade 39
textiles, in slave trade 32–33
13th amendment 185
Thompson, Charles 199
Thornton, John 110–111
Three-Fifths Clause, of U.S. Constitution 64
Tidewater region, of Virginia and Maryland 39–42
tobacco 39, 67, 89–90, 96, 103–105
transatlantic migration 15–24; *see also* enslaved Africans, transatlantic migration of
transatlantic slave trade: chronology of 47–48; Constitutional Convention of 1789 and 64; enslaved Africans in 17, 27, 29, 34–37, 42–48, 64, 185–186; Middle Passage in 6, 10, 15, 21–24, 50, 89; responsibility of merchants and government officials for 45–46
trauma, of slavery 6, 12, 154, 157–162
Treasurer (ship) 4–5, 7, 88, 107–108
Tucker, Isabel (Isabella) and Antoney (Anthony) 5, 89, 109, 153, 162
Tucker, William (captain) 5, 91, 109
Tulsa, Oklahoma 8, 73
"20 and odd Negroes," 1619 landing of 3, 11, 69, 71–72, 75, 89, 197
2019 Commemorative Commission, in Hampton 6
2019 Quadricentennial commemorations, of 1619 69–72
Twi 41, 122, 128, 130

Unsworth, Barry 21–22, 50
Usselinx, Willem 46, 50

vacant esteem, PTSS and 158–160
Vann, Claude III x
Vaughan, A.T. 5, 166
Victor 55
violence 38, 44, 132, 150–151, 160–161, 167
Virginia 1–2, 64, 81, 166; aboriginal cultures

Index

of 4–6, 9–10; Black population, 1640s 58–59; Black population during first century 108–110; Black women's occupations in, slavery and 169–173, 180; census, 1620 108; Christian, V., executed by 167; engendering slavery in 108; enslaved Africans in, homelands of 40–43; land and labor in seventeenth-century 103–104; population distribution by race, ethnicity and gender 170–171; population distribution of women by race and ethnicity 171; as slave society 104; Tidewater region of Maryland and 39–42; tobacco in 104–105; total estimated population, 1610–1720 110; *see also* 1619, Africans landing in Virginia
Virginia Assembly 125–126
Virginia colony 3–6, 10–11, 197–198; African and Indigenous peoples in, Christianity and 59–60; African population, 1619–1649 123; baptism in 115–116; Black population 108–110; Black status in 115–117; Black women in 105, 108; chattel slavery and racialized labor in 59–63; Christianity in 59–60, 125–129, 133–134; colonial law 55, 59–60, 110–111, 115, 117; General Assembly 111–115, 117; history, *Encyclopedia Virginia* on 89–91; House of Burgesses 103–105, 107–108, 125; indentured servants, attempted escape, 1640 55, 58; interracial marriages banned in 117; Jamestown settlement 5, 46, 55, 58, 67, 81, 84–85, 102; Key, E., and 111–118; labor of African American women in 12–13; Lower Norfolk Court in 120, 123, 125, 131–135; Mary in 12, 120–135; racialization in 55, 111; status of children in, mothers and 107–108, 111–115; White women in 12, 103–105
Vonshay Sharpe, Rhonda 12–13
voter suppression 105–106
voting rights 6–7

wa Thiong'o, N. 186
Waldstreicher, David 64
Warner, Mark 182
Warrasquoke 3–5
wars 33–36, 39
Washington, George 1
Watts, William 130–132
"We Shall Overcome" 79
"We the People" 197, 199
West, Francis 5
West Africa 8, 28–29, 31, 34, 42, 50, 122, 138–139
West-Central Africa 19–21, 40–41, 45
western Africa 27–29, 36–37
westward expansion, of U.S. 66
Wheatley, Phillis 65, 98
"When All Africans Could Fly" 76
Whitaker, Alexander 125
White Christian European perspectives, in fallacy of 1619 183
White Founders 64, 184, 189–194
White Lion (ship) 1–5, 7, 69, 88, 90, 107–108, 117
White supremacist ideology 71, 77
White women 12, 103–105, 174–177, 180
Whitney, Eli 66
Wilder, Doug 1
William (child of Isabel and Antoney) 153
Williamsburg 116–117
Williamson, Mary 132–133
Wilson, John 126
Windward Coast 42
women 42, 132; condition of the mother 111–115; European, transatlantic migration of 15, 17, 23–24; mothers 11–12, 17, 44–45, 107–108, 111–115; violence against 160–161, 167; in Virginia, population distribution by race and ethnicity 171; in Virginia, race and ethnicity in occupations for 171–172; White 12, 103–105, 174–177, 180; *see also* Black women; enslaved African women
Works Progress Administration (WPA), Slave Narrative Collection 137–151

Yeardley, George 6, 82
Yoruba 20, 33, 42, 45

Zimmerman, George 187

www.ingramcontent.com/pod-product-compliance
Ingram Content Group UK Ltd.
Pitfield, Milton Keynes, MK11 3LW, UK
UKHW041957140426
5217IPUK00015B/845